REDISCOVERING
LOVE

REDISCOVERING

LOVE

WILLARD GAYLIN, M.D.

VIKING

VIKING
Viking Penguin Inc., 40 West 23rd Street,
New York, New York 10010, U.S.A.
Penguin Books Ltd, Harmondsworth,
Middlesex, England
Penguin Books Australia Ltd, Ringwood,
Victoria, Australia
Penguin Books Canada Limited, 2801 John Street,
Markham, Ontario, Canada L3R 1B4
Penguin Books (N.Z.) Ltd, 182–190 Wairau Road,
Auckland 10, New Zealand

First published in 1986 by Viking Penguin Inc.
Published simultaneously in Canada

Pages 289–90 constitute an extension of this copyright page.

LIBRARY OF CONGRESS CATALOGING IN PUBLICATION DATA
Gaylin, Willard.
Rediscovering love.
Bibliography: p.
Includes index.
1. Love—Psychological aspects.   I. Title
BF575.L8G39   1986   152.4   85-41065
ISBN 0-670-81120-3

Printed in the United States of America by
R. R. Donnelley & Sons Company, Harrisonburg, Virginia
Design by Ellen LoGuidice
Set in Sabon

To Betty,
my partner, companion, friend, and wife.

All of my books have been written with her.
This one was written for her.

RE-STATEMENT OF ROMANCE

The night knows nothing of the chants of night.
It is what it is as I am what I am:
And in perceiving this I best perceive myself

And you. Only we two may interchange
Each in the other what each has to give.
Only we two are one, not you and night,

Nor night and I, but you and I, alone,
So much alone, so deeply by ourselves,
So far beyond the casual solitudes,

That night is only the background of our selves,
Supremely true each to its separate self,
In the pale light that each upon the other throws.

—WALLACE STEVENS

ACKNOWLEDGMENTS

The Hastings Center has been my intellectual home for over fifteen years. While its primary research interests are in ethics and the life sciences, it has influenced my thinking in all areas. One cannot analyze such problems as the right to death, fair allocation of human body parts, *in vitro* fertilization, surrogate motherhood, genetic engineering and the like without focusing on the meaning of life and love, of duty and responsibility, of purpose and pleasure. Those are the subjects of this book. My gratitude to Dan Callahan and my colleagues at the Hastings Center for creating an environment which encourages thinking about the difficult and the important.

My children constitute a cadre of tough but loving "in-house" editors. My gratitude, with love, to Jody and Andrew Heyward, Ellen and Clinton Smith.

Gerald Howard, my "professional" editor, provided the kind of editorial guidance that honors his profession and performed this difficult task with gentleness and humor. I am grateful for this new friend.

It is impossible to acknowledge my wife's contribution to this book. As in all things in my life, it is difficult to know where "she" begins and "I" leave off.

WILLARD GAYLIN, M.D.

CONTENTS

REDISCOVERING LOVE

INTRODUCTION

Love is a central condition of human existence. We need it for survival; we seek it for pleasure; we require it to lend meaning and purpose to ordinary existence. We suffer its loss with grief and often despair. Yet, we understand so little about the nature of love. What is romantic love? Is it related to filial love? To parental love? Is there a common thread that binds these contrasting experiences? If so, what are these threads, and how can we identify them? What is the relationship between the need for love, falling in love, and loving?

Since romantic love is the primary concern of this book, one must somehow relate love to the nature of sexuality, itself a complicated and confusing aspect of human experience. Is there a difference between sexual appetite and other appetites? Is sex pure instinct, a drive we share in common with a host of lower forms of animal life? What is the nature of human passion? Is commitment the antagonist of passion? Can lasting attachments survive in an age that elevates pleasure and personal fulfillment over duty and responsibility? What is pleasure, anyhow? And, for that matter, what do we mean by commitment?

These are but some of the questions which confront me daily in my professional life as a psychoanalyst. Love and relationship, love and its loss, the joy and the agony of love, are the stuff of the psychoanalytic experience. One would think that love would dominate the literature of psychoanalysis. It does not. Since much of the confusion about love in our time is, as I intend to explain, a product of conflicting attitudes unwittingly introduced by psychoanalysis, it seems imperative to bring a psychoanalytic sensibility to the task of sorting out these conflicts and answering these questions. This book is my attempt to do just that.

How does one study a subject like love from a psychological point of view? Most psychological and sociological research starts with an exhaustive search of the literature. One turns to the scientific publications in one's field to draw on the wisdom of those who have preceded and to avoid where possible rediscovering the wheel. You will note, however, as you read this book that I am more likely to quote literature than "the literature." This fact warrants some explanation.

Modern studies of human psychology are divided among a variety of fields: psychoanalysis; psychiatry, both child and adult; clinical, social, and laboratory psychology; pediatrics; sociology; cultural anthropology—and on and on. Most of these fields aspire to scientific respectability, and in science the nature of evidence is clearly biased toward a data base, objectivity, measurement, replicable research, and the like. The feeling and experience of so complicated an emotion as love (and it is more than an emotion) resist this type of research.

Psychologists have tended to use empirical methods to study the simpler behavior of simpler creatures. So we have the elegant observations of B. F. Skinner based on his work with pigeons, and Konrad Lorenz's studies on the goose. We can learn much from these studies about bonding, the nature of learning, and the simple emergency responses of fear and rage. All of this we share with lower creatures, but the way in which our intelligence and imagination are likely to modify the experiences makes generalization from animal to human extremely hazardous. Nonetheless, animal studies are of great help to the psychiatrist in understanding human behavior. They are least helpful, unfortunately, in those areas that are exclusively human. Love as we know it bears no relationship to anything perceived by these lower creatures, although it may be at least analogous to phenomena in higher primates.

The research methods of animal psychology are empirical and often precise. But precision is of little help here. Elegant, high-technology acoustical instruments help us little in understanding the aesthetics of music. Listening and analyzing and feeling and responding are still the methods of musical criticism. Research people understand the value and the limits of their methodologies. As a result the finer human emotions such as love and the feeling (subjective) aspects of these emotions have not been extensively studied by empirical methods. When they have, the results have generally been less than inspiring.

The psychoanalyst uses a somewhat less "scientific" method than the animal psychologist. He studies the proper subject, the human being, but of necessity in a smaller number of cases, hoping to find generalized information from his admittedly dangerously small sample. Nonetheless, Harvey pressed a single thumb against a single set of veins (his own) and discovered the basic principle of the circulation of the blood for our entire species. Psychoanalysts, however, have other problems when confronting love. They have been primarily interested in psychopathology. The same may be said of psychiatrists. They both fix things. They are more likely to study the inability to love or the results of the absence of loving. These studies are all helpful in approaching the experience of love, but only in an oblique fashion.

And so it goes with all of the scientific disciplines. Human love is unlikely to be a primary research interest for most modern social scientists. They recognize the limits of their current empirical disciplinary tools in dealing with love, but for one reason or another they are reluctant to return to the intuitive and analytic methods of their great nineteenth-century forebears.

The world of philosophy and theology has no problem with analytic reasoning. Here there is an exhaustive literature on love. But much of modern philosophy has for its own reasons turned away from considerations of love. The philosophers who did attend to love are rarely contemporaries, and therefore they did not have an opportunity to apply philosophical reasoning that has been informed by the Freudian view of human behavior predominant today. Still, they supply a background of centuries of consideration of love that is an indispensable guide to understanding the experience of love.

Some authors feel that all rational analysis, not just the scientific methodology, does a disservice to the mystical elements that are central to the experience of love. M. C. D'Arcy in his sensitive book *The Mind and Heart of Love* cautions against the "sin of animus" or reason in approaching the human experience:

> The mind is acquisitive and insists on making its own all that it meets in experience. But as the common man and the poet and the saint have all agreed, there is something very incomplete in the life of science and philosophy. The scientist and the philosopher preside over a dead world; they leave aside the world we all love, of colour and movement and intimate, personal intercourse. Their world is the world of things, and even persons are marked, like the poor Jews in concentration camps, with this stigma. They live to give a Roman holiday to the mind; at the very

best they make up its beatitude. Animus is a selfish lord;
he takes more than he gives.[1]

To write about a subject so subjective, so amorphous, so
unquantifiable, and at the same time so paradoxically vast
and intimate as love inevitably demands, even of a psychoanalyst, the necessity (and courage) of utilizing experiential
data from his professional *and* his personal life. Love is at
the center of both my personal and my professional life. The
meaning, the value, the purpose of my life are defined in
terms of my relationships and my work.

Yet, it is difficult for a psychoanalyst to reveal himself, to
expose even minimally his emotions and the data of his
personal past and present—in public print. Some of my more
orthodox colleagues would charge it is "unprofessional."
Psychoanalysis, as a branch of psychiatric medicine and a
form of treatment for mental illness, demands the utmost
discipline in protecting the patient from the personal emotions of the analyst and the burdens that might be imposed
by the knowledge of the facts of his everyday existence.

The most arduous aspect of a young psychoanalyst's professional training is not to master the theory but to master
himself, to control even his protective emotions of love,
identification, tenderness, empathy, and compassion. As he
must not be judgmental, neither must he be reassuring. There
is no place for pity any more than anger in a process where
to know all is—if not to forgive—to dynamically understand all. Forgiveness and understanding may only be different terms from different philosophies allowing for the
same exculpation of guilt and responsibility.

To write for the general public on any subject, even the
most detached from one's life and experience, is, of course,
to reveal oneself. No one knows this better than the psychoanalyst, who sees in all fantasies and all creations the

hand and the heart of the creator. For this reason some in my profession abjure any writing outside of professional journals.

Of course, Freud often wrote simply, directly, and honestly to a general audience and, while not acknowledging so, utilized the most intimate details of his personal life and fantasies in the exploration of his theories. On the other hand, Freud had no true colleagues in his field, only disciples. There was no profession of psychoanalysis, no orthodoxy, no "church."

Professionalization brings rules, and rules are not merely arbitrary restrictions but limits founded generally on experience and good judgment. Nevertheless, certain subjects must be experienced as well as analyzed to be understood; the emotions are a prime example. Since human emotions defy quantifying methods of investigation, they demand the kind of subjective analysis that, according to the basic assumptions underlying psychoanalytic theory, inevitably introduces the values and the bias of the observer. The value systems of an author of the experience of love are pertinent, and knowing them offers some protection against what may be idiosyncratic to his experience.

Simply by identifying myself as a psychoanalyst I reveal a set of assumptions that inform your understanding of my assertions. Most people today understand the basic assumptions of psychoanalysis. We believe in an unconscious. We insist that behavior is dynamic, a result of forces and counterforces. We have a developmental bias that sees the present as inextricably linked to the past, and linked in a way that is quite different from that assumed by a behaviorist. Knowing that I am a psychoanalyst, a psychiatrist, and a physician contributes to your understanding of certain professional assumptions I am likely to make.

There are also ways in which I am an atypical representative of our time and in which my personal experience places me at the limit of the bell-shaped curve for my sex, cultural background, and generation. I fell in love at sixteen (although the concept of "falling in love" was one I did not acknowledge and could not have understood at that time), married my childhood sweetheart at age twenty-one, and have shared a common life with her in the community of marriage for over thirty-five years. I am, in addition, both an optimist and a romantic, and while my use of these terms will become progressively clearer through this book, it may be assumed prior to definition that neither optimism nor romanticism has much currency in the current intellectual marketplace.

I am unconcerned about contamination of my judgments by my experience, protected by the Freudian assumption that such contamination is an essential part of all judgment, that all experience is idiosyncratic, and that self-knowledge and frank admission are the only alternatives to an unachievable "objectivity."

Throughout this book I will be drawing on my feelings and those of others. In the area of the feelings, the anecdotal, the experiential—my own as well as others'—has respectability. Were you and I capable of discussing our mutual colleague John Doe, we could combine our reactions to his abandonment by his wife with our own feelings of rejection and come to some compassionate understanding of what he was experiencing. But as C. S. Lewis has said, "I am driven to literary examples because you, the reader, and I do not live in the same neighbourhood; if we did, there would unfortunately be no difficulty about replacing them with examples from real life."[2]

I am driven to literary examples for all of the above reasons, but also out of my respect for the essential truth that seems best encompassed by fiction. The creative artist is a servant of our souls. Blessed with a sensitivity beyond the rest of us, and further endowed with a capacity to communicate his understandings through words or paints or musical notes, he enriches our lives by illuminating that which we dimly recognize. The great writer is a magician who seems able to read our minds, to have experienced our past, and to share our most intimate sensibilities. It is comforting to know that "someone else" knows and understands. We are not alone with our pains and joys. We are, the artist tells us, experiencing the universal, and that too is comforting.

I do not exempt my own words when I consider the limitations of reason in approaching experience. I depend on the reader to confront my revealed experiences with his own. One must experience to understand experience.

Walt Whitman, that most romantic of American poets, advised us well:

When I heard the learn'd astronomer,
When the proofs, the figures, were ranged in columns before me,
When I was shown the charts and diagrams, to add, divide, and measure them,
When I sitting heard the astronomer where he lectured with much applause in the lecture-room,
How soon unaccountable I became tired and sick,
Till rising and gliding out I wander'd off by myself,
In the mystical moist night-air, and from time to time,
Look'd up in perfect silence at the stars.[3]

I ask the reader to look, not at the stars, but into himself.

1 ❧ REDISCOVERING ROMANCE

T he subject of love is so venerable and awesome, the literature of love so vast and imposing, that the writer or researcher inevitably approaches it with trepidation. Is there any lode of value left in these ancient mines that has not already been uncovered by the hundreds of prospectors who have previously explored these cavernous depths? Is there even a nugget of truth or insight remaining to be discovered? Is it not implicitly arrogant to assume that you will find something of substance that has been overlooked in this overworked abyss? After all, the human condition, and the human experience of love that is so fundamental a part of it, has not essentially changed in the five thousand years or more of written records. Can there be anything beyond the alternative images of love suggested in Plato's *Symposium?* Can there be anything more to add to the insights of generations of medieval and Renaissance philosophers, to the visions of the romantic poets and novelists? Can there be anything *new* to say?

The concept of love must be continually reexamined. Each generation, utilizing the tools, the language, the philosophy, and the biases of its time, ought to reexplore the central conditions of human existence. Certainly love is in that category. Love—along with justice and virtue—must be reconsidered in our time as it has in each preceding generation in order to draw conclusions that are relevant to the special conditions, perceptions, needs, and sensibilities of our current existence.

Love, as I have said, is at the center of my life and of my practice. People do not come to psychoanalysts for self-improvement; nor do they come because they are sick. Many of the sickest will either not acknowledge the fact or will not see their despair as a product of their own action. People come to a psychoanalyst for one reason and one reason alone. They are suffering and want surcease. The sources of their distress are varied, but inevitably they are reducible to questions of self-confidence and self-worth.

Love and work are the nutrient sources that sustain all pride and self-assurance. Despite the ongoing gender revolution, issues of love and loneliness are still the dominant forces driving women to treatment; problems of work more often motivate male patients. Work and its rewards have become in great part the substitutes for love and relationships in the support system of the male ego.

Given the fact that our daily experience is saturated with problems of love and loving, one would assume that the concept of love would be at the center of psychoanalytic theory. This is far from the case. In an unanticipated development, psychoanalytic theory created a loveless world. Psychoanalysis enshrined the sexual drive, the libido, as the primal factor governing human activity. The sexual instinct was declared to be the central motivating force and the exclusive source of energy for all human activity.

In the process of elevating sex, love, that central passion which had focused the attention of centuries of students of the human condition, was reduced to a derivative, a relatively unimportant epiphenomenon. The unpredictable result of this strange set of priorities was not just a reduction of love but also, ironically, a trivialization of sex. Surely this was the opposite of what Freud had in mind. Yet, nonetheless, it is traceable to certain components of early Freudian theory that still prevail. While Freud cannot be held accountable for this distortion, modern psychoanalysts must bear some responsibility.

It is a cliché of psychoanalysis that the only thing worse than a fantasy frustrated is a fantasy fulfilled. We modern psychoanalysts have suffered the misfortune of surviving the victory of our philosophy, and now we must suffer the humiliation of living in this unlovely world that is, in great part at least, our own creation. While the final score is not yet in, the results so far of this so-called "sexual revolution" are less than reassuring. The Freudian view of human behavior laid the positive groundwork for the liberation of the sexual aspirations of women from both an oppressive personal sense of guilt and the shame and humiliation of social stigmatization. But the only empirical results of that illegitimate offspring of Freudian philosophy, the sexual revolution, seem to be the spread of two new sexually transmitted diseases, genital herpes and AIDS; an extraordinary rise in the incidence of cancer of the cervix; and a disastrous epidemic of teenage pregnancies. For the abandonment of love, Freud holds some responsibility; for the trivialization of sex, he must not be blamed.

D. H. Lawrence, that ultimate romantic, that twentieth-century product of a nineteenth-century temperament, also lived to be misunderstood and misinterpreted. Where Freud reduced love to an adjunct of sexual instinct, Lawrence elevated sex to the religious level of romantic love. When he talks of sex, therefore, he means the passion that comes in the bonded fusion of love:

> Now when brilliant young people like this talk to me
> about sex: or scorn to: I say nothing. There is nothing to
> say. But I feel a terrible weariness. To them sex means,

just plainly and simply, a lady's underclothings, and the fumbling therewith. They have read all the love literature, *Anna Karenina,* all the rest, and looked at statues and pictures of Aphrodite, all very laudable. Yet when it comes to actuality, to today, sex means to them meaningless young women and expensive underthings. . . .

That is all sex means to them: just the trimmings.[1]

The loving couple, in Lawrence's words, were a representation of the angelic. "An Angel's got to be more than a human being. So I say, an Angel is the soul of man and woman in one: they rise united at the Judgement Day, as one Angel."[2]

Freud at the same time was trying desperately to place human nature into the context of the burgeoning field of modern science which was expected to replace both religion and romance in the mind of twentieth-century thinkers. While Freud himself was too complex and too questing a figure to have degraded human relationships to the oversimplified definitions of our day, by stressing the biological he laid a foundation for the reductionistic view of *Homo sapiens* as simply an elevated form of animal, one in a continuum. That the human being is an animal is indisputable. That we are simply one in a continuum of other animals is ludicrous to anyone trained in understanding human behavior. We are a glorious discontinuity, as different from the rest of the animal host as God, if He exists, is different from us.

Freud and Freudianism have contributed to some of the current confusion about human relationships and purposes, but they are not alone. Freudian psychodynamics were not only a product of Freud's intelligence and imagination; they were also derivatives of the powerful culture forces of his period, the late nineteenth century, a time of enormous transition. These intellectual tides continued into the twentieth century, shaping other fields of inquiry besides psychoanalysis and influencing other thinkers besides Freud. The absence of any serious consideration of love is an omission that transcends the limits of the psychoanalytic discipline. Little concern for love (or for emotions, values, or even morality) has been evident in the modern world of philosophy, which was, after all, the dominion where theories of love resided for centuries.

A violent aversion to the romanticism of the nineteenth century was characteristic of the sweep of intellectual forces at the turn of the century. The most powerful voice in the academic world was not Freud's; his time was yet to come. If anyone may be thought of as the primary spokesman of that period it was Schopenhauer, that great exponent of the power of nature and will, and an implacable antiromantic.

Freud's debt to Schopenhauer has been acknowledged, but the extent to which Freud borrowed from the body as well as the spirit of Schopenhauer's work has yet to be fully analyzed. In placing sexuality at the core of all love, in seeing sexuality as a pure biological drive exclusively in the service of procreation, in his contempt for the romantic tradition which attempted to free humankind from the limited definitions of biology—in all of these, Schopenhauer was a coauthor with Freud of the libido theory.

The death of the romantic tradition in which love flourished was to be hastened by the explosion of scientific knowledge at that time. Modern science (organic chemistry, modern physics, human physiology, etc.) was born in the German-speaking world of the late nineteenth century. If philosophy was gloomy, science was not. This was the heyday of scientific optimism. The culture of science anticipated a technological solution to all of human misery and all our worldly problems. If not today, then surely tomorrow. There would be no place for romance, since there was no need for mystery. The application of knowledge gained through scientific methods would dispel not only the mysteries of an earlier period but the superstitions which thrived on such ignorance. Religion was an illusion whose future was doomed by greater sophistication and greater understanding. Thus, the nineteenth century laid the groundwork for the death of God and the death of the romantic in the twentieth century, and in its peculiar anthropocentric optimism laid the roots for our current paradoxical times of spiritual hunger in the face of unparalleled material comfort.

In America and the western democracies of Europe the enhanced respect for, even adulation of, the individual would lead to a society that, with all of its injustices, was more humane and probably more just than any of its antecedents. But it laid the groundwork for an overvaluation of the individual—an individual separated from his attachments and freed of the bondage of love—which would ultimately allow individualism to decay into narcissism. And it would allow for the dangerous degradation of the community that would ultimately demand the kind of reappraisal that is currently evolving.

The adored and pampered individual would be more concerned with being loved than loving; with receiving rather than giving. Pleasure would be reduced to fun, and sex would be equated with appetite. The vocabulary of rights would replace that of duties and responsibilities as the basic language of moral philosophy at the same time that philosophy was becoming less interested in morality at all. The elements of a psychology, a philosophy, and a culture of individualism were all in place.

The average person rarely reads philosophy and is unaware that he is in the process of any kind of revolution. Fashions change, life-styles change, growth and aging are

ultimately recognized within one's lifetime; but few participants in any society are aware of the strong cultural tides
that wash across, and are changing, the very lands in which
they live. The Victorians were fond of saying that the last
thing a fish is likely to discover is water.

What is the average person today aware of? A painful
sense of a promise unfulfilled. A confusion because, while
all the right forms are in place, the stuff and substance seem
to be missing. We have seen in our time and in our country
a relief (for most of us) from the specific anxieties of severe
poverty, but we are left with a curious and vacuous plea-
sureless existence. The technological world has turned out
to be a hard-edged and cold place. Work has come to be
reduced to its elements. No one starts or finishes anything.
Entertainments, while universal and quick, seem slick and
superficial. They come to you, you don't have to go to them;
and while this seemed like an improvement it somehow or
other, without our knowing why, diminished the pleasure
inherent in the activity. It was more fun to play baseball
than to watch it. In pursuit of quick pleasure we forgot that
patience and pain are often essential components of profound pleasure. In addition to this corruption of the concept
of pleasure, there was an abandonment of the joy in duty,
obligation, and commitment. Getting without giving is really not much fun.

The individual in pursuit of his individualism seemed reduced instead of being enhanced. We had lost touch with
the larger concept of community. The ethnic ghetto, while
not to be romanticized by nostalgia, at least suggested that
we were a part of something. For one reason or another,
ethnic identifications, church identifications, loyalty to party,
to ideology, to religion, to union, all became attenuated.
The talk is still there—"I'm Polish and proud of it"—but the
very talk and the fact that it is reduced to bumper stickers

denies the sense of a continuity and involvement with community.

One product of this heightened individualism was the diminution of our attention to the importance of relationships in general. The goals of life were increasingly cast in terms of individual expectations instead of social roles, in terms of what we would receive rather than what we might give. Self-actualization, self-fulfillment, doing your own thing, letting it all out became the catchphrases that identified the process.

Why did not our psychologists and sociologists save us from this drift into a joyless narcissism? Why did philosophy not remind us of the verities of love and community? The answer is that the social sciences and philosophy were subject to the same cultural forces and had been corrupted by the same delusions.

The scientific disdain for the subjective eventually was to corrode the importance of sociology and psychology. Since human imagination and human pursuits are not encompassable by purely empirical methods, the psychologists were driven to study animal behavior, and the sociologists, in pursuit of quantification and measurement, forgot the glories of the intuitive insights of such of their forebears as Max Scheler, Max Weber, and Emile Durkheim. Contempt for the intuitive led to an overvaluation of that which could be measured.

If love could be packaged in a container, but the love within could not be measured or quantified, we would have to study the container. Its dimensions could be recorded. We all—philosophers, artists, poets, musicians, and social scientists—became clever packagers. Since our most respected methodologies involved quantifying, measurement, and objectivity, then only those things which could be explained within those dimensions would be studied. It was as though we had designed the tools first and then directed ourselves to those tasks for which the tools might be usable.

In discovering technology, we abandoned mystery. In reducing life to the rational we denied the miraculous elements inherent in our species. Romance was relegated to the young, the very young. And we all began to feel very old. We had lost the youthful passion which should survive until death in a questing creature. We had lost it sometime in late adolescence. How could the material world have been predicted to be so joyless? The cry of the poet in *Faust* seems particularly and painfully timely today:

> Then give me back those years long past
> When I could still mature and grow,
> And when a spring of song welled fast
> Out of my heart with ceaseless flow,
> When all the world was veiled in mist,
> When every bud a miracle concealed,
> And when I gathered myriad flowers
> Crowding the valley and the field.
> Though naught was mine, I had enough in youth,
> A joy in illusion, a longing for the Truth.
> Give back the surge of impulse, re-create
> That happiness so steeped in pain,
> The power of love, the strength of hate—
> Oh, give me back my youth again![3]

The sexual revolution not only was a contributor to these trends that reduced passion to appetite and dissolved romance in reason, but was itself a product of these powerful directives that emerged within the twentieth century. A technological revolution was in progress. It was to grant new powers to the human species. The same powers that were directed to dispel the mysteries of the universe seemed to demand that we demystify ourselves. Religion elevated us above the slithery creatures of this earth; the biological and social sciences would establish our kinship. In a peculiar way we reduced ourselves in our expectations. The sexual revolution saw us passing into something that might be called earthworm envy. To those of you unfamiliar with the exotic and delightful potentials in the sexual life of the nematodes, let me explain.

An earthworm is so constructed that one end is male and the other is female. It is quite possible for the male end to be copulating with the female end of another earthworm. Similarly it is possible for the female end of the earthworm to be copulating with the male end of the second earthworm. Finally if the earthworm is alone there is no reason it cannot copulate with itself, and it does.

If human pleasure and human sexuality were to be reduced to an animal level, then why not the level of the earthworm? For if human sexuality is only the gratification of animal instinct, how much better to have the multipotentials of the slimy round creature whose androgyny goes far beyond our feeble attempts through fashion and hairstyle.

But of course human sexuality is not reducible, or must not be reduced, to animal instinct. Human passion is more than just animal lust. What it is, and in what way it is more, must be understood and appreciated. Love in all its aspects, even at the most "animal" level of pure lust, is always influenced by that extraordinary element known as the human imagination. This is the sensibility which transforms human love into something beyond mating or maternal care, something magically and uniquely human.

Romantic love is sexually influenced, but it is transformed by human imagination beyond the potentials of a higher primate, let alone a nematode. It is felt at its most extreme in the exquisite experience of first love, which Turgenev compares to a revolution:

> Sanin and Gemma were in love for the first time, and all the miracles of first love were happening for them. First love is exactly like a revolution: the regular and established order of life is in an instant smashed to fragments; youth stands at the barricade, its bright banner raised high in the air, and sends its ecstatic greetings to the future, whatever it may hold—death or a new life, no matter.[4]

What has all this to do with sexual appetite? Of course romantic love is triggered by that appetite, but we dare not reduce love to instinct or animal appetite. Consider the following scene and try to imagine anything remotely approaching this experience in any other creature. In Mark Helprin's novel *Winter's Tale,* Beverly Penn is dying. She is consumed with a passion that she presumes to be sexual appetite. Peter Lake has broken into her house to rob her of her riches. He watches in amazement as she, instead of resisting, "removed the clasp from the towel that was wrapped about her, and, while leaning back on the pillows as if she were about to suffer a medical examination, undraped herself. She breathed heavily—the feverish breathing—and stared straight ahead." She instructs him to make love to her.

> "If you don't make love to me," she said, "I don't think anyone ever will. I'm eighteen. I've never been kissed on the mouth. I don't know anyone, you see. I'm sorry. But I have a year." She closed her eyes. . . .
> He pulled her in and swung her over and began to kiss her forehead and her hair. At first she was as limp and shocked as someone who has begun to fall from a great height. It was as if her heart had stopped.
> She had not counted on affection. It startled her. He kissed her temples, her cheeks, and her hair, and stroked

her shoulders as tenderly as if she had been a cat. She closed her eyes and cried, much satisfied by the tears as they forced their way past a dark curtain and rolled down her face. . . .

He talked to her for hours. He talked himself dry. She leaned back on the pillows, pleased to be naked in front of him, relaxed, calm, smiling. He talked hills. He talked gardens. What he said was so gentle, strong, and full of counterpoint and rhyme, that he was not even sure that it was not singing. And long before he was all talked out and exhausted, she had fallen in love with him.[5]

Beverly had fallen in love, without ever having been made love to. She had been beguiled by affection, that gentlest component of the amalgam called love, an amalgam as uniquely human as language and literature. The scene, more than mere description, exposes the fallacy of equating human love with an instinct or a drive.

To lay readers, many of whom think of Freud as the founder of a cult of love, it may come as a surprise to discover that love, as a concept, barely exists in the psychoanalytic theory; the word "love" is rarely used. When relationships between people are scientifically examined—which is not often, since the modern Freudian has been more concerned with intrapsychic phenomena than with interpersonal—there is talk of "attachments." By using a word like "attachments" psychoanalysts wittingly or otherwise maintain a separateness that is contradictory to the definition of love that I intend to propose. Barnacles attach. Human beings do more than that. Surely love and the intermingling of human beings is more than simply an attachment.

"Between two people, love itself is the important thing, and that is neither you nor him. It is a third thing you must create,"[6] wrote D. H. Lawrence. It will be my argument that loving does create that "third thing." The fusion of two lovers, intensified over time, breaks down the barriers of the ego, fusing the separate senses of self into a common identity.

The ancient Christians came close to the discovery and enunciation of the phenomenon of fusion in love. But their concern was with the love of man for God. Aware of the Augustinian injunction demanding a clear separation between the nature of God and humanity, and frightened of accusations of heresy, they found a solution by referring to the "glue of love." According to Saint Bernard:

> The union of God and man is brought about not by confusion of natures, but by agreement of wills. Man and God, because they are not of one substance or nature, cannot be called "one thing"; but they are with strict truth called one spirit if they adhere to one another by the glue of love. But this unity is affected not by coherence of essences, but by concurrence of wills. God and man because they exist and are separate with their own wills and substances abide in one another not blended in substance but consentaneous in will.[7]

But man and woman are not of different natures and different essences, and it may be that we ought now to reconsider romantic love in terms of the fusion that was denied in the religious love of its Christian antecedents. In human love there is a "coherence of essences"; we are "blended in substance."

Irving Singer in his invaluable book *The Nature of Love* considers the possibility of merging among people and dismisses the idea:

> The notion that people can merge with one another is, however, a strange idea, elusive, baffling. In everyday life, we realize that one person's experience may have something in common with another's. . . . But we would not ordinarily speak of merging in our personalities, of being or becoming one another. We are distinct individuals,

each living his own life, each responsible for what he
does. . . .
      Let us assume that the concept of merging makes sense.
But how could merging possibly occur in the world as we
know it? By means of magic.[8]

In the biological and psychological world from which I
operate, there is no such creature as a "distinct individual";
human beings are collective creatures, and merger, or fusion
as I prefer to call it, is possible through the "magic" inherent
in the psychoanalytic concept of identification. I will later
describe why the romantic elements were stripped from love
by the reductionism of Freud's early libido theory, and how
we may now restore romance to its rightful place in loving
without abandoning essential psychoanalytic assumptions.
This can be accomplished by building on more sophisticated
current psychoanalytic concepts of identification. The idea
of a nonmagical, nonpsychotic capacity for fusion of our
identities with those of a loved other will be central to that
argument.

The romantic element must be restored to modern life. It
must be added to our relationships to reinstate human love
to its central position in human experience. Further, romance must be rediscovered in our time in order to overcome the mounting sense of isolation, purposelessness, and
ennui. We need something to make sense of an everyday
existence that does not seem to do so now that it has been
stripped of its fundamentalist religious role as a transition to
a better afterlife. We have lost our hopes for heaven. We
need a new good story for our times, a meaning for the
everyday—particularly in an everyday that for most of us
will involve heavy investment of time in the routine and the
mechanical. We need a new here-and-now gospel. We tried
finding it in ourselves. But the individual self is a small and
lonely place. We must find it in communion with others. I

have faith that it can be discovered through love and commitment.

In *Androcles and the Lion,* Shaw makes his most profound statements about faith and commitment. Lavinia, the Christian martyr, is determined to die. The Captain, who is enamored of her, tries every means of persuading her to go through the token conversion required by the Roman state. It is not necessary, the Captain tells Lavinia, that she believe, but simply that she say she does, for after all he really does not "believe in Jupiter and Diana, no more than the Emperor does, or any educated man in Rome."

She answers the Captain saying that what might have been called her faith "has been oozing away minute by minute while I have been sitting here, with death coming nearer and nearer, with reality becoming realer and realer, with stories and dreams fading away into nothing."

> The Captain: "Are you going to die for nothing?"
> Lavinia: "Yes, that's the wonderful thing. It is since all the stories and dreams have gone that I have now no doubt at all that I must die for something greater than dreams and stories."
> The Captain: "But for what?"
> Lavinia: "I don't know. If it were for anything small enough to know, it would be too small to die for."[9]

The most profound aspects of human life will ultimately defy absolute definition and will only be understood by that combination of learning and experience that William James referred to as "knowledge of" and "knowing about." If the nature of love could be encompassed within any single book or any individual philosophy, we would not have the thousands of books, poems, novels, the philosophies and fictions that constitute the literature of love. Yet further books will continue to be written about the nature and experience of love. The proper "knowing about love" is crucial to enable us to fulfill the promise of the experience.

We examine where we came from in psychoanalysis, not only to discover where we are going (to the existentialist we are going nowhere) but to enhance the experience of the present. That of which we are aware is the present with its satisfactions or dissatisfactions; the expectations and the realities; the promise fulfilled or promise betrayed. More and more there is a sense of the lovelessness, the pleasure-lessness, and the purposelessness of modern life. There is a desperate need to reexamine the experience of love.

If psychoanalysis has in part contributed to the neglect of the emotional life in general, the concept of pleasure in the specific, and the principle of love and commitment in particular, it is imperative that those of us in psychoanalysis utilize the insights that unwittingly led us into this condition to help in leading us out of this darkness. It is important to begin thinking in a psychoanalytic way about love—not "cathexes," not "attachments," not "object relationships," but love. In that process we will rediscover romance.

2 ❧ THE NEED FOR LOVE

The premises of psychoanalysis rarely acknowledge any role for the accidental as a determinant in human behavior. It is not by "accident" that I start my case for love by seeking its biological roots. Biology, for those of us trained in its discipline, often becomes a form of religion, particularly when the person exposed to it is not committed to a traditional religion. In this religion *Homo sapiens* is the mysterious and wonderful god in whose service we labor and from whose marvels we draw inspiration and excitement. Most of the major modern influences on my thinking have derived from biologically trained authors.[1] I exclude here for the moment the indirect but profound influence of literature and fiction. I see the imprint of biology on my ideas, on my values, and on my unexamined assumptions, as I see the influence of my natural parents and my cultural antecedents.

In addition, training in modern medicine molds the young physicians in ways that inevitably distinguish their thinking from that of those whose primary training was in philosophy, sociology, or psychology. In the course of this training they will experience the grandeur and the fragility of our species. Through their ignorance they may suffer the grief of costing a patient his life, and with their knowledge they may experience the transcendent joy of saving a life. Both happened to me, and I will remember the details of each event until the day I die. My frame of reference is essentially medical, and the general assumptions that shape my argument are derived from that model.

From the start it is crucial to understand that love is not an embellishment to survival nor a refinement on the human condition. It is not the icing on the cake; it *is* the cake—or to be more precise, an essential ingredient thereof. Love is necessary to sustain human life, and beyond that, necessary to ensure the specifically human qualities of that which survives.

In order to survive, human beings need warmth, water, oxygen, a fuel to energize them (the caloric input of foods), certain specific essential elements (vitamins, trace minerals, salts, amino acids, and the like)—and *people*. And not just any kind of people. As will shortly be argued, they must be caring or loving people. The human infant will surely die without the presence of caring adults, and to develop the specifically human ability to be caring and loving, the infant must experience a minimum quantity of these qualities during the first years of life.[2]

To understand the need for love it is necessary to appreciate some features of our biological nature that distinguish us from lesser creatures. Most of us have little occasion to examine our functions except when they cease to work. We take for granted the miracle that is the human body and the magic that is in its potential. Were I to describe the complexity of so simple an activity as walking, it might occupy six to eight pages. Most of us do the complicated alternation of flexions and extensions of muscles, of articulations and movements of joints, of readjustments of balances without thinking about it. After all, "everybody" can walk from the toddler stage upward. Human locomotion is accepted as ordinary, for one is not used to thinking of everyday and ubiquitous events as miraculous. When a person loses or damages normal locomotion through stroke or injury and attempts to "relearn" to walk, he becomes conscious of the extraordinary and complicated simultaneous steps that must be taken.

Locomotion is hardly a higher function, nor is it uniquely human. Upright locomotion has a special significance in the freeing of our hands for the use of tools and weapons. But our locomotion is no more complicated than that of the porpoise or the ocelot. There are, however, attributes which are so exclusively a product of our species and so special in their applications as to distinguish human beings as separate from the continuum from amoeba to ape that defines the animal kingdom. The human being is not king of the animals; he is *sui generis,* a being apart and above.

In an age of science there is a natural propensity to see ourselves as being simply one part of the animal host.[3] We think this way because we are applying the categories we invented called anthropology, paleontology, and comparative anatomy, which seem to suggest such a continuum, while at the same time the very identification of these sciences clearly suggests a discontinuity. We explore with such sophistication a past that only *Homo sapiens* could even conceptualize. The past as an entity—independent of the concept of its nature—is only recognizable by the human imagination.

Obviously a more religious period clearly perceived human beings as a discontinuity:

And God created man in His own image, in the image of God created He them. And God blessed them; and God said unto them: "Be fruitful and multiply, and replenish the earth, and subdue it: and have dominion over the fish

of the sea, and over the fowl of the air, and over every
living thing that creepeth upon the earth.[4]

While the Old Testament makes sharp distinction between
man and God (it is the New Testament that flirts with fusion), it also makes clear that we are not one among the
many—but something perhaps halfway between. And so we
are.

Once, in a heated but informal discussion, I casually said
that the distance between man and the apes was greater
than that between the apes and the amoeba. This conclusion
was certainly not clearly thought out nor even analyzed. It
was intuitive and probably intended to be provocative. To
my embarrassment the remark was repeated in the presence
of a friend of mine, a distinguished biologist. I was not at all
sure I could defend the position. To my relief my biologist
friend responded to the statement with the indifferent casu-
alness of someone hearing the obvious restated.

We are unique in dozens of ways. For the purposes of this
book it is only necessary to focus on three distinguishing
aspects of our species: the nature of human imagination;
our freedom from instinctual fixation; and the prolonged
dependency period of the human infant.

I am using the broad and somewhat crude category that I
label "human imagination" to encompass the special ingredients which, in a more specific and detailed analysis, could
be said to compose human intelligence: the capacity for
learning, analytic reasoning, the capacity for synthetic reasoning or creativity, the capacity for knowledge and its ac-
cretion and transmission from one generation to another,
true language, fantasy, abstraction, long-range anticipation
(the discovery of the future), and so on. In other words, by
imagination I mean those special functions of the human
brain beyond just simple intelligence that make human

thought and perception different from thought and
tion in all other animals, and human experience ι
Our imagination enables us alone among creatures to create
the very world we will live in and helps to determine what
we ourselves shall become. In the words of the distinguished
human geneticist Theodosius Dobzhansky: "By changing
what he knows about the world man changes the world that
he knows; and by changing the world in which he lives man
changes himself. . . . Evolution need no longer be a destiny
imposed from without; it may conceivably be controlled by
man, in accordance with his wisdom and his values."[5]

The second unique element of the human condition is our
freedom from instinctual fixation. The argument about
whether the human being is truly free is one that has been
debated by philosophers throughout history and in modern
times by such psychologists as B. F. Skinner.[6] Indeed, psychic determinism—the concept that we are not free but that
the present is hostage to the past—is one of the few points
of correspondence between Freudian dynamic psychology
and behaviorism. Both, in a sense, deny certain traditional
concepts of freedom and autonomy, seeing the human being, while not trapped by a genetic code, at least constricted
by his early conditioning and experiences.

Whether people are truly free and autonomous, whether
choices are available, whether we can form rational decisions or merely offer up rationalizations for decisions that
are predetermined by our history, we do know that there is
something, call it freedom or not, that distinguishes human
behavior from all other behavior. It is the degree to which
we are freed from instinctual patterning; the degree to which
we can for good or for evil alter our most profound biological directives. A little girl is in the present devoted to her
mother, or not devoted, by the sum total of her experiences
with her mother and all others in the past. A duckling is

"devoted" to its mother by conditions of bonding. If a horse passes the duckling's visual field before Mama Duck, it will be the old gray mare to which Donald will bond.

Where nature dictates to most animals, it only advises or cautions to us. There are certain extreme limits beyond which we dare not tamper with nature, but for the most part, not only may we dare, we are invited to. This is an old idea that must be rediscovered in each generation.

There is a terror of doing "the unnatural," corrupting God's work or intruding on His prerogatives. Across the generations, one sees this response to new and dramatic scientific developments, whether they involve genetic engineering and *in vitro* fertilization or, in an earlier day, attempting to plot the courses of the planets. There is something frightening, if not heretical, in such transgressions on the natural order, particularly where human nature—and the human position in the order of things—is at stake. I sometimes call this irrational element the Frankenstein Factor.[7] There are, of course, rational fears involving the direction in which science may take us, but the special element of anxiety that intrudes when we feel we are fooling with Mother Nature derives from a misunderstanding of our contract with her. Mother Nature wants us to tamper; she designed us with that capacity. We cannot confine human behavior within some limits defined by our nature, because it is of the nature of human beings to change our nature, to be mutable and protean.

As the great Renaissance thinker Pico della Mirandola eloquently reminded his generation:

> Neither a fixed abode nor a form that is thine alone nor any function particular to thyself have I given thee, Adam, to the end that according to thy longing and according to thy judgment thou mayest have and possess what abode, what form, and what functions thou thyself shalt desire.

The nature of all other things is limited and constrained within the bounds of law prescribed by Us. Thou, constrained by no limits, in accordance with thine own free will, in whose hand We have placed thee, shalt ordain for thyself the limits of thy nature.[8]

The same problem was considered in the empirical and homely style of the medieval talmudic scholars when they asked: "If God had intended man to be circumcised why would he not have created him so in the first place?" And the answer which is given is that man alone among creatures is created incomplete with the capacity and privilege of sharing in his design with his Creator.

For good and bad there is some undeniable form of freedom that is built into the nature and the condition of human life. When I make the case for the biological roots for loving, I am not some Pollyanna oblivious to the almost daily reports of children beaten and tortured by their parents. That which is kind and loving can be as selectively destroyed by us and our culture, as it can be enhanced. This option only adds renewed impetus to the need to fully understand the biological underpinnings of human behavior.

The third unique biological aspect of *Homo sapiens* is the prolonged and extreme dependency of the human infant. This condition may seem peculiarly concrete and trivial in comparison with the first two, but it is certainly not. Indeed, it was the one that Freud selected as the central biological condition shaping human experience. Despite his relative neglect of the early dependency period of childhood, Freud was keenly aware of the crucial impact this must have upon the child.

In the last ten or fifteen years of Freud's creative life he attempted a massive reevaluation of his theory out of which were to emerge some of his most profound, startling, contradictory, and inspired statements. In *Inhibitions, Symp-*

toms and Anxiety (1926) Freud cites two crucial factors in human development, one psychological and the other biological:

> The biological factor is the long period of time during which the young of the human species is in a condition of helplessness and dependence. Its intrauterine experience seems to be short compared to that of most animals, and it is sent into the world in a less finished state. . . . The dangers of the outer world have a greater importance for it, so that the value of the object which can alone protect it against them and take the place of its former intrauterine life is enormously enhanced. This biological factor then establishes the earliest situation of danger and creates the *need to be loved* [italics added] which will accompany the child through the rest of its life.[9]

The "object which can alone protect it" is obviously Freud's reference to the loving parent. The uniqueness of man in the prolonged state of his helplessness has been emphasized and confirmed by such distinguished modern biologists as Adolf Portmann:

> The most striking among those marks of our civilized state is the peculiarity of our early development. Instead of continuing in the protection of the mother's body as long as would accord with our superior brain development, we are born as helpless creatures—in contrast to the state in which most mammals are born. Instead of beginning our life with well-developed limbs and the ability to move as freely as grown-ups of the species—like deer, calves, foals, like elephant cubs, young giraffes, whales, dolphins and seals—we have a special extrauterine first year very different from all further development, during which we gradually learn both to stand and to talk through social contact; we also learn purposeful action, the specific human fashion of controlling environment. None of these three facilities will be fully achieved if so-

cial contact is lacking or inferior. That is one of the reasons why biologists are eager to bring up both the correspondences and the differences between the behavior of man and of the animals most closely related to him.[10]

Why is the child born so helpless and why does he remain that way for so long a time? What possible reason would Freud have to place this in the peculiar position of biological primacy that he does? And, finally, why is this so crucial a factor in a consideration of love?

The human infant must be born "prematurely"—at least in comparison with other mammals—because of that extraordinary organ the human brain. Given the peculiar nature of the human pelvis forced on it by our upright posture the fetus must be born in an unreasonable state of unpreparedness for life. The rapid growth of the human brain demands birth at nine months of gestation. Otherwise it could not pass through the birth canal. The human brain weighs roughly 350 grams at birth, but by the end of the first year of life it will have grown to 825 grams! That is over half its potential brain growth; the normal adult brain weighs 1,400 grams. In other words, the one-year old, at 10 to 15 percent of his adult body weight, has nearly 60 percent of his brain matter. This explains the truly astounding rate of learning of which the child is capable.

At one year of age, the human infant more closely resembles what one would expect a mammalian fetus to be at birth, although on closer examination one realizes that he will, by any standard of measurement, remain dependent for a greater proportion of his life potential than any other creature. The unparalleled physical helplessness of the human infant explains why many biologists have referred to the first year of life as a secondary stage of fetal existence.

There is another group of peculiar animals that are born

tiny and helpless and, indeed, have an extrauterine stage of development. These are the marsupials, best represented by the kangaroo. The tiny kangaroo emerges from the birth canal, attaches itself within a protective pouch to the nipple of its mother, and stays glued there, like a parasite, during its final periods of gestation. The pouch truly is an extra-uterine equivalent of the placenta. But the human fetus has no protective pouch. Obviously there must be some equivalent mechanism to protect the equally vulnerable human fetus. A loving and caring concern for the infant must be biologically and genetically inherent in the parental adults as the human equivalent of the marsupial's pouch. This is what links the arguments for the biological need for love to a biological capacity for love. No animal infant so constructed could survive if it were not assured of an adult community committed to its care. The need for love is the ultimate proof of the caring nature of our species.

The loving response of the parents to the child cannot be an accident of culture. There have been only thirty thousand years or so of developed culture in the two million years or so of human existence, which suggests that a precultural—and therefore natural and unlearned—biologically indicated or programmed concern for the young or the infant must be part of the genetic endowment of the human species. There must be some constant biological mechanism to protect so vulnerable a young. The loving responses of the adult organisms to the helplessness of the baby must represent that. Otherwise no species so peculiarly designed could have survived to a point of evolution of culture.

The biological capacity to love is an essential assumption that must emerge from an understanding of the dependency state of the human child. Why, however, would Freud rank this dependency as the preeminent biological factor in hu-

man development? Freud was interested in the psychologi
cal need to be loved in the adult rather than the physical
need for love on the part of the infant. Here too we must
return to the unique psychological and intellectual nature of
the human child.

If gestation is considered to extend through the year beyond birth, it is of an extraordinary and peculiar kind. It is
the gestation of a sensitive, perceptive, and aware "fetus"
who while helpless to protect himself is all too capable of
understanding the perilous nature of his position. This infant is capable of neither fight nor flight, the usual emergency mechanisms built into animals, and he knows that.
He is, however, capable of clutch and cling, and beyond that
capable of eliciting a self-sacrificing devotion from his parents, who can save him. And he knows that, too. This aware
"fetus" with his huge brain is learning lessons which will be
indelibly marked upon him and will be sustained into adult
life. Among those lessons, perhaps the most crucial is the
link between helplessness, love, and survival.

At the turn of the century, this loving response to the child
was assumed by psychologists to be so obvious as not to
warrant analysis or investigation. This caring nature was
usually subsumed under the heading of a "maternal instinct," a term most often associated with the great psychologist William McDougall. It is wrong to think of it either as
an instinct, which by implication has a fixed and immutable
course of development, or as necessarily exclusively maternal. In all adults there is a response to the helpless and the
childlike, and this means all adults in proximal relationship
to the child, not just parents.

Paternity, unlike maternity, is a relatively new and sophisticated self-discovery. In those early days before the discovery of biological paternity, there must have been something

which allowed the father, or male members of the tribe who saw no kinship with the child, to respond to it with affection. Even during desperate periods the child was not seen as an object to satiate the hungers of starvation. Besides the teleological arguments, our everyday experience indicates the vulnerability of most of us to the suffering of a child or even for that matter to the needs of anything that bears childlike features. We respond to creatures that are soft, cuddly, large-eyed, floppy, with a small nose and mouth—a puppy, a kitten, a harp seal.

In the past I have proposed the following. Imagine the possibility of a species that is endangered in precisely the same way that the harp seal is today, but is dramatically different morphologically. Rather than looking soft and cuddly with soulful eyes, a typical characteristic of the infant harp seal, this animal looks like a giant cockroach with a hard, brittle shell, beady eyes, and antennae. It is conceivable that there would still be some diehard nature lovers campaigning to preserve this endangered species, but one feels confident in predicting that in their campaign they would not show a picture of the endangered pups as part of their appeal for support.

The awareness of paternity, enlarging the sense of oneness and identity so central to loving, is capable of enhancing the paternal feeling to a point that rivals the maternal. It may not have the lasting power of a maternal bond that is supported biologically and psychologically through the hormonal changes of pregnancy and nursing, and that is further reinforced by the mother's being assigned the role of primary caretaker, but it is strong when culturally permitted to develop.

One can trace the discovery of paternity through the evolution of myths. The predominance of early myths of maternal gods in primitive societies is seen as indicating the universal assumptions that maternity is the essential and exclusive blood relationship. It is, after all, not an easy thing to discover the causal relationship between copulation and conception nine months after the fact. Certain contemporary primitive cultures still do not accept a relationship between the two.

Similarly the almost inevitable conversion of most cultures from maternal to paternal gods is usually interpreted as being coincident with the discovery of the role of copulation in procreation. The discovery of paternity had to await the development of animal husbandry, farming and agriculture in general. A human concept of paternity could be discovered more readily through observation of the shorter gestation period of animals, or simply from the fact that isolated penned female animals did not reproduce. This knowledge could then be extended into the human experience. At this point an equally false but opposite image emerged, which conceptualized the blood relationship as deriving exclusively from the father. The model was obviously that of the planted seed in the soil. The male sperm represented the germ, the essence, the seminal part of the organism, the seed. Now the maternal body would be reduced to the role of the nurturing earth, supporting the development of the child but not biologically or genetically linked to it. In this misconception, the concept of patriarchy was born.

Once established, paternity allowed for the development of that love that is a product of all the symbolic implications of biological parenthood. Beyond "blood of my blood; flesh of my flesh" there is the sense of linked identities that comes with accepting and experiencing the awesome responsibility for the survival of another human being. C. P. Snow poignantly describes the experience of a new father on first viewing his child:

Soon afterwards she rang and asked the nurse to bring the baby in. When she did so, I stood up and, without finding anything to say, stared at him for what seemed a long time. The nurse—she had a smooth and comely Italianate face—was saying that he was not a whopper, but a fine boy, "all complete and perfect as they say": I scarcely listened, I was looking at the eyes unfocused, rolling and unstable, the hands waving slowly and aimlessly as anemones. I felt utterly alien from this being in her arms: and at the same time I was possessed by the insistence, in which there was nothing like tenderness, which was more savage and angry than tender, that he must live and that nothing bad should happen to him. . . .

I stood and watched her holding the child. Partly I felt I could not get used to it, it was too much for me, it had been too quick, this was only a scene of which I was a spectator. Partly I felt a tug at the fibres, as though I were being called on in a way I did not understand; as though what had entered into me could not yet translate itself into an emotion, into terms of anything I could recognise and feel.[11]

I myself was astonished that this experience could be replicated across a generation, and have reported on my intense response to viewing my first grandchild. I had seen this child within hours of his birth and with that seeing knew, not just understood, the meaning of biological imprinting. His image coursed through me like some secret message to an internal computer, readjusting all the patterns of my consciousness. To the lifetime of experiences that had shaped my characteristic perceptions and behavior a new experience had been added of such magnitude that a new sensibility existed. I knew that from that time an image would be unshakably within me—no, a part of me—and, that in some way I did not understand would inevitably alter, in some way I could not predict, all my awareness and all my judgments.

None of this was thought out. Something had changed, and I instantly knew it without having any inkling of what had changed. I suppose the closest thing would be its antithesis. After a shared lifetime with a spouse, one must feel at the moment of her death, beyond mere grief over the loss of a companion, a sense of oneself suddenly incomplete, bereft of some vital part. Something would seem torn away; a ragged edge would be left, a wound, and all things forever would be different after that. So too was this. Except here something had been added, and an almost painful sense of fullness was present, a sense of "too much" that made me seem stretched to the limits of sensitivity and vulnerability.

This loving and caring capacity is a complex one. We are all aware from the daily headlines of the "unnatural" behavior of the strong toward the weak, of the powerful toward the helpless. One must again keep in mind that among the three central aspects of human nature with which I deal in this chapter, one is the capacity to recreate ourselves in new images. Unfortunately, in some of our kind all traces of love, tenderness, or conscience even toward their own children are missing, and, sadly, they tend to produce children with similar deficiencies. This is what is meant when Dobzhansky alludes to the powerful role of culture in human genetics. This is why I have referred to human development as being the one exception to the Mendelian rules that dominate all other animal behavior. In the human animal acquired characteristics *can* be inherited. In this peculiar fashion *Homo sapiens* operates under Lamarckian laws.

Nonetheless, the evidence for parental caring as a biological and natural phenomenon is overwhelming from at least two areas. One is the experiential one and the other is the transcultural examination of myths. Across cultures the sacrifice of a child has been seen as the ultimate test of faith, whether it was the sacrifice of Isaac that was demanded as a test of Abraham's faith, the death of Iphigenia which Artemis set as the price for Agamemnon's victory over the Trojans, or the Christian concept that the ultimate demonstration of God's love of man was the sacrifice of His Son. Certainly there were times when life was held less dear than now; times when death of the young was so inevitable that only a religion of assured reconciliation and reunion could bring comfort to the multitudes. Still, the persistence of the symbol of the sacrifice of a child as a test of faith across cultures and down through time is testament enough of the value that has almost universally been placed on the life of a child.

A biological mechanism for initiation of maternal caring responses—showing a strong relationship between human mothering and that of herding animals—has recently emerged from some extraordinary work on human mothers. In certain herding animals it had been known that contact with the mother was necessary to initiate maternal responses. These studies indicated that the maternal response of a goat, for example, is not an automatic phenomenon but is dependent on the initial contact with her kid. If a goat is allowed to maintain contact with her kid for the first few days after delivery and then is separated from it she will, despite the separation, resume nurturing her kid on its return. She will do so only on the presentation of her own infant, rejecting a strange one, even to the point of kicking it to death. If she is allowed to remain in the presence of her kid for only a few hours and then separated, sufficient inducement for mothering will still occur, but it will be much more erratic. The mother will then seem incapable of distinguishing her infant from others. She will indiscriminately accept and nurture all young. If she is deprived of her child immediately postpartum she will then reject all infants, including her own, refusing to mother any. In the goat, at least, it seems that the presence of the infant is a necessary stimulus to the very mothering response which in the adult is essential for the child's survival and development.[12]

Using this as a model, neonatologists Klaus, Kennell, and their group, tried to determine if the enforced separation of a human mother from her infant when the infant is born prematurely could have harmful effects on human mothering attitudes. And, indeed, they found this is the case: "Observations in human mothers suggest that affectionate bonds are forming before delivery, but that they are fragile and may easily be altered in the first days of life. . . . Maternal behavior may be altered in some women by a period of separation just as infant behavior is affected by isolation from the mother."[13]

This introduces a new note to the traditional view of early bonding as applied to human beings, making it less parasitic and more symbiotic. Human biological bonding in this view then becomes a model of mutual influence and nourishment where giving and taking are indistinguishable, closely approximating the form of adult love. In addition, the difference between the human mother and the goat is vastly greater than the similarity. The *biological* mechanism for bonding is the exclusive determinant in the goat. In the human being it is one small component, enforcing no imperative behaviors and easily overpowered by psychological and sociological factors. The difference noted in human mothering was only statistically significant, still representing a minority of the mothers.

In very few areas of human behavior is there the fixity of instinct that exists even in higher primates. Psychology and culture are countervalent forces that overwhelm all but the most rigid of genetic determinants in human beings. At this point, I cannot honestly think of any behavior (beyond such primitive infantile maneuvers as sucking) that can transcend a powerful enough environmental influence.

The need for loving, genetically founded on our early state of profound dependency, demands the reciprocal presence of a propensity for giving love on the part of the adults of our species. This seems to me an irrefutable assumption derived from the obvious nature of our biology. A significant question remains. In its essence, is "love" in parental loving the same as "love" in the romantic or sexual context which concerns us here? I am proposing that it is, and will demonstrate later the common elements that underlie all loving.

Having said that, a cautionary note is indicated. The need for love is not the same thing as loving, nor, for that matter, is it the same as falling in love. This would seem to be an obvious statement, but in our current life and culture a great confusion exists. We must unpackage these similar products and examine the critical and different elements of each.

A narcissistic need to be loved seems to have preempted the primary role of active loving. There are almost antithetical distinctions between the need for love and the need to love. An excessive need to be loved is only the persistence of a state of anxiety, a diminished self-confidence, that requires the constant reassurance inherent in expressions of love or adoration. A capacity to give love implies the generosity of a full spirit and a confident ego. The fact that so many in our culture are more concerned with whether they are lovable than whether they have love to offer is evidence of the passivity, immaturity, and anxiety that characterize current relationships.

The reception of love is experienced as intensely pleasurable. In a truly narcissistic state, the "pleasure" seems that perverse form of pleasure that evolves from the alleviation of pain or anxiety. Whether that is true pleasure is an interesting question. Certainly there is a kind of elation when one knows that one has been saved. There is a form of joy in rescue, relief from burden and surcease from pain. If we are to call these "pleasure," then they represent a different form of pleasure from that which is involved in the act and giving of love.

To many, receiving love effortlessly, as a child does— undeserved love, unearned love—is the glorious ideal. It is my contention that it is a less nourishing and less profound experience than the often painful and arduous experience of supplying the love. Obviously much of our attitudes about loving and being loved will be conditioned by our concept of pleasure, for while love is surely more than that, it is at least in great part a form of pleasure. Thus the concept of pleasure that one maintains will in many ways determine one's attitude toward love.

3 ❧ THE NATURE OF PLEASURE

During the spring of 1984, readers of the literary pages of newspapers and magazines were treated to an impassioned and somewhat hysterical discussion of an esoteric event that had occurred in the world of intellectual history some eighty years before. With the publication of Jeffrey Masson's *The Assault on Truth*[1] a critical switch in Freudian theory, which had been part of the training of every psychoanalyst and part of the general knowledge within the psychoanalytic community, was revealed as though a literary detective had discovered a hidden diary, exposing some deliciously salacious fraud.

Something important and unique had indeed occurred. Freud had made a dramatic about-face in his theory of the etiology of neurosis. This was not, however, as modern debate would suggest, some capitulation to bourgeois sensibilities, but a courageous if somewhat wrongheaded turning away from a primary attention to the environment and interpersonal relationships in order to discover the nature of the internal life of the individual. In terms of its reflections on human development this about-face would prove to be a triumph. For the understanding of emotions and for the psychology of love it was to be a disaster.

Why should such an intellectual and distant event be of any interest today? Freud's theory of neurosis was an extension of his view of normal human development. Since his view of human nature was to become *our* view of human nature, it was to change the way most of us perceive and judge ourselves, our motivations, and our relationships. Without going into the technical details of Freudian theory and at the risk of oversimplification, let me summarize what had happened.

Psychology at the turn of the century was a derivative of the new physiology emerging from the laboratories of Wilhelm Wundt and Hermann Helmholtz and the other titans of the nineteenth-century science of human behavior; its other roots extended from the field of clinical medicine. Concepts of vision, perception, and cognition were developing as extensions of neurology, physiology, pathology, and anatomy. Freud was trained in this rigorous German tradition and brought to it for good and bad a poetic vision, the imagination of a creative artist, and "the mind of the moralist."

He was a man interested in large theories, and as such he was as close to the philosophic tradition as he was to the psychological tradition which was then emerging. Nonetheless, he started with the simple tools of a clinician: patients in pain, his observation of them, his attempts to change them, and the deductions one could draw from both success and failure. While he brooked little criticism from others he was constantly in an anguish of self-doubt, changing his theories, evaluating them, and even contradicting them.

In the beginning of his career Freud concluded—on the basis of the pathetically small number of patients available to him—that all neuroses were the products of undischarged, encapsulated, unacceptable and therefore repressed ideas, wishes and impulses. These "foreign bodies" trapped in our memories were poisoning the psychic life of the individual.

As Freud put it, the neurotic was "suffering from reminiscences."

In his early observations the source of these ideas seemed to Freud invariably sexual. The neurotic individual, he proposed, was the victim of a sexual seduction early in his childhood, which when reactivated symbolically in adult life led to a neurosis. After courageously establishing the theory that all neuroses were due to premature childhood seductions—anathema to the Victorians, who were reluctant to publicly acknowledge a sexual life for women, let alone children—Freud was forced by self-criticism to reconsider his basic theory.

While traumatic premature seductions did occur and obviously could contribute to neurosis, three separate sets of observations made it apparent that they could not be the generalized and exclusive cause of neuroses. First he discovered there were "normal" people who either had fantasies of early seduction or actual experience of seduction. If normal people have the same experience as sick people, then that experience cannot alone be sufficient to explain the sickness. Secondly, he became aware of the power of fantasy; many of the "seductions" reported to him were not real but had been fantasized and as such were expressions of the child's own unconscious desires. And finally he became aware that many of the fantasies or statements about early sexuality were iatrogenic—that is, doctor-caused. Freud discovered that many of his patients told him what they sensed he wanted to hear. They were what we today would call transference phenomena.

If certain people exposed to sexual seduction became neurotic while others experiencing the same traumas remained healthy, there must be something in the constitution, the genetic aspects, of human sexuality that responded differently to the trauma, making some resistant to neurosis and others vulnerable. It was necessary then to examine the genetic nature of human sexuality and to seek the sources of psychopathology in the internal complex of the individual.

Freud abandoned the emotive and motivating power of the real world. He did not totally exclude environmental agents in causing neuroses, but from that time on they were to become peripheral and incidental precipitating factors. The internal world became the real stage for acting out of human conflicts. Freud had ironically and perhaps unconsciously returned to his roots in German idealism.

The "libido theory"[2] was the masterpiece of his revised theory and the cornerstone for much of modern psychoanalysis. With this theory, all human behavior could be related to the driving force of the sexual instinct and the counterforces that kept it in check. And Freud meant *all* behavior. Friendship, love, creativity, affection, attitudes toward work, character traits (such as stinginess or sloppiness), religion, and culture are all merely derivatives of the sexual drive. According to Freud, since sex is the only energy source that drives human behavior, all behavior must be sexual behavior in one disguise or another.

The power of the libido theory is that in one grand scheme it provided a mechanism for understanding normal human development, pathology, culture, and nonpathological behavior of all sorts. The *intrapersonal* life of the individual was to become the exclusive focus of the psychoanalyst. Conflict became the central thesis, and particularly intrapsychic conflict. One unfortunate result was that in concentrating on dynamics, conflicts, and ideas (penis envy, Oedipal complex, fixation points, defense mechanisms), the world of emotions was slighted. Of course, the emotions were present—how could one ignore anxiety?—but they were incidental fallout, derivative not causative, and therefore scientifically "uninteresting." Fear was a "product" of repressed libido; anger was conveniently ignored; and pleasure was the name for the discharge of libidinal tension. The attachments, the interrelationships, between people were neglected.

One of Freud's greatest early conceptions was that all human behavior was motivated—all behavior had a goal and a purpose. But even this insight was to suffer from the demands of the libido theory. Now, according to Freud, not only was the energy for all behavior sexual, but the only purpose, the only goal, of behavior was sexual.

The patients could have told the modern psychoanalysts otherwise. They do not come to treatment to resolve some ideational conflict, particularly when it exists in an internal and unconscious world of unawareness. They come because they are in pain. Pain is emotional, and not incidentally is usually generated in relationships. Nonetheless, the libido theory thought it had the answer.

Crucial to the libido theory was this peculiarly narrow concept of motivation. What drives human behavior? Freud saw all human behavior as being driven by pleasure. But in his definitions he trivialized pleasure. He cast the human being as a totally hedonistic animal, instinctually driven like some migrating bird or rutting beast. He defined pleasure exclusively in something akin to physiological terms, ignoring the transcendent power of human imagination to mitigate and modify even thirst and hunger. Pleasure, according to the libido theory, was neither more nor less than the experience of sexual release; pain was simply impounded or frustrated sexual release. It has been described by many as a hydraulic principle. The backup of sexual energy (seen almost in a fluid form) created pressure and tension, demanding release. The pleasure then was in the release and relief of this tension.

The drive for instinctual (sexual) gratification was labeled the pleasure principle, and for a preponderant time in psychoanalytic theory was viewed as the sole motivating force from which all human behavior was presumed to derive (and is still so viewed by many psychoanalysts today). This construction was more suited to explaining the mechanisms of urination and bladder function than the complex subject of human pleasure and human motivation. In addition, it was based on an archaic and faulty model of energy. Pleasure as seen by Freud was almost a peripheral neurological function. How could it explain the poetic sources of pleasure available to the human imagination? In Whitman's words:

> Grand is the seen, the light, to me—grand are the sky
>   and stars,
> Grand is the earth, and grand are lasting time and space,
> And grand their laws, so multiform, puzzling,
>   evolutionary;
> But grander far the unseen soul of me, comprehending,
>   endowing all those,
> Lighting the light, the sky and stars, delving the earth,
>   sailing the sea.
> (What were all those, indeed, without thee, unseen soul?
>   of what amount without thee?)
> More evolutionary, vast, puzzling, O my soul!
> More multiform far—more lasting thou than they.[3]

There is no way the libido theory can account for the sense of joy and pleasure described here by Walt Whitman. Nevertheless, despite all its limitations, the libido theory provided such a stunning framework for future research, allowing many theoreticians to construct new concepts of human behavior, both normal and pathological, that it concentrated the attention of psychoanalysts from that point forward. And they took the bad with the good. Many of the early psychoanalysts had serious questions about the energy components of the libido theory, including Karen Horney, Clara Thompson, Erich Fromm, Abram Kardiner, Sandor Rado, and others, and for these doubts they were driven from the temple of the orthodox community of psychoanalysis. Surprisingly, what was little attended to even by these renegades was the degradation of the concept of pleasure inherent in this theory.

Freud was too keen an observer of human behavior to underestimate the power of work, creativity, friendship, and even love. How could all of this be derived from sexual instinct? To this end, Freud traced a genetically determined line of development for the libido, and established points along the way to which he could attach such "derivative" phenomena as character traits, and any seemingly nonsexual interests.

Since the child is incapable of sexual pleasure from sexual intercourse, Freud postulated that it is incapable of pleasure in relationships at all. The only thing a child is capable of enjoying is itself, or to be more precise, parts of itself—its mouth, its anus, its genitals. Not being an earthworm, it cannot have intercourse with itself, so infantile pleasure is mediated through such activities as eating, defecating, exhibitionism, voyeurism, and the like.

It is only with maturation that we bring all these "polymorphous perverse" mechanisms together, unify them in a drive toward sexual gratification through intercourse, and free ourselves from our attachments to our own parts and to ourselves. Only after we have freed ourselves from our "autoerotism" will we be able to love or to have sexual desire for another. These fractional elements of early sex become the "fixation points" from which all other energy-consuming activities derive. Freud then elaborates an intriguing repertory of mechanisms to relate pleasure to early infantile pleasure.

If one has a character trait of neatness or tidiness, it can be a "reaction formation" against the primitive infantile pleasure in smearing feces. Alternatively, if one has this same primitive desire, one need not react against it but can "sublimate" it—that is, elevate it to a higher purpose, perhaps by becoming a painter or potter, engaging in a socially acceptable form of smearing and messing. Friendship is nothing more than an "aim-inhibited" form of the sexual drive. So, too, character traits, occupations, interests, eventually religion, and *all* human activities can be related to the vicissitudes of the sexual instinct. Same stuff, simply different disguised end points.

But the pleasure described in the libido theory simply will not do. It does not adequately explain human sexual behavior, with its un-animal-like dependence on romance, idealization, and imagination. It certainly does not begin to encompass the complex nature of human pleasure. And it contributes nothing to the understanding of love, as Wallace Stevens observes:

If sex were all, then every trembling hand could make us squeak, like dolls, the wished-for words.[4]

Surely there is a pleasure beyond the pleasure principle.

Pleasure Beyond the Pleasure Principle

Pleasure is a feeling of well-being, a joyous feeling, a good feeling, a feeling of satisfaction—but if nothing else, it is first a feeling. Feelings and emotions are not things that are inherent in all animal creatures. There are organisms that do quite well without any of them.[5] I am fond of citing the amoeba, which has, one feels safe to presume, no feelings. Nonetheless the survival probability of the amoeba is greater than that of the human race. The amoeba has a much simpler mechanism for surviving. It is an empiricist. It attempts to ingest all subjects with which it comes into random contact. It is not motivated. It moves about at random and eventually it will bump into "something." It will attempt to absorb that something as a nutrient. If the something is not absorbable and not a nutrient the amoeba will eject it. If it is, the amoeba will ingest it, satisfying caloric needs. One need not speculate about emotion, drive, motive, purpose, intention, planning, or cognition here.

As one ascends the ladder from lower animal forms one sees the emergence of something I will call sensations, as distinguished from feelings or emotions. I reserve the use of the term "feelings" for that aspect of the emotional life that is felt or perceived—feeling proud, touched, ashamed, hurt, disgusted, loathsome, happy, sad, etc. I will refer to the appreciation of the modalities of heat, pain, cold, etc. as sensations.

The sensation of pain exists in some very primitive animals, and so does something, I suppose, that has to be called pleasure, although I am reluctant to grace it with that term. That is, there are animal forms which are hedonically regulated—their actions are controlled by primitive pain and pleasure. These animals are engaged in purposive or motivated behavior; they avoid those things which are self-destructive and seek out those things which enhance survival. This need not involve thinking. Hedonic regulation may be as simple-minded as the controls of a thermostat. The stimulus of painful hunger initiates behavior to procure food. Eating relieves the pain or tension and produces the sensation of satiation, or call it, if you will, pleasure. The same model will suffice for sexual tension and gratification. Between the two we have the basic ingredients for individual and species survival.

Hedonic regulation can direct through a positive response—can we call this pleasure?—to the color or smell of a plant that is particularly nutritious, but for the most part this does not require pain or pleasure. It can be automatically and instinctively controlled. One sees this in the heliotropic response of plants to light, and in the response of maternal birds to the open jaws of the young. One can appreciate the mechanical and essentially simple-minded quality of this apparent loving care of the nestlings (it is certainly not parental solicitude) by observing its corruption. When a cuckoo chick displaces the much smaller warbler chick from its nest, the massive open mouth of the giant cuckoo baby drives the confused small parent songbirds to distraction and ultimately to death in their attempts to feed this monstrous usurper of the rightful space of their own progeny.

The kinds of pain and pleasure that produce hedonic regulation undoubtedly occur at a very early level of development. It is conceivable that a mutation could occur which was anhedonic—that is, some animal form that loved toxins and loathed nutrients could be born. The Darwinian assumptions allow for such a development. But that unfortunate mutation could not survive past the first generation and would not be able to transmit its genetic code and create a new species.

What I call true emotions or complex emotions await a more sophisticated anatomy and physiology than are possessed by, say, a clam. They require at a minimum the presence of distance receptors. For true emotions we must have in place some organ of sight, hearing, smell, or sensitivity to vibrations. This alone allows for anticipatory warnings which underlie the basic *emotions* of survival, fear, and rage.

An organism without distance receptors but with a central nervous system that could mediate pain (and pleasure, although both are not necessary) would experience the dangerous situation at the moment of contact. When the shark's teeth bit into the animal's flesh the sensation of pain would occur and it would know that it was in contact with a "maladaptive" situation. While I would not deny the helpfulness of this, its limitations are obvious. Such defenses as simple sensate pain are more useful against self-inflicted wounds than against predators. Certain tastes become disgusting—through Darwinian selection—because they are toxic; the disgusting taste serves species survival.

To return now to the case of the shark and the pain, if an organism is capable of seeing the shark in the distance or smelling it or hearing it, the organism can identify the predator at a time when escape is still possible. By "identify" I do not mean an anthropomorphic capacity to conceptualize something as "shark" or even "predator." At the simplest level the shark smell, sight, sound, or vibrations will directly initiate the action of flight. Nonetheless, as one ascends the ladder there will emerge species that will be freed from the fixed instinctive flight or fight. Intervening emotions of fear or rage will allow for delay, decision, choice—some emotional modification of the instinctual pattern. Distance receptors anticipate the event and enhance survival by buying time and offering options guided by these emotional indicators.

Emotions not only alert us but activate the process necessary to fulfill the act of survival—muscles are tensed, blood is redistributed, all of the processes to facilitate the fight or flight response are set in motion. Another intriguing aspect of emotions is that they may be transmitted, one to another.

One sees this in herding animals. It is not necessary for every member of the herd to sight the stalking lion. The sensation of fear generated in one will mobilize fear in the others. In group animals—and *Homo sapiens* is a group animal—feelings are contagious. Emotions are powerful motivators of behavior, providing an edge on survival. They also are an instrument of communication with our own kind. They bind us together into survival units.

In the area of emotions the human species is in a class by itself. We do not just possess the emergency emotions of fear and rage. We have subtle small passions. We have pride, shame, and guilt. We feel hurt and touched. These smaller emotions significantly modify the emergency emotions of fear and rage, and commingle with our intelligence in guiding our actions. One of the most mischievous false perceptions is the casting of emotion as the enemy of reason. Feelings are a necessary adjunct to—not the antagonist of—our freedom from instinctual fixation and our intelligence. Because we have so many options for actions that are not dictated by automatic responses, we depend on these emotional signals to indicate the best immediate response, and if it turns out our judgment was incorrect, the emotions will guide us to alternative behavior to modify the unproductive response after the fact.

Anxiety will keep us from diving into a dangerous current. Shame, at the fact that we are allowing our friend who cannot swim to be carried away, will overcome our fear. Pride in ourselves for having saved his life will influence our behavior in some future event, which may have nothing to do with river currents, but through our power of abstraction will be seen as possessing the same balance of self-risk and service.

Just as our emotions influence our reasoning, our intelligence informs our emotions. With the advanced intelligence of the human species, we do not have to wait for the distant receptors to operate. We can learn through experience that certain waters at certain times of the year contain sharks and are dangerous—and we can avoid them. Beyond personal experience, we can learn this through our studies of the habits of sea creatures; we can analyze, predict, and generalize about shark behavior. Nor do "we" have to do it. We may learn it from others who have learned it, even if such knowledge was acquired in a previous generation. This is another example of that capacity to transmit knowledge from one generation to another which I have called the "Lamarckian" aspect of human genetics, the aspect that so profoundly differentiates our species from all others.

No songbird whose nest has been usurped by the cuckoo is ever going to "wise up," or be able to relate his sad experience for the edification of his fellow songbirds. Songbirds are protected as species by other mechanisms. If the cuckoo is too successful it may destroy the generation of songbirds that supports it, and in so doing limit its own species' chance for survival.

The wonder of language and accumulated knowledge permits us to avoid dangerous places. It allows us to build natural defenses to avoid even the potential of danger. We can build shelters, develop the science of meteorology, manufacture weapons that will defend us from much stronger creatures, and change the conditions that define that which is dangerous. Of course, our imagination and intelligence will also allow us to perceive and anticipate falsely as well as correctly, and this can lead to paranoia, isolation, and potential self-destruction in a nuclear war.

Human emotions are of a different order from those of the lower creatures. In addition, all considerations of human emotions must acknowledge the extraordinary influence of the human imagination and intelligence on even our simplest emotions. If fear can be mitigated by knowledge, or overcome by shame or pride, then what must be the case with pleasure and love? There is no pleasure that cannot be influenced by guilt, that is not vulnerable to fear, that cannot be intensified through idealization and imagination, or that is not defined in part through a value system "inherited" or instilled by our parents and our culture. One certainly can understand this in relation to the complexity of love, but it is also relevant in the primitive pleasure drives. Human eating and human sexual appetite are simply not reducible to the level of animal instinct or capable of being understood in that limited context.

Certainly one cannot think of a "maternal instinct" in human beings that is not modified by knowledge and imagination. It is possible that an advanced ape may feel the same kind of maternal, protective "love" that a mature woman does. It is unlikely that out of that love the mature ape can do something that in the short run seems destructive—such as allow a stranger to inflict pain on her child—to satisfy the long-run survival of her infant. It is not just that the ape does not have the intelligence to conceive of surgery, for example, but the nature of the maternal instinct, if present, will be relatively fixed and unmodifiable, and therefore not susceptible to imagination and knowledge. Consider the concept that surgical amputation of a cancerous limb that to all outward appearances is perfectly functional may be necessary, and therefore desirable, to save the life of the child even while destroying its locomotion. Every phrase of this statement is beyond the ape's potential for understanding, and would be resisted by the ape mother's maternal instinct.

Pleasure, then, is one aspect of human emotionality—a form of joy, delight, satisfaction—that obviously is not directly analogous to the pleasure of any other animal. Certainly it cannot be reduced in the way that Freud attempted to the level of the most primitive animal instinct. If pleasure and pain were exclusively the products of instinctual release or instinctual frustration, we would be reduced not to the level of an ape but to the level of a mouse.

A further failure or limitation of the pleasure principle was its naive assumption that pleasure and pain are polar phenomena. There is no question that the great pleasures of human existence inevitably involve pain. When I examine my own life and list those things which have given me pleasure, first and foremost has been the experience of raising my children, although that is being challenged at this point by the immense pleasure of relating to grandchildren.

The great joys of raising children to maturity, and the multiple interactions with them in the process, have also encompassed some of the most painful experiences of my life: the vulnerability; the need to discipline; the pain of disciplining; the terror of that extended self which is the child, and over which one has so much less control; the fear of letting go; the paternalistic awareness of superior judgment, and yet the need to allow the child the autonomy to become an adult; the experiencing of the child's anguish even when one knows the triviality and unworthiness of its cause. The list can be almost indefinitely extended by every parent. The most painful experiences of my life have been involved with the fears, the expectations, the angers, the guilts, and the responsibilities of loving and raising my daughters.

In my first attempt to understand the mechanisms of pleasure (as part of a general examination of the nature of feelings) I recognized at least two major difficulties. Coming out of the field of medicine and psychiatry I am better conditioned to evaluate something that does not work than something that does. Psychiatry as a branch of medicine has always been more successful in dealing with pain than with pleasure, with sickness than with health. I am not sure, however, that our experience is much different from that of others; it is generally easier to analyze failure than success. Unfortunately, we are then likely to define success as the absence of failure, pleasure as the alleviation of pain—sexual pleasure as the experience of the relief of discharging sexual tension. Surely, there is some positive sense of pleasure. We have all experienced it. We know what it feels like to feel good. We even know that mystical experience of feeling good when we have no idea what has happened or what has changed or what justifies the feeling. A feeling of transcendent pleasure can occur seemingly unrelated to any event.

The second problem in defining pleasure is the diversity of forms in which we may experience it. Yet to make any sense out of the abstract concept of pleasure, we must find some common ingredient that binds together such diverse activities as skiing, reading, eating, having a massage, or writing a poem. A favorite quotation comes from the writings of that titan of eighteenth-century American letters Jonathan Edwards. I find this quotation extraordinarily appealing because although the source of pleasure is remote from our modern experience, the expression of pleasure is readily identifiable today:

> The whole book of Canticles used to be pleasant to me, and I used to be much in reading it . . . and found, from time to time, an inward sweetness that would carry me away in my contemplations. This I know not how to express otherwise than by a calm, sweet abstraction of soul from all the concerns of this world. . . . The sense I had of divine things would often of a sudden kindle up, as it were, a sweet burning in my heart; an ardor of soul, that I know not how to express.[6]

Most of us today do not share Jonathan Edwards's delight in the Canticles or even his religious convictions. But the abandonment of a belief in God elevates the role of pleasure. If this world is all we have, this world must be worth having. Peter De Vries, in coming to terms with his daughter's death, is comforted by the discovery of a taped message from his dying daughter, quoting his own words back to him:

> I believe that man must learn to live without those consolations called religious, which his own intelligence must by now have told him belong to the childhood of the race. Philosophy can really give us nothing permanent to believe either; it is too rich in answers, each canceling out the rest. The quest for Meaning is foredoomed. Human life "means" nothing. But that is not to say that it is not worth living. What does a Debussy *Arabesque* "mean," or a rainbow or a rose? A man delights in all of these, knowing himself to be no more—a wisp of music and a haze of dreams dissolving against the sun. Man has only his own two feet to stand on, his own human trinity to see him through: Reason, Courage, and Grace. And the first plus the second equals the third.[7]

Despite the differing forms of pleasure, there does seem to be one basic ingredient common to all. Those activities which give us pleasure will, in one form or another, enhance and expand, enlarge and elevate our sense of self. By "enhance" I do not mean simply "intensify" but, as the dictionary says, "to make greater, as in . . . value or attractiveness; to heighten, improve, and augment." Pain can, in one peculiar sense, also intensify our self-awareness, but it will eventually destroy the sense of self. While I have said that pain is an essential component of complex pleasure, certainly I am aware that pain and pleasure as end points are different phenomena.

With the attempt to see this common binding definition of pleasure as a form of self-enhancement in mind, it is worth looking at some categories of sources of pleasure. It is logical to start with the simple form of sensory pleasure—the basic elemental pleasure that comes from eating, orgastic release, stroking, the scent of a flower, and the like. Even here at the simplest sensory level it becomes difficult to avoid the secondary elaboration that almost inevitably complicates all human experience. The things that "delight" the eye of the animal are probably limited to the sight of a prey, a mate in season, and possibly the view of a parent or offspring. But the human eye perceives as it sees and integrates its simple perception into a matrix of experience and sensibilities, permitting an exclusively human delight such as Gerard Manley Hopkins expresses:

Glory be to God for dappled things—
For skies of couple-colour as a brindled cow;
For rose-moles all in stripple upon trout that swim;
Fresh-firecoal chestnut-falls; finches' wings;
Landscape plotted and pieced—fold, fallow, and plough;
And all trades, their gear and tackle and trim.
All things counter, original, spare, strange;
Whatever is fickle, freckles (who knows how?)
With swift, slow; sweet, sour; adazzle, dim;
He fathers-forth whose beauty is past change:
Praise him.[8]

All human sensory functions can be elaborated, symbolized, and enriched by association and imagination. In this category I wish to include the pleasure of eating, for example, as distinguished from the pleasure of dining, which would inevitably have an amalgam of other associations; the simple pleasure of being stroked, independent of the meaning of that stroke and from whom it is received. That the pleasure is enhanced when the stroke is a sign of love will be part of the argument that will evolve on the nature of love. Similarly, human visual and auditory pleasures are rarely exclusively "sensate." Beyond that, the pleasurable stimulus is most often itself an artifact of human imagination. In the following scene from Antonia White's *The Lost Traveller,* Clara is attending the opera with her father:

> In spite of all his warnings she could not help being disconcerted that both Venus and Tannhäuser should be so elderly and so very fat. But the smell of scent and dust, the glimmer of white shirt fronts and creamy shoulders in the vast dim house, the sense of being present at some extraordinary ritual soon produced a kind of intoxication. She forgot everything and let herself drown in the sensuous, easy music.
>
> When the lights went up, she and Claude blinked at each other as if waking from the same rapturous dream.[9]

I hesitate to label even those unadorned sensate pleasures as "simple," because in many ways they are the most fundamental pleasures of life. It is crucial that orgastic release or slaking of thirst be intense pleasures. They support survival. One might think of these as primary pleasures, although again "primary" seems to give them an ascendancy over the other pleasures for which I have already indicated a bias. Perhaps "primitive" is best, because they are pleasures that we can associate with lower animals. Because they are primitive and because they are in a certain sense simple does not mean they can be ignored or minimized. After all, the absence of such pleasures militates against *any* pleasure. The more complex pleasures are luxuries whose presence is contingent on the preexistence of minimal conditions of survival. When there are pain, grief, and despair because of actual want and actual deprivation, when there is no surcease from the onslaught of the elements or the pain of hunger, all else becomes luxury and meaningless.

A second source of pleasure is that inherent in play. I put this second because it, too, is something we share with lower animals. That animals enjoy play is obvious to anyone who has had a pet. If you have had the misfortune of sharing a beach house with a retriever, or even a neighbor's retriever, you know the insatiability of their joy in retrieving anything thrown, and can appreciate the close linkage between the nature of their play and a fundamental biological function. Of course, it is chancy when generalizing about animals to talk about domestic animals. They are so much a part of the human existence that their very genetic natures have been modified to accommodate our needs.

Unwittingly, by suggesting the retriever, I have stumbled on an example of such accommodation. What possible use could retrieving—that is, the act of fetching and carrying game undamaged back to a person—have if there were not the presence of a "person"? Why shouldn't the dog, if hungry, devour the bird for food? The retriever is an artifact, in a sense a plaything, of the human being. Nonetheless, it too enjoys the play. The retrieving tendency is so much a part of it that even in conditions where hunting is unthinkable—a beach house on Cape Cod, for example—the retriever will delight in retrieving anything. If you should fall victim to its seductive appeals and throw a ball or a piece of driftwood into the water you are doomed to an afternoon of nagging that is not dissimilar to the nagging desire for attention of a two-year-old. The joy in retrieving is no less genuine for being the genetic creation of man.

Yet animals do play, and play may serve for them the same function as it was originally intended to serve for human beings—as an initiation into activities that are essential for life, as a sharpening of tools, as a testing of aggression, and as a learning of limits of tolerated behavior within a group for those animals which are group animals. Play for adult humans has an obvious further function as an alternative to, or simulation of, competitive areas of life that may now be too distressing or dangerous. As in the tourneys of the medieval world we can joust with blunted spears while savoring victory or nursing a defeat that is less than life-threatening. We can also test ourselves against limits without the humiliations and risks inherent in such activities in the real world.

It is somewhat distressing to see the corruption of play as a form of pleasure in human beings by an intensification of the competition to a point of potential humiliation. In some play, competition heightens the pleasure, and in addition is one of the safest and most culturally satisfying means of siphoning off the rage and frustration of everyday life.[10] But we have found ways of increasing the competition to a point of sacrificing the pleasure. In a society in which everyone feels insecure and every element of activity must be perverted into a reassurance rather than a form of pleasure, winning becomes all. The ugliness of some spectator sports has made them only too similar to a Roman circus, only now death is more likely to come to the spectators.

The competitive aspect of Little League, for example, has been attacked from a number of quarters. I have not found the competition of Little League that intense or objectionable. I know of no one more naturally competitive than young boys. Screaming, ranting, and hysteria—violence threatening to emerge at every point—is a characteristic of young boys at play. It is not a characteristic of young girls at play, a gender difference that has been noticed and is beginning to be analyzed.[11] My chief objection to Little League is that it corrupts the children's game that was intended to serve all of the purposes of play, including the release of aggression, by converting it into a performance. The child no longer is driven by his own needs and pleasures. These are compromised by the presence of an audience of parents who will either approve or disapprove his "performance." Here we see a prime example of the proclivity of our time to degrade the natural and normal into a narcissistic preoccupation with being approved and being loved.

A third category of pleasure is discovery. To really appreciate the joy in discovery one has to have had the opportunity to observe a toddler. The almost frantic delight in poking, pulling, hammering, emptying, examining, upturning, climbing—the incessant activity that is the toddler's day—is enough to exhaust the average adult merely by observation, never mind repetition. Experiments done many years ago in which trained athletes attempted to replicate the activities of toddlers during the course of an average day exhausted the athletes beyond their capacity when the toddlers were obviously just getting warmed up.

Discovery, some compulsion to move on and find more, takes us well beyond the mere sensate. Discovery joins our intellectual need for knowledge (whatever may feed that) with some built-in pleasure system that gives delight in the seeing, feeling, touching, and sensing of the new. This delight in new experience is an essential part of the human being. One sees it not just in the unrelenting probing of the one-year-old, but in her imitative play, which leads not only to performance skills but eventually to language. And one sees it in the incessant "whys" of the three-to-five-year-olds. This delight in discovery nurtures intellectual curiosity. It is the primal trait underlying scientific curiosity and is what Dr. Johnson called the "hunger of imagination which preys incessantly upon life."

Discovery can totally abandon sensation and still produce

pleasure. There is a form of pure discovery that exists in the intellectual world, the discovery that involves no motion, only imagination. No acrobatics, only mental acrobatics.

Our intellect frees us from the limits of our own experience. It allows us to transcend our own world, our own time, and even our own identity. We can travel to foreign lands, to distant times, or identify with the heroic despite the humbleness of our current position. If I am honest, when asked to list the books I have enjoyed most, as distinguished from those I most value, one book that must head the list is Stevenson's *Treasure Island*. I read this book at least once a year from the time I began reading (seven or eight) to an age so advanced I am almost ashamed to admit it. I remember during college, when I was neurotically avoiding my assigned readings, reaching for *Treasure Island* like an anxious child groping for his "blankie" or favorite stuffed animal and finding comfort in it. I do not particularly recall covering it with a plain paper wrapper, but I am sure that in the pseudosophisticated milieu of the undergraduate I would have been more ashamed to be caught reading it than the hardest of hard-core pornography. The mere thinking of *Treasure Island* during the course of writing this book drove me to it again. It is still wonderful!

What was the allure of this book to me as a child? Something exotic vested in the different space and different time; the concept of the sea, which in my Midwestern childhood I had never seen; the romance of good and evil; and above all the heroic sweep of the adventure with an adolescent boy (and how I identified with Jim Hawkins) at its center. I have a grandson now, who in anticipation of a movie or a book wants to know if there are any "bad guys" in it. I know precisely what he means. He does not like to be frightened, so it is not the presence of a villain that he wishes. If there are "bad guys" then there must be "good guys." Their presence will guarantee conflict and adventure; there must be (in children's books) a clear moral dimension—the triumph of the good; there must be a heroic, as distinguished from an everyday, dimension. He is looking for those elements that have been stripped from twentieth-century experience, the heroic and the romantic.

When I ask women friends of my generation (to control the variables of a different time and culture) what books they have enjoyed most, the book most often mentioned is *Little Women*. The difference between these two books is really quite startling. In children's literature, identification is essential, and the prepubescent child is relatively limited in this capacity. A twelve-year-old girl wants a heroine, not a male protagonist (that is why we had Nancy Drew and Tom Swift as parallel series) and she wants her to be between twelve and twenty-two, not an old lady of thirty-five, like her mother. Certainly there is romance in *Little Women*, and there is the exotic element of an earlier time frame, although the book was in its time a successful contemporary novel. But it is not heroic. Its drama is in the relationships, its suspense is in the character developments, and its romance is in the discovery of love. All point to some difference in gender needs.

Beyond gender difference there may also be a time-of-life difference. Most children read little nonfiction. They prefer fiction, or romantic biography, which to them can be a form of fiction. As adults, many of us turn to history, current affairs, and philosophy. I believe the answer may lie in the smallness of the child's world and the largeness of the adult's. To the child, exploding with new passions emerging at rapid-fire rates, and growth so rampant that a new body seems daily emerging, life seems a conspiracy of constraint. The child's life is hedged in by school bells and bedtimes. He is bursting out of his skin in a world of "not-nows" and "not-for-yous." He is too big for the confinement of his scheduled existence and must escape into the larger world of fantasy through fiction. As adults, the world is too much with us. We are becoming aware of our smallness in relation to the larger order; we are frightened by how little we matter in the scheme of things and how little time we are allotted. We want to understand the nature of existence, and through understanding, to define and confine it. We want to rationalize and humanize our experience. We want to expand the shrinking self by reducing the larger world around us.

All children originally have joy in discovery. It is part of the common developmental experience. One can even see a purpose in this pleasure. Discovery is probably an essential ingredient in the process which will lead a child away from the protection of the mother into the larger world. As a child goes through the period from one to two, her play becomes progressively more independent of the protective parent. I do not mean simply that she will no longer need the parent to play with her, since for the most part the baby plays by herself anyway. The one-year-old is reluctant to play by herself, because she is reluctant to *be* by herself. She needs that security—the reassurance of the parent in the room, within eyesight or earshot—to allow her to indulge her autonomous pleasures in discovery. As she gets older that very need to discover will give her the courage to move from one room to another, to become so absorbed and occupied in an activity that she will automatically and unknowingly distance herself from her parent. Discovery then becomes part of the process of separation that leads to autonomy and maturity.

The two-year-old is a bundle of curiosity, explorer, adventurer, philosopher, and scientist. What in God's name happens to this questing creature? How is it that as our pleasure in the sensual and physical world seems to expand as we grow through adolescence, so many of us will lose this other source of joy? I suppose they could be alternatives; that one replaces the need for the other. But why? Why should they not supplement? In many people's lives they can. The people I know who enjoy discovery and the world of ideas seem equally at home with the world of physical pleasure. Surely they need not be alternate sources of pleasure.

Perhaps there is a natural attrition of pleasure in discovery. Intellectual discovery is said by some to atrophy with aging, although I doubt that. One finds in some of the aged— as their choice for physical activity becomes limited by illness or the limitations of aging; as their sexual drive is attenuated; as their sensate capacities wane—a salvation in the intellectual sphere. If there is not a natural attrition of pleasure in discovery, then it must be some artifact of our education or cultural system. Something is wrong. To deliver to an educational system such an incredibly curious creature as the average five-year-old, and to have delivered back to us after twelve years of education the average seventeen-year-old, seems to suggest a certain complicity on the part of the educational process. Even allowing that there may be a natural biologically determined diminution in all delight in life (which might mitigate the pain of our eventual need to abandon existence), seventeen seems too early an age for the process to have started.

Very closely related to discovery is our fourth category of pleasure, which I will call expansion or mastery. Human beings have innate pleasure in a sense of growth and improvement. They are frustrated by a sense of stagnation and distressed by a sense of regression. There is an elation in athletic endeavor when one has the sense of one's body having done well. There is excitement, whether it be in dance, basketball, gymnastics. It is one of the reasons that golf is such a frustrating game. It seems so easy to move up one notch, to reduce that small difference—just one stroke a hole—that separates the champion from the masses, and yet it is so difficult.

Just as with discovery, mastery can have a purely intellectual component. From earliest days children seem to love problem-solving. Again, am I carping if I ask why they don't enjoy that most delightful of problem-solving activities that is the mental gymnastic known as mathematics? I do not think that by labeling it gymnastics I am stretching an analogy. What we enjoy is the nimbleness of our mind when we are fortunate enough to have it work in such a way. The pleasure of sensing our mind in operation is in every way the equivalent of the joy we receive in sensing our bodies. Problem-solving enlarges the sense of ourselves in the same way as working and mastering things. It does not matter if the enhancement occurs via utilization of the intellectual or the physical self; the perceiving self which is enlarged is the same. Obviously this sense of enlargement or enhancement is a perceptual, not an actual, phenomenon. It is here that I reveal my Freudian roots, for I assume it is the internal reality, the perceived event, that is important. Whether we are actually doing much better is irrelevant.

There are many things we do that are masterful but that give us no particular joy. We are all master breathers, and the mechanism of breathing is intricate and magnificent. The moving of the diaphragm which creates a negative vacuum which allows for the influx of air; the stretching of the intercostal muscles (between the ribs) which allows for the expansion of the rib cage and the dilation of the lungs; and the biological and chemical transections along the lung membrane—all exercised so beautifully many times a minute, yet producing no pride or pleasure. We are unaware, we are not in control. It is a gift from nature. It is a part of us but not a product of ours. It is not of our doing and therefore there is no pride and there is no joy.

Someone who has lost a natural capacity and through sheer force of will has taught himself to relearn it—to feed himself after a stroke or to walk with the aid of a prosthesis—will experience the same joy in these processes as in the solving of a chess problem or catching the backhand corner with a blistering first tennis serve.

Mastery offers a perfect opportunity to expose the foolishness of using pain and pleasure as polarities. With mastery it is easy to see that most things which involve the greatest pleasure also involve pain. Here without the pain there would be almost no pleasure. Perhaps no activity better expresses the confusion between pleasure and pain than running. It is often difficult to determine whether it is an activity of self-punishment or elation. Perhaps it is both, as it seems to be in N. Scott Momaday's description:

> He was running, and his body cracked open with pain, and he was running on. He was running and there was no reason to run but the running itself and the land and the dawn appearing. . . . He was running and a cold sweat broke out upon him and his breath heaved with the pain of running. His legs buckled and he fell in the snow. . . . And he got up and ran on. He was alone and running on. All of his being was concentrated in the sheer motion of running on, and he was past caring about the pain. Pure exhaustion laid hold of his mind, and he could see at last without having to think. . . . He was running, and under his breath he began to sing. There was no sound, and he had no voice; he had only the words of a song. And he went running on the rise of the song.[12]

The "I did it" phenomenon is significant only when there

is the sense that the thing that was done was difficult to do. Otherwise, where is the achievement? There is pleasure in attending a concert, but I am sure it is less great than the pleasure in having written the music. Even attending the concert is not a totally passive phenomenon. What we are hearing is music, not just sound. It is not exactly the same as smelling a flower. We are collaborators with the composer, albeit junior ones. Hearing music involves a complex synthesis of intelligence, imagination, sensitivity, conditioning. We are cooperating with the composer in a shared emotional experience and a shared pleasure. The agonies, though, that went into the effort of creation inevitably influence the nature of the "did" in the phrase "I did it," and therefore the nature of the pride and pleasure in composition and creation of music must be more profound than that of mere listening.

Perhaps a more homely example than the complex one of music would be the pleasure one has in seeing a superbly executed piece of cabinetry. Having fumbled my way through carpentry to many a disastrous result, I can testify to the joy in my few successes. Part of the joy in woodworking involves the hundreds of hours spent in the painstaking and boring tasks of sanding and finishing necessary to produce the perfection of fit and finish that goes into a beautiful cabinet. It is the awareness of the sweat, toil, perseverance, and agony involved in the process that endows the words "I did it" with so rewarding a quality. The implication is that it was not easy, and having done it I have proved something about myself and my worth.

I suspect that in using both cabinetry and music I have slipped into what, while closely related to mastery, is still entitled to be a category of its own, creativity. The fact of having done something well is expanded in joy when it is not simply useful but special and beautiful. I am hesitant to list creativity as a category of pleasure because it is not part of the universal experience. Perhaps I am being too elitist here and using "creativity" in too elegant a sense. We cannot all be creative artists, and I can only imagine what it must be like for Mozart, Shakespeare, Yeats, Tolstoy, Rembrandt, Cezanne, Dickens, or Austen to examine their finished products. There are lesser forms of creativity, and we need not reserve that concept for those blessed few in each generation who have that gift, that consummate genius, of high artistry. While we cannot all be artists, we can involve ourselves in activities that test us to the limits of our own creativity. Many do this with hobbies, whether it be wood carving or gardening or cooking.

Involvement in hobbies is perhaps the best example of another peculiar form of pleasure: an immersion in activities to a point of losing the sense of time, of perception, and even seemingly of self. It is a joyous experience. It is the opposite of the boredom and the drudgery that characterize the lives of the clock-watchers of the world. At first consideration this concept of immersion in things may seem a contradiction to my basic principle of pleasure, that of enhancement, but I don't think so.

This total immersion in an activity allows us to transcend our awareness of our bodily needs, pains our trivial sensate discomforts. The sun is setting and we are unaware of it; our back is aching but we will only suffer from that later. I am always astonished by what immersion can do to the sense of pain. I am not a particularly stoic person. Things that strike me as frightfully hot and not handleable are picked up with insouciance by my wife, who will disdainfully take the casserole that I have just dropped with a shout of anguish, cradle it in her hands, and slowly serve me from it. Nonetheless, after a hard day's work of spring cleaning and pruning in my rose garden, I will come in to shower and notice that my exposed arms and legs are covered with cuts and scratches. I have done thirty years of battle with a wall of climbing roses. Those of you who are gardeners know that roses are ungenerous and ungrateful flowers. They are demanding and spoiled, want constant attention, need severe discipline and control, and retaliate if they are neglected. In conquering that wall of old climbers I have a sense of power and mastery and find myself immersed in the activity to a point where I, like some miniature superman, have altered my threshold for pain. What happens with immersion is the profound involvement of self with thing. To be immersed in an activity is to sense ourselves in a new environment, like floating in water. The environment of the activity allows for new awareness of ourselves through a new surrounding medium.

Closely related to immersion in things is cohesion with others. What does one make of the pleasure that is achieved by playing in an ensemble or orchestra, or singing in a choir or being a part of a team in a sport? Here the individual's effort is not always distinguishable from the effect of the total group. Indeed, the kind of pleasure I am describing is best understood when it is not separable. For the purpose of this argument, do not think of the pitcher on a baseball team, but rather of a rower in a scull or a member of the team in a tug-of-war. I want to distinguish here between the soloist, with whom I am not concerned at this point, and the choir. This, too, on initial consideration seems to be a denial of my basic thesis of pleasure as an enhanced sense of self. But here again I think not. What happens is rather than disappearing into the crowd, we are allowed the privilege of joining it and identifying ourselves with this larger unit of achievement. Knowing the limitations of my own voice, the awareness that the awesome and thrilling sound emerging from that chorus is in small part my own creation produces a sense of pride and joy that is extraordinary.

We find a form of self-enlargement through joining with our fellows. We are *not* lost in the group or intimidated by the masses as we may be when we are trapped in a traffic jam or caught in a mob scene. Those are self-reducing and humiliating experiences and no pleasure. The mighty sound of the chorus is different. We hear our voice extended. We become expanded into and one with the group.

This thrill is similar to that in all cooperative effort. It is the excitement of sitting in a scull pulling hard, pulling together where your own backbreaking effort is indistinguishable from those fore and aft of you. The great sense of power and motion is compounded by the fact that you are all pulling together in one united purpose, and at times the whole scull seems to be moving by your own individual effort. Cohesive and joining activities of all sorts are profound delights and come close to that fusion that I am proposing as the central condition of loving.

Before dealing with love, the ultimate form of pleasure, I wish to consider that which, for want of a better term, I will call the transcendental experience. This is the sense of being lifted, almost physically, out of oneself. In the same way that immersion in an activity or cohesion with a group allows us to expand the limits of self by including the activity of others in our sense of self, the transcendental feeling allows for an even larger attachment, beyond groups, things, people, world. This transcendent feeling is experienced by most people in terms of nature and natural settings, as in this scene from Trollope:

> The night had come on, with quick but still unperceived approach, as it does in those parts. . . . The night had come on, but there was a rising moon, which just sufficed

to give a sheen to the water beneath her. The air was deliciously soft—of that softness which just seems to touch one with loving tenderness, as though the unseen spirits of the air kissed one's forehead as they passed on their wings. The Rhine was running at her feet, so near, that in the soft half light it seemed as though she might step into its ripple. The Rhine was running by with that delicious sound of rapidly moving waters, that fresh refreshing gurgle of the river, which is so delicious to the ear at all times. . . . Alice felt that the air kissed her, that the river sang for her its sweetest song, that the moon shone for her with its softest light—that light which lends the poetry of half-developed beauty to everything that it touches.[13]

The transcendental feeling is that awesome, almost over-whelming experience at seeing an extraordinarily beautiful sunset, or the first sight of the anticipated sea as one comes over the hill and it unexpectedly thrusts itself above the horizon, overcoming us with its proximity and grandeur. It is the heart that leaps up as it beholds the rainbow in the sky. It is, in part, the mystical joy that some experience through religion. It is a religious feeling in the broadest sense. I have avoided using that term because in some minds the adjective "religious" has the strict connotation of belief in a specific divinity, rather than awareness of the divine in general. What both senses of the word affirm is our sense of being a part of a continuity beyond the limits of our personal existence that will connect our limited life span to an ongoing and endless process. It makes us a part of a cosmos. It affirms our place in the larger order of things, and we are excited and enhanced by this.

A transcendental feeling can also be experienced through the arts. There is vast variation among individuals both in the potential for the feeling and in the kind of art likely to elicit it. I personally experience this transcendental feeling with architecture, music, and poetry, and practically never with prose literature (the intellectual stimuli dilute the pure feeling). Those of you who have felt moved by music know precisely what I mean. If you have not, I can only compare it to the feeling which you may have felt with exposure to the awe and beauty of nature. There are certain notes and combinations of notes that have nothing to do with intellect, rationality, or ideation, that inevitably cause a kind of chill across the back of my neck and give me an almost literal feeling of being lifted out of my seat. They produce the effect with such regularity that sometimes when I am half-listening to music in the background while doing other things—really not listening at all—I experience a strong alerting of consciousness. The notes just prior to the section to which I am particularly vulnerable intrude into awareness and will interrupt the flow of concentration on my "primary" activity, diverting my attention to the music. The feeling is of being lifted out of myself, yet through that I paradoxically experience an enlarged sense of self. It is as though being rid of *specific* feelings allows *pure* feeling— whatever that might be—to come through.

Being moved by the arts is a form of the transcendental emotion that brings us in contact with some essential self beyond measurement and specificity. It is experienced at its purest by most of us in the nonliterary forms of the arts. It is a tone of feeling that is separated from ideas, thoughts, and perceptions. I find that the poetry which moves me most is that in which the specific meanings are often obscured by language, mood, or imagery. Here the ideas serve the mood. The messages, if present, are unobtrusive and tangential. The very obscurity that offends some readers by disturbing their sense of rationality and logic serves my primary purpose by subduing everything to the sound and feeling. In the hands of a master, like Wallace Stevens or Osip Mandelstam, the idea will somehow magically emerge out of the evoked feelings and images. When an impressionistic fusion of meanings and half-meanings, tones and sounds all blend in one effect, when one finds difficulty in teasing out the specific instrumentation that elicits the mood, it is then that poetry becomes a form of music through words.

I do not offer the preceding as a particularly definitive list nor an ultimate statement on the nature of pleasure. Saint Augustine has his own. He lists the earthly pleasures he enjoys, before announcing the subservience of these earthly pleasures to the love of God. What is so captivating in Augustine is the lack of pomposity. One senses his love of earthly pleasures, and in that recognition we honor him more. A sensualist who abandons earthly delights seems more saintly than an ascetic who does:

> The eye is attracted by beautiful objects, by gold and silver and all such things. There is great pleasure, too, in feeling something agreeable to the touch, and material things have various qualities to please each of the other senses. Again, it is gratifying to be held in esteem by other men and to have the power of giving them orders and gaining the mastery over them. This is also the reason why revenge is sweet. But our ambition to obtain all these things must not lead us astray from you, O Lord, nor must we depart from what your law allows. The life we live on earth has its own attractions as well, because it has a certain beauty of its own in harmony with all the rest of this world's beauty. Friendship among men, too, is a delightful bond, uniting many souls in one.[14]

I am delighted that Saint Augustine starts his list with sensate pleasure and ends with the joy of bonding with our fellow creatures. I am not sure that I would have thought of revenge as one of the great pleasures, but of course it is. It not only supplies one with a sense of power, usually a reversal of power (the worm turning), but restores a sense of moral rightness to the world, of justice triumphant. There's an exhilarating experience, and oh, how sadly rare these days. In so subjective an area as pleasure, each person, drawing from his or her own experience, may wish to add or subtract from any lists drawn up by others. Ultimately pleasure, like humor, is essentially unanalyzable, and like all of the emotions is best understood through experiencing it oneself or sharing the experience with another. It is the "you know how you feel when" phenomenon.

One significant omission from my discussion is the good feeling that is related to the relief of stress. I do not classify that as a pleasure. It is, I am aware, a good feeling to be liberated from pain, but I believe that the results of rescue are closer to reassurance and renewed hope than to primary pleasure. On the other hand, there is unquestionably joy, elation, and even an enhanced sense of self that is secondary to "being saved."

Perhaps I can make the same distinction here that I have made between being loved and loving. These pleasures secondary to relief, rescue, or reassurance may be called "narcissistic" pleasures as distinguished from what I will call "true" pleasures. In the very labeling I suggest my bias for the true pleasure.

Narcissistic pleasures are the pleasures contingent on reassurance and status. They are secondary phenomena of a primary response which is more closely related to survival needs than to joy and quality of life. Narcissistic pleasures, when carefully analyzed, serve to relieve anxiety. They include most of the quick-fix pleasures of modern life. The narcissistic pleasures are passive. They come to us. We do not have to earn them. A compliment, an honor, even a good review can give a momentary sense of well-being and enlargement, but it is not the stuff of either real security or real pleasure. Narcissistic pleasures do not stick to the ribs; they are not nourishing. We are temporarily rescued by them from self-doubt, but they cannot build self-esteem or self-confidence. They must, in some way, be distinguished from true pleasure. Of course, there are tilt-points in our lives where reassurance, support, reward—the "positive reinforcements"—will encourage the development of self-confidence. But they operate by encouraging the activities or the relationships which are the true materials out of which we build the sense of self. Narcissistic pleasures are the extras. Have the "jimmies" on the ice-cream cones if you like, but they are not true nutrients. As adjuncts they may serve a purpose, but used as alternatives to true pleasures they will deprive us of those aspects of experience that nourish pride and self-esteem.

Too many of us awake in the twilight of our lives, surrounded by the products of our pursuits of narcissistic pleasures: the status symbols of cars and jewels and furs, of titles and trophies, of honorary memberships in dreary places, and honorary listings on unnurturing rolls. We awake, if at all, often too late, and wonder not just what joy or passion remains, but whether any ever existed for us. Relief from distress and insecurity is part of the mechanism of pain and pain avoidance, which while related to pleasure is still a separate entity. We must not in our anxious pursuit of narcissistic pleasures ignore the true pleasures that alone lend significance to an existential life.

I raise this here because in the traditional Freudian dynamic, pleasure is cast exclusively in terms of the relief of distress as experienced by discharge of the sexual instinct. According to the libido theory, pleasure is that which is experienced by discharged libido, as pain is represented in its frustration. This conceptualization has trivialized and degraded the concept of pleasure. No concept of pleasure so mechanistically designed could ever encompass so complex an example of pleasure as human love. The redefining of pleasure is the necessary first step in the rediscovery of love.

4 ❧ THE NATURE OF LOVE

She knew a great deal about pulleys and hoists but nothing about love. She went to the library to look up love as she had looked up the mechanical advantages of pulleys. Surely great writers and great lovers of the past had written things worth reading. Here were some of the things great writers had written:

> Love begets love
> Love conquers all things
> Love ends with hope
> Love is a flame to burn out human ills
> Love is all truth
> Love is truth and truth is beauty
> Love is blind
> Love is the best
> Love is heaven and heaven is love
> Love is love's reward

"Oh my God," she said aloud in the library and smacked her head. "What does all that *mean*? These people are crazier than I am!"

Nowhere could she find a clear explanation of the connection between "being in love" and "doing it." Was this something everybody knew and so went without saying? or was it a well-kept secret? or was it something no one knew?[1]

Walker Percy's character Allison here expresses a perplexity that often results from attempts to "understand" love without experiencing it.

The essential error in the libido theory was not just in the narrowness of its definition of pleasure, which was problem enough, but in its assumption that love, any form of human love, could be explained exclusively in terms of sexual gratification, in terms of "doing it."

While love is a form of pleasure it is also something beyond pleasure. To see human love only as an extension of the sexual drive that *Homo sapiens* shares with fish, birds, and insects is to do disservice to the complexity of human emotion and to the very special place of the human being in the order of animal life.

One cannot condense caring, compassion, empathy, identification, fusion, maternal or filial love, or even sexual or romantic love into mere variations and disguises of orgastic release. Even pure sexual passion in human beings is not an instinct turned on in the male by mechanical receptors triggered by mechanical stimuli issuing from the female at certain times of the year. Hume was speaking precisely to this when he said: "Love between the sexes begets a complacency and goodwill very different from the gratification of an appetite."[2] The human sexual drive emerges in an elaborate matrix of idealization, anticipations, memories, cultural biases (only a Maori is likely to find those ritually scarred warrior faces sexy, or a mandarin those crippled bound feet), and romantic mythology.

By clinging to an antiquated concept of instinct that never operated in human beings as it does in the lower species, we grossly underestimated the uniqueness of our species. We have been supplied with an alternative to instinct, and that is intelligence and choice. We are autonomous creatures for good and bad, and that autonomy, influenced by our imagination, shapes every aspect of our existence, including our biological drives.

Freud liberated sex from the hypocrisy of Victorian morality. In so doing he acknowledged the power of the drive in human beings and its ubiquitous operation across class barriers, gender distinctions, and all ages. In addition, he discovered sexual aspects and sexual gratifications in a host of seemingly nonsexual activities. What Freud saw was there; he was an extraordinary observer. He then made the assumption that all behavior, beyond having the capacity to contain covert sexual aspects, was in essence sexual. And that was an error.

There are other powers that drive our behavior as urgent as the sexual; there are, for example, those emotions that serve our survival. Freud was aware that the woman dreaming of a gun might well be dreaming of a phallus. He should have been equally aware that a woman dreaming of a phallus might really be thinking of a gun. The great insight of Freud is that all things are not what they seem to us to be, not that all things are sexual. We are motivated by sexual drive, but we are also motivated by aspects of power and dependency, the two major means of survival. In any activity involving one, we may see the shadows of the other. Much of our involvement with power is sexual, but much of our sexual activity is a power play. When the man in the street says "If you're not careful, you're going to get it in the ass," or "Boy, was I fucked," or "Up yours," he is not talking about the giving and receiving of anal sexual gratification. He is talking about the power struggle in terms of a society in which power is symbolized in the masculine genital instrument. All activity may involve a conflation and a confusion of major drives. Sex is not all; survival is something. Sex is similarly not all in considerations of love.

Rather than attempting to see all love as a form of sexual

drive it would be better to see the sexual drive as one dominant element of a specific category of loving called romantic love. There are three powerful human capacities that through combinations and permutations form all aspects of human love. One of these, certainly, is sexual passion. All love *may* have a sexual component, although the evidence is not as convincing as most psychoanalysts would have one believe. Another is the potential for empathy, sympathy, identification, and unselfishness, feelings and attitudes that I group under the rubric of caring. The third essential component of human love is a concept that I have yet to expand upon—the capacity for fusion. These three motivating forces powerfully influence human behavior and in their combinations define all human love.

As in moral discourse, in which complexity and contradiction arise when basic principles of approximately equivalent power come in conflict (for example, truth-telling versus compassion or lifesaving), it is the occasional conflict among these three driving forces (passion, caring, and fusion) that leads to contradictory definitions of the nature of love. Is commitment the antagonist of passion? Is passion the enemy of reason? Is passion a binding force or a disruptive influence in human affairs? Some of these seeming contradictions about the true nature of love which have been argued about since classical times can be resolved by approaching love in its various forms as a different balance or commingling of these three powerful directives, where different proportions lead to very different behaviors that often seem contradictory.

The Two Aphrodites

When considering the nature of love, most scholars are likely to return to Plato's *Symposium*.[3] The *Symposium* is written as a conversation among friends at a banquet, conversation in which various theories of love are suggested. All are ultimately rejected as inadequate or incomplete until, typically, Socrates offers his last word. In the final theory of Socrates, love is elevated beyond desire or passion into a yearning for some ideal, some good that transcends the physical entirely.

In our non-Platonic world of the late twentieth century, greater understanding may come from focusing on two of the "incomplete" definitions of love offered in the *Symposium*. One is the concept of the two Aphrodites, and the other is the myth of Aristophanes.

At the banquet, Pausanias distinguishes two contrasting aspects of love that he defines as the earthly and heavenly Aphrodite. The details of his argument are unimportant for us. What is important is that a crucial division between two seemingly contradictory aspects of love was introduced into the arguments of the *Symposium*. In the classic literature predating Plato, these two contradictory images had already been recognized. On the one hand, love is the passion which is in opposition to and threatens order and rationality. It is therefore a destructive force driving human beings beyond reason. It is the residual animal aspect of our nature striving for gratification and requiring restraint. It is not far from the uninhibited libido which Freud describes. This "earthly aspect" of Aphrodite is expressed powerfully and beautifully in this chorus from *Antigone:*

> Love, unconquered in the fight, Love, who makest havoc of wealth, who keepest thy vigil on the soft cheek of a maiden; thou roamest over the sea, and among the homes of dwellers in the wilds; no immortal can escape thee, nor any among men whose life is for a day; and he to whom thou hast come is mad.
> The just themselves have their minds warped by thee to

wrong, for their ruin: tis thou that has stirred up this present strife of kinsmen; victorious is the love—kindling light from the eyes of the fair bride; it is a power enthroned in sway beside the eternal laws; for there the goddess Aphrodite is working her unconquerable will.[4]

Throughout ancient mythology the concept of a disuniting, malicious, and even maddening Eros is a constant presence, often visualized as a blind cupid, an impish and mischievous boy, the hermaphroditic agent of a capricious and potentially destructive aspect of human nature. Some of the great Greek tragedies deal directly with love and passion (*Medea*, *The Hippolytus*), while others that deal centrally with issues of justice (surely *Antigone* is not primarily a story of sexual love), obligation, and guilt and innocence nonetheless pivot on a plot structure of love. One sees this in the *Oresteia*, whose tragic events are precipitated by the seduction and elopement of Helen, or the great dramas that focus on the destiny of Oedipus. A sexual act—even though preordained by the gods—is the common event that initiates a chronology of doom, suffering, guilt, and repentance.

The concept of a maddening Eros was not idiosyncratic to the Greeks. It was pervasive in classical literature, and would only be replaced with the conversion of the Roman Empire to Christianity. In that masterpiece of Latin literature the *Aeneid*, Virgil describes the awesome destructive power of the unfortunate Dido's passion:

What good are shrines and vows to maddened
    lovers?
The inward fire eats the soft marrow away,
And the internal wound bleeds on in silence.
Unlucky Dido, burning, in her madness
Roamed through all the city, like a doe
Hit by an arrow shot from far away

By a shepherd hunting in the Cretan woods—
His flying steel had fixed itself in her;
But though she runs for life through copse and glade
The fatal shaft clings to her side.[5]

In this concept of the earthly Aphrodite, love is clearly
meant to represent the passions as the enemy of rationality.
The same conflict may be seen in other myths, as in the
contrast between Dionysus, the god of sensuality, hedonism,
excess, and abandon, and Apollo, who represented balance,
control, temperance, and beauty. It is the traditional battle
of instinct versus reason, impulse versus control, and was, I
believe, the essential model that Freud used throughout his
lifetime.

Coexisting with these powerful indictments of the earthly
Aphrodite was a literature with as lengthy and impressive a
pedigree that acknowledged the cohesive and civilizing aspects of love. This is perhaps expressed most eloquently in
the writings of the fifth-century-B.C. Greek philosopher
Empedocles.[6] Here, love is not in conflict with reason but in
contrast with strife. Aphrodite is the bonding, compassionate, and unifying force in nature. Aphrodite is visualized as
the antagonist of Ares, the god of war and destruction.

When one updates the terminology of Empedocles, he
begins to sound extraordinarily modern. The concept of
two life forces, called Love and Strife, not closely identified
with any gods but simply as brute forces which dominate us
and are in constant antagonism, has a late-nineteenth-
century vitalistic air. One is a unifying and binding force,
while the other is aggressively selfish and destructive. Love
is not disorder and chaos but peace and harmony. It is strife
that represents danger and irrationality. In this tension one
is reminded of such terms as "anabolic" and "catabolic,"
and Freud's own ultimate contrast of a life force and a death

wish. In Empedocles the sexual act itself is seen as the individual and physical expression of the general and spiritual unifying force of love.

This same apparent distinction between two possibly oppositional views of passion, this duality of love, was to confront philosophers throughout the ages and to be resolved by each in his own way, reflecting not only personal values but the dominant traditions of the time. One sees in the confessions of Saint Augustine his personal turning from the earthly to the heavenly, from lecher to lover of God. But here the heavenly Aphrodite is irrevocably separated from love of woman and physical desire.[7]

Plotinus, the Hellenistic philosopher who founded the Neoplatonist school, saw three aspects of love—the godly, demonic, and passionate. He revived the idea of the earthly and heavenly Aphrodites; the former ruled over love on earth and the latter held sway in the world of Platonic ideals. One sees the two forces recognized in the late writings of Freud, where he chooses to cast the life forces as a duality between Eros and Thanatos, sex and aggression (love and strife).

The two Aphrodites may be visualized as two of the three vital component forces that I suggested at the beginning of this chapter: caring and sexual passion. But I am reluctant to grant even this distinction. Certainly caring is the essential binding force in human affairs, but while passion may be irrational, divisive, and destructive at times, that is not its normal role in the human species.

Sex among human beings is rarely pure unadulterated instinct. The most passionate lovers may like to think so, but they do not behave like a rutting bear or a bitch in heat. All human sexuality is shaped by emotion and imagination, by reality and fantasy. One sees pure sexual drive unadulterated by other human sensibilities exclusively in animals and in the animalistic behavior of such people as rapists, for whom sex may be totally separated from affection or even knowledge of the other person. But even here one may be surprised. Careful study of rapists shows that sex is frequently a secondary factor in the attack. Rage and fear of women may motivate the rapist more than lust.

With the sexual liberation of the last twenty years the emptiness and unfulfilling nature of sex unattached to love is beginning to be appreciated by large parts of the population. It is now easier for many young people to go to bed with each other than to form trusting or intimate relationships. It is easier for them to expose their genitals to a stranger than to expose their feelings. It has become less frightening, and it is socially condoned. The resulting confusion is just beginning to be sorted out in psychoanalysts' offices around the country.

Isolated and detached sexuality has existed for some time in certain byways of our culture. One subculture of the male homosexual community has an obsessive need for a sexual—more exactly, a phallic—experience stripped of all human association.[8] This desire for anonymous sex leads to the groping bathhouse behavior, or public-toilet activity, where one man may compulsively be penetrated by or perform fellatio on twenty to fifty "partners" in a night. In this kind of sexuality, the anonymity is a major part of the excitement. Another human presence intrudes on the fantasy—it is the isolated phallus that is desired. In this frantic drive, sexual pleasure is totally incidental to some secret scenario of power and humiliation, dominance and submission, anxiety and reassurance. The driven behavior is barely sexual, and certainly not gratifying, as is evidenced by its insatiability. Sexuality divorced not just from affection but from human contact (the heterosexual equivalent to this has been described by Erica Jong as the "zipless fuck")[9] turns out to be sexual in its form only. The real motive forces behind these activities are part of the complex domain of male competition, dominance, submission, and dependency cravings.

In human beings the sexual instinct is rarely expressed, or I should say enjoyed, independent of other emotional inter-relationships with the partner. We don't have sex, generally speaking, with people who repel us. Why they repel us will be determined by a number of very subjective judgments which may prove to be illusory, ephemeral, or self-deluding. One man's meat is frequently another man's poison. And "What in the world did she see in him?" is asked by someone at most marriages and all divorces.

Some researchers assume that there is a pure sexual appetite, equating it with hunger. Most of us in the privileged western world have separated the experience of eating from anything remotely resembling the behavior of a hungry animal. Recently I dined at a somewhat pretentious restaurant. Suppose we examine the strange ritual of which I was a part as a detached observer might:

I was seated on a chair carved out of an exotic African wood (mahogany) in an imitation of an eighteenth-century design (Chippendale), whose seat was covered by a fabric woven from the secretions of oriental worms (silk). The table was covered by a material woven from the flax plant (linen), and on it were placed various arrangements of objects of hard, translucent ceramic made by firing pure clay and glazing it with variously colored fusible materials (china). On one of these was my first course: the puréed livers of chickens seasoned with a wine made in Madeira, nutmeg and clove from the East Indies, truffles from Italy, peppercorns and garlic from God knows where, etc., etc., etc. Need I go on? By the time I adequately described the flatware, the salt cellar, the pepper mill, and the vase of

flowers and took us through the full seven courses, not forgetting the string quartet in full formal attire that played in
the background throughout the dinner, I would have written an entire and other book. What in the world does any of
this have to do with the experience of a lion tearing at the
throat of an antelope or an ape eating a banana? If eating
has been so elaborately transformed by human imagination
in modern culture, sexuality, which is infinitely more complex and metaphoric, no longer bears any relationship to the
exercise of automatic animal instinct.

To repeat, then, when human sexuality is expressed as
pure appetite independent of the nature of the partner we
tend to label it as pathological and perverse; we perceive
such sexuality as being beyond human norms. Such indiscriminate sexual behavior usually represents a compulsive
utilization of sexuality to fulfill other unconscious needs
(such as rape as an act of rage at women). The sexual act,
even when it is not a part of romantic love, is always modified by imaginative aspects of the human psyche. The sexual object must be attractive—whatever that means to us—
must be of a certain age, style, manner, or personality to
elicit desire. The rat seeing and smelling a receptive female
rat is not concerned with aesthetics, relationships, or status
factors.

For the most part, romantic love demands even more than
the complicated version of sexual desire that I describe. It
involves a fusion of the sexual drive with those caring aspects previously discussed as the fundamental element in
parental feelings toward the child.

While Freud seemed to build his definitions of sexuality
along the lines of animal instinct, he was aware of some
problems in so doing. As there is more than one Aphrodite,
there are multiple Freuds. In his theory of psychopathology,
in the libido theory, he was consistent in seeing man as

selfishly driven by a sexual instinct that must be controlled and civilized. Parallel to this, however, were a series of writings which indicated Freud's bafflement and confusion over behavior that seemed to be inconsistent with the uni-instinctual, driven, survival-oriented creature he had created. How was he to explain unselfish behavior, self-sacrificing acts, generosity, guilt, shame, and conscience?

The conflict goes back to the time of the very discovery of the unconscious by Breuer and Freud in the book *Studies in Hysteria.*[10] It was here that the concept of "repression" was first enunciated. Both Breuer and Freud shared a sense that the women patients they were then studying suffered from reminiscences; that buried in their unconscious were thoughts which were unacceptable and were causing neurotic symptoms through the displacements of their affect. In other words, the emotions of the trapped ideas of childhood were reappearing in adult life in the disguised form of a neurosis.

The key question which separated Breuer and Freud was how an idea got into the unconscious. Breuer assumed that ideas simply slipped in when the patient was in a state of diminished awareness. Freud could not accept so lackadaisical and haphazard, so chancy, a concept. He was profoundly deterministic in his philosophy and rational in his analysis of human behavior. He decided the ideas were "repressed"—that is, they were pushed into the unconscious because they were unacceptable. But what in the world makes an idea unacceptable? Freud simply decided that they were unacceptable because they generated the emotions of shame, disgust, and loathing. At that time he didn't question where shame, disgust, and loathing would have come from. He defined the source neither as a culturally determined set of values nor as inborn. Eventually, though, he was to settle on the latter.

In the major trajectory of the Freudian theory of neurosis, these questions about shame, disgust, and loathing were simply dismissed. They were seen as character traits, which later would be derived from the instinctual drive in the same way that I have described certain pleasures as being derivative. They were reaction formations or sublimations: the instinctual drive turned topsy-turvy and embracing its opposite, or the instinctual drive disguised as a socially acceptable activity.

I am not sure this is an answer that will satisfy anyone today. It never completely satisfied Freud. He attempted to explain the unselfish aspects of human behavior in a series of papers devoted to an understanding of creativity, religion, and civilization itself. One of the most extraordinary of these was also one of the earliest, *Totem and Taboo*,[11] published in 1913. For years this remained a relatively neglected masterpiece. Only in the last dozen years or so have psychoanalysts returned to it with enthusiasm. The book was underestimated because Freud—sharing the ignorance of his day—falsely assumed a Lamarckian (as distinguished from Mendelian) mechanism of inheritance; he assumed that acquired characteristics could be transmitted, and he constructed the central argument of this book on this false concept. When one strips the work of its faulty genetics and biology, its conclusions still emerge as sparkling, brilliant, and creative.

In attempting to understand what forces support the kind of behavior that allows people to live together in groups, Freud conceived of a relatively independent set of genetic determinants that guide human behavior. These emotions limit our selfish impulses and set constraints on our instinctual drive. These totems and taboos civilize individual human behavior, and in so doing make possible communal living. He visualized these taboos as part of the *genetic* endowment of the species. Presuming that in the early prehistory of our species we learned the necessity for constraints on our sexual desires, particularly our incestual desires, he assumed that this knowledge, incorporated over generations, eventually—in a Lamarckian mode—became a part of the genetic makeup of the human being.

This was an astounding conclusion to be drawn by Freud, as it was not at all consistent with the assumptions of the libido theory. In the libido theory, you will remember, everything was derivative of the sexual drive. Now these limitations and restrictions on the selfish pursuit of the sexual instinct, these taboos, were held to be as inherent and genetically part of the species as the sex instinct itself. The foundation of a biological moral nature specific to *Homo sapiens* was now laid.

With this theory, for the first time, social living, community, love, and unselfishness become not an accident of a culture that by sheer luck managed to survive our destructive drives for pleasure, but part of our nature. This work goes beyond that. It defines a new unit of survival, a new biological entity. No more is the individual a thing in itself. It is *the group* that becomes the basic unit of life. By defining the group as a genetic necessity, Freud introduced a new view of humanity in which compassion, care, and even love have to be inherent attributes. *Totem and Taboo* firmly placed the individual in a network of other human beings who are necessary to support his survival and through whom he defines his identity. No more can the psychological unit be an isolated individual; now it is an interdependent and interrelating group of individuals.

Thus, conscience, love, self-sacrifice, unselfishness, need no longer be perceived as antagonists to our need to survive, but can be seen as being directly in the service of survival. What this book recognizes is that the human being as individual alone is a self-deception. We, as much as goats and sheep, are group animals—and perhaps more so, given the protracted dependency of our young. We are probably best visualized as something halfway between a herding animal and a colonial animal like coral.

Take the individual human being at birth away from the group and he cannot survive. Take the infant away from the group under a certain age and he may *survive,* but that which survives will be something less than fully human and have less of the features we tend to define as human, i.e., a capacity for creativity, conscience, and love. In *Totem and Taboo* Freud defines *Homo sapiens* as an obligately social animal just as I did at the beginning of this book. He did this prior to all the major research in psychology, psychoanalysis, and pediatrics that demonstrated the disastrous effects of isolation on the human infant.

We know, of course, that what is considered to be disgusting or shameful is massively determined by the culture. Some things we eat are loathsome and disgusting to cultures that share our planet at our time. We also know that the way we dress would have been shameful and repugnant to a previous generation of our cultural antecedents. We are certainly not genetically different from the Victorians, yet the topless bathing suit would have been unimaginable then even for men, let alone women. Even those aspects of our culture that we consider the most sacred will be considered profane by other cultures. The very rituals and symbols that constitute our religions can be perceived as disgusting. As we examine with loathing and incredulity the religion of the Aztec sun worshipers with its dependence on human sacrifice involving the excision of the living human heart, we might remind ourselves that other cultures might consider with disgust a religion that has the torn body of a man nailed on a cross as its central symbol of worship.

Perhaps Freud should have paid more attention to the cultural milieus which shape our attitudes. To ignore cultural influences on perceptions and behavior today would be a flagrant dereliction. But Freud was asking a more profound question; he was investigating not the nature of that which *causes* shame and disgust but the nature of the shame and disgust itself. Since there are emotions designated shame, disgust, and loathing as a natural part of human response, they must have been built there to some end. It was this teleology that led Freud to assume instinctual and genetic factors that bind people together in a countervailing effect to those selfish drives for personal survival.

He also defined in this book those taboos that he presumed to be universal, and therefore species-bound, as distinguished from those that are culturally determined. He decided that the incest taboo was a universal phenomenon. There has been some questioning of this assumption,[12] but one suspects that if it is not universal, there are others that are. Reactions of disgust and loathing to excrement, for example, seem to extend across all cultures.

In the Freudian psychology, we see the imprint of both the destructive and the cohesive Aphrodite: the sexual drive and the in-built morality that constrains it; the drive for pleasure and the mandate for caring.

We are good by nature. We have goodness and the genetic directive toward it within us just as we have the capacity for evil. Which will survive in any given generation, in any given culture, or in any given individual will be dependent on the culture, not on our nature. These biological directives for personal gratification and unselfish caring may have existed in some kind of perfect balance at some early time in our history, although the story of Adam and Eve in Genesis would suggest an awareness of the conflict very early in our recorded history. We know that we are instructed by nature to experiment and to recreate ourselves in whatever images we deem desirable. We are free to change our natures. The way we define ourselves will become a major determinant of what we become. For that reason if for no other it is important to keep in mind that caring for others, unselfishness, and commitments are as basic a part of our biological directive as the drive for sexual pleasure or for any pleasure.

That sexual drive is not the central "life force" should be apparent from everyday experience. There are survival needs that inevitably preempt sexual appetite. We know, for example, that when anxiety meets sexual drive, it is sexual drive that usually disappears. Any boy or girl literally caught with his or her pants down knows how quickly sexual appetite atrophies. The most throbbing and pulsating of erections on the most ardent of teenage boys will prove as evanescent and ephemeral as a zephyr and will vanish in an instant at the sound of the footsteps of the girl's parents.

The erosion of libido in times of despair or deprivation is also a recorded phenomenon. Rather than libido occupying the seat of power, it is simply one agent operating on a multiply motivated and multiply determined human being. Beyond pleasure there is the need for individual survival and the emotional forces that support it—fear, rage, and pride; and the need for group survival and its supporting emotions—guilt, shame, empathy, and caring. Since the individual and the group share a common destiny, sex and love ultimately serve both. It is not surprising that sexual passion can drive us to both the noblest and the basest actions.

The Myth of Aristophanes

The myth of Aristophanes as presented in the *Symposium* is a parable for that central and necessary condition for loving that I call fusion.

Aristophanes proposes that originally "primeval man" was round, with four hands and feet and with back and sides forming a circle. Because of men's arrogance they made an attack upon the gods and Zeus decided to punish them. He split them asunder "as you might divide an egg with a hair." The myth then continues:

> Each of us when separated is but the indenture of a man, having one side only like a flat fish and he was always looking for his other half . . . and when one of them finds his other half . . . the pair are lost in an amazement of love and friendship and intimacy, and one would not be out of the other's sight, as I may say, even for a moment . . . for the intense yearning which each of them has for the other does not appear to be the desire of intercourse but of something else which the soul desires and cannot tell, and of which she only has a dark and doubtful presentiment. Suppose Hephaestus . . . to come to the pair lying side by side and say to them . . . "Do you desire to be *wholly* one? For if this is what you desire, I am ready to melt you into one and let you grow together. . . ." There is not a man among them when he heard this who would deny or would not acknowledge that this meeting and melting in one another's arms, this becoming one instead of two, was the very expression of his ancient need. And the reason is that human nature was originally one and we were whole, and the desire and pursuit of that whole is called love.[13]

It is ironic to see old mythic stories being reborn in technological and modern language. The concept of originally being one with another and of the birth of the self by cleavage from another, the poetic myth of Aristophanes, finds renewal in the psychological theory of a modern-day psychoanalyst, Dr. Margaret Mahler.[14] She has postulated that originally the child has no awareness of the self but sees himself as one with the mother. She then describes the emergence of self-awareness, the discovery of the self, as a process of "hatching out" of the mother-child pair.

The developmental scheme of psychoanalysis can be seen as tracing the individual's first discovery of herself through a separation from her mother, then passing through a period (the autoerotic) in which the only important relationship is with the self, and finally entering maturity by overcoming the narcissistic preoccupation with self to find a larger self through relationships with others. Freud *defined* normalcy in terms of one's capacity to escape from self-involvements and to form heterosexual relationships. The genital person, i.e., the person capable of going on from "autoerotism" to "object relationships," is in Freudian terminology the healthy or normal person.

The capacity of the adult to return to an earlier state of oneness with another, which I call fusion, is the essential and necessary condition which underlies the capacity for all forms of loving. It is the presence of fusion that relates the love of parent to love of child, to love of spouse, to love of God, country, or ideal. The common ingredient of all love is the merging of the self with another person or ideal, creating a fused identity.

It is axiomatic in almost any psychology that a normal person ought to know who he is. The cliché of the "madman" who thinks he is Jesus or Napoleon states the condition precisely. While these delusionary figures represent a minority of psychotic patients, surely they represent the ultimate distinction between the normal and the psychotic.

In almost all definitions of psychosis one of the distinguishing features will be a loss of self-boundaries—the inability to know where the self begins and ends. Except in the very first days, and perhaps hours, of an infant's life (and only then in certain theories of child development), loss of ego boundaries implies serious psychopathology. It is with that general understanding that I wish to take exception in the special conditions of loving. To borrow a memorable lyric from the thirties associated with Russ Columbo, "You may call it madness, but I call it love."[15]

This very blurring of boundaries is what I mean by fusion and what I place as the central phenomenon of loving. Freud in the end was not at all sure whether in addition to fusion occurring in "madness" it could not also exist in "love": "At the height of being in love the boundary between the ego and the object threatens to melt away. . . . A man who is in love declares that 'I' and 'You' are one and is prepared to behave as if it were a fact."[16] Finally Freud persisted in his demand for a healthy reality testing, and hedged his observation by utilizing the phrase "threatens to melt away."

As I stated in Chapter 1, Irving Singer, in *The Nature of Love* had considered the idea of merging, only to dismiss it, stating: "*We are distinct individuals* [italics added], each living his own life. . . ."[17]

It is here that I, from a biological position, disagreed with Singer. I do not think of the human being as a "distinct individual." I have already discussed the dangers of seeing the human being as akin to an amoeba, as a true individual. The psychologist must recognize the communal nature of human existence. The reality of the psychological world is closer to the imagination of the poets than the analysis of realist philosophy.

It may be that Singer was overly influenced by Erich Fromm's *Art of Loving*.[18] This splendid book emphasized love as protection against isolation. In so doing, while it illuminated much about the nature of loving, it tended to diminish love, to reduce it to being simply a protection against isolation rather than having the primary role in human emotions, indeed in human survival, that I believe it holds. Of course, human beings are sensitive to the dangers of isolation, but that is the secondary phenomenon.

Singer argues that in all accounts of love there is one point on which realists and idealists tend to agree. They usually begin with the loneliness of man. But Aristophanes did not begin with the loneliness of man, and in Freudian psychology we do not begin with the loneliness of man. We begin with the mother-child dyad. We see the newborn individual as imagining a world of oneness, all fused within herself. She is torn from this original state of allness, of magical omnipotence, when she is forced to identify an independent self—a helpless and dependent one at that—separate from her mother. I am speaking, of course, as a Freudian psychologist, and Freudianism is, whether it is recognized or not, an idealistic philosophy. Perhaps in his attack on idealism Singer would include Freud.

Singer says: "Let's assume that the concept of merging makes sense. But how could merging possibly occur in the world as we know it? By means of magic."[19] And here one again sees the difference between the logical truth of the philosopher and the psychological truth of the psychoanalyst. The "real" world that we live in (according to my biases and Freud's) is not the "actual" world out there (a distinction that the psychoanalyst Erik Erikson makes)[20] but the "real" world of our perceptions. That is the reality to which we respond; that is the reality that shapes our personal heaven and hell. The threats we perceive, the joys we experience, our victories and defeats, are only loosely related to the objective world of facts and verifiable truths. We live by the perceptions that we each construct out of the actual stuff of facts.

The actual world is redesigned in our own perceptions in order to fulfill our own unconscious fantasies, needs, and desires. That is the nature of "psychological" truth. Never mind that you are actually beautiful, thin, and brilliant. Think of yourself as ugly, fat, and stupid, and you might as well be. Your reality will reside in what you think you are; and tragically, those self-defined placards we hang around our necks will determine the judgment of others about our "true" natures. Think of yourself as ugly and eventually you will be so considered. Think of yourself as beautiful and it is extraordinary to what degree people will treat you as a beauty. I think of a woman I know who by every objective criterion would be defined as plain, but who nonetheless managed to be attractive and exciting—and here I mean sexually, not just intellectually—to almost every man who had the pleasure of her company. She generated a sense of her sexuality through her own feelings about herself. She hung a sign around her neck that said "desirable," and indeed she was.

The concept of fusion as I will use it literally means the loss of one's identity in that of another; a confusion of ego boundaries; the sense of unsureness as to where I end and you, the person I love, begin; the identification of your pain with my pain and your success with my success; the inconceivability of a self that does not include you; and the inevitability that your loss will create a painful fracture of my self-image that will necessitate a long and painful rebuilding of my ego during a period of grief and despair. It is what Hemingway's lovers in *For Whom the Bell Tolls* experience:

> "Afterwards we will be as one animal of the forest and be so close that neither one can tell that one of us is one and not the other. Can you not feel my heart be your heart?"
>
> "Yes. There is no difference."
>
> "Now, feel. I am thee and thou art me and all of one is the other. And I love thee, oh, I love thee so. Are we not truly one? Canst thou not feel it?"
>
> "Yes," he said. "It is true."

"And feel now. Thou hast no heart but mine."
"Nor any other legs, nor feet, nor of the body. . . ."
"But we will be one now and there will never be a
separate one." Then she said, "I will be thee when thou
art not there. Oh, I love thee so and I must care well for
thee"[21]

Singer traces the dangerous attraction the concept of
merger held for the religious philosophers of the Middle
Ages. I say "dangerous" because the concept of merger, or
fusion as I would have it, had clearly been defined as heresy.
"Attachment," "joining," "being glued together," were all
permissible, but one could not melt into the loved one, since
the loved one was always God, and the natures of man and
God must be maintained as distinct. Yet, love was at the
center of concern of Christian philosophers in the Middle
Ages, and no one attempting to define the essential qualities
of love could avoid the concept of merging. The medieval
Christian mystic Gerlac Petersen says:

> Thou givest me Thy whole Self to be mine whole and
> undivided if at least I shall be Thine whole and undivided
> . . . for this means nothing more than that Thou enjoys
> Thyself in me and I by Thy grace enjoy Thee in myself and
> when in Thee I shall love myself, nothing else but Thee do
> I love, because *Thou art in me and I in Thee, glued to-*
> *gether as one and the selfsame thing,* which henceforth
> and forever cannot be divided.[22]

Despite the theologically authorized use of the concept of
adhesion and gluing, it is clear that what is meant here goes
beyond the attachment of two separate entities; it is the
fusion into "one and the selfsame thing."

When Saint Theresa compares spiritual betrothal and
spiritual marriage—i.e., the actual consummation—there is
no question that she goes beyond just joining of two indi-

viduals into the merging (heretical or not) of substance and
to the merging of selves:

> Here it is like rain falling from the Heavens into a river or
> a spring; there is nothing but water there and it is impos-
> sible to divide or separate the water belonging to the river
> from that which fell from the heavens. For it is as if a tiny
> streamlet enters the sea, from which it will find no way of
> separating itself, or as if in a room there were two large
> windows through which the light streamed in: it enters in
> different places but it all becomes one.[23]

The passage is surprising only in that it was not con-
demned as heretical. This is the same Theresa who brings
such an erotic flavor to so many of her discussions of love of
God. Anyone who has seen the Bernini sculpture depicting
Saint Theresa being impaled by the Heavenly Rays knows
that while Bernini carved the statue in the form of purest
spiritualism, an erotic luminescence nonetheless emerges.
How could it not? Listen to her own description of the
experience which inspired the sculptor:

> In his hands I saw a great golden spear, and at the iron tip
> there appeared to be a point of fire. This he plunged into
> my heart several times so that it penetrated to my entrails.
> When he pulled it out, I felt that he took them with it and
> left me utterly consumed by the great love of God. The
> pain was so severe that it made me utter several moans.
> The sweetness caused by this intense pain is so extreme
> that one cannot possibly wish it to cease, nor is one's soul
> then content with anything but God. This is not a phys-
> ical, but a spiritual pain though the body has some share
> in it—even a considerable share.[24]

Images of melting into one another's arms, commingling
as in waters, lost in whirlpools of desire, merger, and fusion—"I am my beloved and my beloved is me"—abound in
mystical religion, poetry, and the literature of love.

I have often wondered at my own predilection for the term "fusion" over a term so similar as "merger." "Merging" was the term more commonly used in the religious literature. For many reasons, it ought to come more naturally to a Freudian. The primary definition of "merger" in the dictionary, "to lose or cause to lose one's identity by being absorbed, swallowed up, or combined," could have come directly from the psychoanalytic literature describing the nature of identification through introjection (swallowing up) and incorporation (combining with). Yet, "fusion" is my choice, perhaps because the dipping, plunging, sinking, liquid roots of "merge," while perhaps appropriate for spiritual love, seem less appropriate for other love than the "melting by heat" that is implied by fusion. Perhaps it is simply that in our modern terminology "merger" has the connotation of something pedantic, dull, statistical, and corporate, whereas "fusion" has the frightening but awesome connotation of nuclear power.

In attempting to draw the antecedents of a concept of fusion from my own roots—that is, from Freudian psychoanalysis—I run into the frustration, and the joy, of being a Freudian. How lovely it would be to be a disciple of Whitehead, of Hegel, of Kant. These were men who were systematizers, who knew what they believed, who developed arguments one upon the other where each work built on the work preceding it, who wrote *texts,* scholarly texts, annotated texts. That was not Freud's style. His creative mind transcended his obsessive nature. Ideas poured out: the same ideas in different terms; complementary ideas; contradictory ideas. A concept like instinct was first defined in one context, then redefined to satisfy another argument, then defined in totally different terms, as though the first definitions were not still extant; then, finally, recognizing the chaos of multiple definitions of the same term, Freud attempted to accommodate all definitions under the umbrella of yet another definition. Anyone who wishes may find antecedents in Freud to support whatever his psychology fancies.

Another problem with Freud is that being a physician, in the perverse manner of that profession, he built his concept of normality out of his experience with the pathological. The extraordinary aspect of this is that Freud's theory of *normal* development and normal behavior is the richest, most convincing, most sustained, and most enduring aspect of his theory. He was not a very good pathologist. He never really discovered the "causes" of any mental illness. He could not explain why people with identical psychodynamics developed different symptoms and different "diseases." If you have not solved the problem of "symptom choice" you have not solved the problem of causality. Freud's strength and his enduring contributions to the future rest on his superb insights into the development of the normal human being and the institutions of normal life.

The closest Freud came to love and the closest he came to merger or fusion was in the concept of identification. Looking for a theory of identification in Freud is not a matter of teasing out a thread in a complicated tapestry, but more like locating raisins scattered throughout a pudding. It appears haphazardly and randomly. It emerges in the most diverse discussions over an amazing span of time. To come unexpectedly upon a discussion of identification in an area that would seem to promise no reward is a matter of delight. I have already alluded to the fact that Freud saw something close to merger as the first reality in the life of the infant: "Identification is the original and earliest form of emotional life."[25] Freud further utilized the concept of identification in explaining stages of normal development, the evolution of character traits, and the development of conscience (super-ego) and in his explorations of culture.

Freud also discovered identification as a mechanism in that severe pathological state we now call depression. It is not with perversity that I turn to a very early study of a pathological condition to begin my discussion of normal identification, but because I feel Freud came closest here to a concept of fusion.

In *Mourning and Melancholia*,[26] Freud, building on a profound insight of one of his disciples, Karl Abraham,[27] attempted a systematic analysis of a major clinical illness, depression. According to the fashion of his times, he called it melancholia. The key to this analysis was a comparison of the pathological state of melancholia with the normal pro-cess of mourning, which it resembles in many respects. To put it into modern language, it was an attempt to discover the differences between two superficially similar events, grief and depression.

Mourning the death of a loved one is considered normal, despite the fact that it involves some of the same "patho-logical" conditions one sees in depression: a withdrawal from the interests of the outside world, a diminution of all activity, a loss of interest in the sensual life, reduced libido, and finally the emotional state of dejection, sadness, and teariness. Normal mourning has a limited time frame during which it can still be considered normal—although the time of mourning is far longer than is usually thought. Most people are capable of resuming normal activities within months if not weeks. Closer examination reveals that the grief reaction will last for years, and I suspect that in the case of the premature death of a child it can last for a lifetime.

There are many ways in which depression differs from

grief, but only one cardinal symptom is germane to this discussion—the tendency toward self-punishment. The depressed patient berates himself, humiliates himself, and condemns himself. Freud evolved a theory based on some of the distinctions between grief and depression to try to come to an understanding of the dynamics of the depressed state. He decided that in both there was a sense, real or imagined, of the loss of a loved object, and therefore the features common to both were explicable as responses to loss. In addition, in the depressed patient he postulated an ambivalence toward the lost love. In addition to love, the depressed patient felt rage at the loving person who had abandoned him.

Freud then described a complicated set of mechanisms based on this ambivalence. In order to try to hold on to the loved object, the depressed person introjects her—swallows her up, psychologically. This introjection also serves the rage; it is visualized as a sadistic and punitive devouring of the loved object, thereby satisfying the other half of the ambiguity. After the introjection, the ego splits. Half of it remains angry with the love object and maintains its autonomy and independence. The other half, in an attempt to hold on to the abandoning figure, fuses with the loved object and identifies with it. This process was labeled "narcissistic identification," probably to distinguish it from the primary identification that was seen as the original infantile state of fusion with the mother.

The terminology is difficult, and it became even more complicated as Freud redefined primary identification and secondary identification to a point where even dictionaries and texts on psychoanalysis differ on the definitions. None of it is particularly relevant here except for the idea that one can contain within oneself, fused with at least part of the ego, the psychic representation of another person.

What seems like self-punishment in depression is actually

an angry assault on the departed, but since the departed is fused with the self, what happens is an assault on the self! Here is the first demonstration (beyond the infantile) of the human capacity to so identify with another person that self and other become confused. The importance of *Mourning and Melancholia* extends beyond its theory of depression, which has since been severely modified by some researchers and totally abandoned by others.[28] The paper's importance today lies in its introduction of the mechanisms of introjection, incorporation, and identification that were later to be used in studying interestingly dissimilar but related phenomena.

When Freud was prepared to develop his first principles of conscience, and later when he enlarged this to the concept of the superego, identification and incorporation became principal mechanisms. We swallow whole the figure of the punitive father and then behave as though his judging presence were always with us. Fear of the punitive father within guides us to "proper" behavior according to his standards. In the later and more sophisticated model of superego we incorporate an idealized image of the parent within us and so identify with this image that betrayal of its values is interpreted as self-betrayal, which produces a profound sense of guilt or shame.

This concept of identification is so close to one of fusion that one wonders why it was not quickly and readily extended. The fact that the child identifies with the mother or father should have prompted the awareness that a parent can similarly identify with the child. Ironically, when the term is used by lay people these days, it is more often intended in this latter manner. Perhaps this failure to extend the concept of identification was due to the fact that in early theory all character formation was assumed to be limited to the first few years of life. Only with the work of Erikson and others did we begin to appreciate that we could find our "introjects" throughout life.

Identification upward—that is, the child's identification with the parent—is so obvious and apparent a device that we may take it for granted. The fusion is so automatic that it may be seen as something less profound. A little boy "behaves" as his father wants him to behave out of fear of the father, love of the father, or a need to ingratiate and be loved by the father. The same little boy also behaves *like* his father—even if that may not be the way his father wants him to behave—out of a strong and almost mechanistic mimicry. The mimicry is often encouraged. It also may be influenced by some genetic coding that may affect posture, learning rates, or other familial variables. Beyond these, however, is the most powerful of behavior-determining measures, identification. It is a "wholesale" adoption of the forms, habits, and often the values of the parent by incorporation and identification. A son tends to resemble his father in form, manner, and behavior because of genetics (appearance is most likely influenced here) and conditioning, and partly because he *is*, in part, the father. He has incorporated the image of his father into his mind in such a way that it will be a basic building block out of which his identity will be constructed. Of course, he will also incorporate images of his mother, older siblings, and many "significant others" to form the final self.

The child therefore learns his behavior in two ways. Piece by piece, he is encouraged toward or discouraged from developing certain traits by the rewards or disapprovals in the faces and manners of the adults on whom he is so dependent. He also learns in big blocks by incorporating various identities through introjections. To find yourself, with age, recognizing your father's face in the mirror is one thing, but to find yourself relating to your children with the irratio-

nalities you resented in your father is, to say the least, un-
settling. The fusion is there in precisely the way Freud
described it in the dynamics of depression.

Identification "downward" is another thing entirely. And
here fusion is all. One would not usually say I "look like"
my daughters. If any likeness exists, it more appropriately
would be said that they look like me. Similarly, I do not by
incorporation adopt their mannerisms, tastes, or sensibilities. But the confusion about where I end and they begin is
more profound in this direction than in the other. To hurt
my child minimally is to lacerate me. It is not that I have
introjected them, I have "extrojected" (if there were such a
word) *me*. It is not that they are within me. I am within
them. I have in some mysterious way located the essential
me within another's corpus. I am now in the vulnerable and
extraordinary position of having my fate and destiny packaged in a body under someone else's control. If my daughter
does something foolishly and willfully self-destructive, the
pain will be experienced by hapless and innocent me. No
wonder I am capable of such anger with my children. They
carry the helpless me with them on all their foolish and
sometimes treacherous escapades. How dare they risk the
purpose of my existence, my only immortality, my existential "meaning," by endangering themselves? When Catherine
in *Wuthering Heights* says that she does not love Heathcliff
but *is* Heathcliff, I know what she means. She is not just
talking about romantic love, she is talking about the fusion
that is at the root of all love. She is talking about me and my
daughters, as well as me and my wife.

This identification downward can be a disaster. The fusion can be so powerful, so quasi-delusional, that we forget
the primary responsibility of a parent to nurture children to
a point of autonomy. We can encourage their continuing
dependence on us. We can do worse. We can deny them the

right to an independent existence. The child may be viewed as a new self, offering us an opportunity to rectify the inadequacies of our current existence. It is not just that the child will be forced to attempt to become the writer, baseball player, or ballerina that you were unable to become. She or he will become, in this reincarnation, the you that never was. You run the risk of seeing the child not just as an ally or extension of the self, but as a corrected self. The child will cease to be a person. The power of this fusion can be a nightmare for the child, in which the parent obsessively serves his own frustration by rationalizing it as in the best interest of the child. The power of fusion is awesome.

It is obvious that fusions differ in relationships. The ego of the child, in incorporating many models, may be seen as a large circle composed of a number of circles of varying sizes contained within it. The loving couple can be seen as two circles which, while independent, overlap and are therefore linked by the overlapping space shared by both. In the identification downward, it is as though the whole self of the parent were deposited within the circumference of the child. This leads to different relationships between the identifying loved ones and different reactions to loss. The death of a loved spouse is like an amputation. An integral part of you is ripped away. The death of a parent is often more tolerable, because the psychological parent is permanently fused into one's identity. But the death of a child may be seen as carrying away the entire self.

Identification remained for Freud the halfway house, the resting point, in his journey toward love. He never got all the way there. Reluctant to accept fusion as a normal possibility, he never understood the nature of love. In recent years one has seen a healthy movement within psychoanalysis to move away from language and models that are outdated and to build on Freudian insights to elaborate new concepts. Psychoanalysis, one senses, is about to discover love.

The process of identification is essential in understanding some of the contradictions in our caring capacity. Why is it that we seem more committed toward those people separated from us in time—that is, future generations—than toward those people separated from us in space—the tragically dispossessed inhabitants of the Third World? It may be that future generations are appreciated as biological extensions of ourselves. We are able to visualize grandchildren as replications and continuities even when we are quite young. But since few of us have any clear picture of our great-great-grandparents, could we possibly sense an obligation toward our great-great-grandchildren?

The answer may lie in understanding a phenomenon I will call "proximal identification." It is an unpleasant and seemingly ugly one, and when articulated in public offends almost everyone. It is offered as a psychological reality, not a moral principle. I believe that the loss of a limb by my child would grieve me more than the loss of life by my neighbor's child. I am not pleased by this observation. It seems a limitation on my capacities for empathy, but I am convinced it is true. I would go further. I would say the scarring of my child (forget about the total loss of a limb) would cause me more grief and agony, more concern, than the death of a neighbor's child. Further—horrifying but true—I would say that the same scarring would, in the same terms, grieve me more than the death of five hundred thousand children in the sub-Sahara.

Intellectually, of course, I am distressed by the agony and injustice represented by the hunger in Africa. When I visualize this tragedy in the faces of real people, through the graphic representations on television or even only in my imagination while reading the newspapers, a sense of true grief overcomes me. But only temporarily am I emotionally involved. I may maintain my intellectual involvement and moral commitment through relief activities, but my true emotions will not be the same as those caused by the everyday awareness of that scarred or injured child sharing my life. I am not concerned about the possible shock and horror in the faces of those who hear me present this discussion because I refuse to believe I am unique. Having dealt with human suffering on the most intimate level in my work with patients, I know that true suffering has a proximal quality. It is not a new idea. As Hume observed over two hundred years ago, "Pity depends, in a great measure, on the contiguity, and even sight of the object."[29]

Proximal identification does not require the physical closeness to or sight of the object that Hume suggests. As we form our identifications through our kinships they can extend into a future too far for most to visualize and back to a past we never experienced. The chaos in Ireland, taking the lives of hundreds of innocents, will touch the Irish-American more than the loss of thousands of lives in Afghanistan. A terrorist bomb placed on a bus full of Israeli children will break the heart of an American Jew who has never visited Israel. These linkages, ethnic, religious, racial, for good and for bad—with the limitations of empathy that is their obverse—can be seen as deriving from important survival patterns built into our genetic matrix.

While proximal identification may be irrational and "unjust," I see in it a biologically adaptive mechanism. The units of survival in prehistoric times were much smaller than those of today. There were no nations, there was no universality of man; there were only family clusters. Survival of the species, particularly of the dependent human young, demands an overvaluation of and an extreme sensitivity to the needs of those young who are our specific charge.

In the same way that we extinguish and block from consciousness certain physical responses that are intruding on our assigned tasks—the street noises that would intrude on our concentration are simply "not heard"—we extinguish certain pain and empathy responses to matters over which we might have little influence, but which might significantly distract us from matters over which we do have control. The physiological process of extinction allows focusing attention on a primary goal and purpose. Similarly, the psychological extinction of pain beyond the borders of our immediate interest allows focusing our caring nature on those to whom we have primary responsibility. The ultimate in proximal identification is, of course, when the individual is within you and beyond identification. This is the phenomenon called fusion which I believe is central to all loving.

One other major aspect of all loving is an idealization of the loved object, but that will be better understood in the context of a comparison among falling in love, loving, and being loved.

In the passage from Walker Percy with which I began this chapter, Allison went to the library seeking a way to "get away from my everlasting self sick of itself to be with another self and is that what *it* is and if not then what?"

Allison finds the answer, not in the library, but as one should in any good romantic novel, in a relationship with her lover:

> What I need to know and think I know is, is loving you the secret, the be-all not end-all but starting point of my very life, or is it just one of the things creatures do like eating and drinking and therefore nothing special and therefore nothing to dream about? Is loving a filling of the four-o'clock gap or is it more? . . . It might be the secret because a minute ago when you held me and I came against you, there were signs of coming close, to *it*, for the

first time, like the signs you recognize when you are getting near the ocean for the first time. Even though you've never seen the ocean before, you recognize it, the sense of an opening out ahead and putting behind the old rickrack bird-chirp town and countryside, something tasting new in the air, the dirt getting sandier, even the shacks and weeds looking different, and something else, a quality of sound, a penultimate hush marking the beginning of the end of land and the beginning of the old uproar and the going away of the endless sea.[30]

Love *is* more than a filling of "the four-o'clock gap." It is the sense of "an opening out ahead," of "putting behind the old," of "something tasting new" and "looking different"; it is "a quality of sound"; it is "the beginning of the end and the beginning." It is all this and more—and more.

5 ◈ THE EXPERIENCE OF LOVE

One of the avowed purposes
of this book is to salvage the concept of love from our
current obsessive preoccupation with being loved. The pressures, anxieties, tensions, and value systems of our modern
culture have so unsettled most of us that we seek constant
reassurance. In pursuit of this need for approval, we have
come to the misguided notion that love means being told:
You're O.K., I'm O.K.

Love bestowed upon us does provide support for a sag-
ging ego. But love is too rich a resource to be exhausted on
such a narrow pursuit. As pleasure must not be trivialized
by reducing it to simply one more form of reassurance, love
is too essential a component of a full existence to be casually
expended as a narcissistic poultice.

We must reestablish an ascending trajectory of aspiration: from being loved to loving. In that process we will
rediscover the romantic element of love that was excluded
from legitimacy by Freud's aversion to nineteenth-century
romanticism. In distinguishing between being loved and loving, we will encounter a third unique condition, that ephemeral but delightful state called "falling in love." We must
once again confront the two visions of Aphrodite, to consider whether that aspect of love which is erotic and pas-

118

sionate is a necessary antagonist of that aspect of love which is comforting and binding.

A psychoanalyst friend once confided to me that he was confused by the American preoccupation with "popularity," claiming that it was a concept alien to his Germanic upbringing and tradition. What he meant by popularity—what he saw in the distinctly American desire—was the need to be loved in breadth as distinguished from depth. It seemed to him that Americans had an urgency not just to experience the intimacy of love with one individual but to bask in the affection of the multitude. This was exemplified by the frantic preoccupation of adolescents specifically, but also of adolescent adults, with "popularity."

I cannot testify to the cultural differences which he described, but I can affirm that the concept of popularity in our society is but one extension of the massive concentration on the need to be loved. Obviously, by starting this book with a chapter on the need for love and the biological roots that support it, I acknowledge this need as both an essential pleasure and an urgent requirement for survival. Being loved is a major component in the complicated process of giving and getting that forms the scenario of a good love relationship. It should not be used as a substitute for such reciprocity. The need to feel loved, however, can serve as a safe entry point to the more frightening and vulnerable territory of reciprocal love, as for Thomas Hardy's character Sue:

> "At first I did not love you, Jude; that I own. When I first knew you I merely wanted you to love me. I did not exactly flirt with you; but that inborn craving which undermines some women's morals almost more than unbridled passion—the craving to attract and captivate, regardless of the injury it may do the man—was in me;

and when I found I had caught you, I was frightened. And then—I don't know how it was—I couldn't bear to let you go—possibly to Arabella again—and so I got to love you, Jude. But you see, however fondly it ended, it began in the selfish and cruel wish to make your heart ache for me without letting mine ache for you."[1]

But as is often the case, an outsider can be aware of the dynamic of a relationship well before the principals appreciate the roles that they are playing. Jude's wife, the crass but streetwise Arabella, would see the state of affairs:

"He's charmed by her as if she were some fairy! . . . See how he looks round at her, and lets his eyes rest on her. I am inclined to think that she don't care for him quite so much as he does for her. She's not a particular warm-hearted creature to my thinking, though she cares for him pretty middling much—as much as she's able to; and he could make her heart ache a bit if he liked to try—which he's too simple to do."[2]

There is a profound excitement in the alternation of loving and being loved; in the capacity to be caretaker, nurturer, and parent at one moment while at another moment in the same relationship feeling free to be childish, vulnerable, and cared-for. Mature love tolerates, indeed encourages, flexibility; each partner has the pleasure of playing multiple roles. What is disastrous in much of the modern scene is the preoccupation with the passive role—the peculiar elevation of the role of the infant to many levels above that of the parent. The qualities of love I described in the parental role exist almost intact in romantic love, except for the mutability of its form and the changes mandated by reciprocity and maturity.

The element that sometimes mitigates and always complicates romantic love is the introduction of the volatile and demanding sexual drive to this already powerful amalgamation of feelings. The force of lust and the powers of passion and idealization that are inherent in romantic love make it less stable than the more focused parental bond. Romantic love is at best a complex and difficult phenomenon to sustain. When, as is happening in modern culture, it is further endangered by the overvaluation of the infantile role of loved object rather than the mature role of lover, when both parties vie for this crib of honor, fighting to be the center of passivity, when both actors aspire to the role of the basin rather than that of the pitcher, romantic love, seems almost impossible to sustain.

The narcissist desperately craves not only to be loved, but to be loved in a specific and certain way. He wants to be loved for himself, not for what he does. He wants the love to be freely bestowed, not earned, as though in some way any effort on his part would tarnish this love. What does it mean to be loved for oneself alone, not for one's virtues, not for one's actions, not for one's body, not for one's beauty? In a peculiar irony of coincidence, Irving Singer in his chapter on erotic idealization quotes the following lines from a "popular" song with words by Henry Blossom, music by Victor Herbert—obviously a nineteenth-century or turn-of-the-century lyric:

> Not that you are fair, dear,
> Not that you are true, not your golden hair, dear,
> Not your eyes of blue.
> When we ask the reason, words are all too few!
> So I know I love you, dear, because you're you.[3]

In a discussion of narcissism in *Feelings* I had quoted an almost antithetical dialogue between two lovers, using the identical imagery to make precisely the *opposite* point.

"Never shall a young man,
Thrown into despair
By those great honey-coloured
Ramparts at your ear,
Love you for yourself alone
And not your yellow hair."

"But I can get a hair-dye
And set such colour there,
Brown, or black or carrot,
That young men in despair
May love me for myself alone
And not my yellow hair."

"I heard an old religious man
But yesternight declare
That he had found a text to prove
That only God, my dear,
Could love you for yourself alone
And not your yellow hair."[4]

Yeats was, of course, absolutely correct. What does craving to be loved for ourselves—as distinguished from our traits, our attributes, our behavior, and yes, even our possessions and our position—what does that mean? There is no inner self independent of our behavior, our character, and our form. There is only one time to my knowledge when one is loved for oneself, independent of one's behavior. That of course is in the first stage of early infancy.

There is little about the *behavior* of a newborn to delight anyone. His eyes are usually out of focus; he is likely to disturb one's sleep and exhaust one's energies with demands which cannot be fulfilled; his tears of rage are coercive demands—for what we cannot always know; and his tears of pain fail to reveal a source that can be corrected. He violates all the rules. He behaves in a way that will be greeted with dismay and disapproval, even in the young child. He will interrupt our dinners. He will refuse to maintain even a reasonable schedule that seems to be adapted to him. He will pass gas and more in public. He will urinate on visitors we are most apt to want to impress. In a ritual called "burping" he will be encouraged to vomit on one's shoulder. And the burp with the vomit will be received by the relieved parent as a gift of satisfaction and delight. This is, I expect, what is meant by "true love." This represents being loved, not for what one "does," but for what one "is."

It would seem, therefore, that what the narcissist desires is a return not just to an earlier stage but to *the earliest* stage. What an extraordinary route we have come from the age of chivalry. In the troubadour's concept of *fin' amors* we have an image of true love in which the loved one must never be touched. Love must always remain ungratified. There was only one actor in this love—the lover. It was a game of solitaire. It was not only satisfactory but absolutely necessary that the loved object be pristine, detached, and unavailable. Courtly love was all loving, with no possibility of returns.

The nineteenth-century romantics did not completely abandon the concept of the unattainable love. Certainly *La Nouvelle Héloïse* of Rousseau directly continues the courtly desire for unfulfilled love and idealizes the moral (and sexual) excitement of frustrated passion. And Friedrich von Schlegel's *Lucinde* is often cited as the ultimate nineteenth-century expression of love as an unrealizable ideal. These days we tend to view the whole enterprise of courtly love as incomprehensible. We are amused and bewildered by all those bizarre and awkward customs which served an isolated love that was never to be fulfilled. The whole charade seems ludicrous.

Yet, in narcissistic America in the late twentieth century we have a culture that is just as ludicrous in its direct antithesis. With the troubadour the pursuit of love was sufficient without the presence of love. In narcissistic love the pursuit of being loved is sufficient without the act of loving. It is less by any standard. It is a regression from the courtly experience. It is passive versus active. It is receiving rather than giving. It is infantile rather than adult. Men in the twentieth century have voluntarily sought the degraded role that had traditionally been assigned to women. Modern man desires to be an object, a love object.

In the contrast between the courtly and the romantic definitions and traditions of love we may find some sense of where we lost our way. We may find some way of rediscovering love.

The Brontës represent pure nineteenth-century romanticism. Jane Eyre gets her Rochester, and Catherine in a peculiar way gets her Heathcliff, if only in the heightened spiritual sensibility of that age. Again and again and again, Catherines are reunited with their various Heathcliffs across the generations. Still one senses here the residue of the courtly ideal in the power of passion unfulfilled. It is only with Heathcliff that Catherine achieves the fusion that identifies true love:

> "If all else perished, and *he* remained I should still continue to be; and all else remained, and he were annihilated, the universe would turn to a mighty stranger; I should not seem a part of it. My love for Linton is like the foliage in the woods: time will change it, I'm well aware, as winter changes the trees. My love for Heathcliff resembles the eternal rocks beneath—a source of little visible delight, but necessary. Nelly, I *am* Heathcliff! He's always, always in my mind—not as a pleasure any more than I am always a pleasure to myself, but as my own being."[5]

To me, as a boy growing up in twentiety-century America, *Wuthering Heights* with its pure romanticism was less accessible than *Jane Eyre*. As a teenage boy I could find excitement in the unfulfilled passion of Jane, not dissimilar from my own unfulfilled passions. And after all, wasn't Jane herself also a teenager, or close enough? And Jane was aggressive and spunky, and—like a Horatio Alger hero—she would ultimately have to triumph. Jane offered the romance of adventure as well as that of a love I could not yet comprehend. The optimistic victory of Jane was what I as a teenager demanded.

In my first go-round with *Wuthering Heights,* I left it unfinished. It was too mushy, too ethereal, too static, too mystical for me. In addition, early in the novel before its repetitive decline in successive dreary generations, I was horrified to realize that Heathcliff, the only character in this novel an adolescent boy could possibly identify with, could not prevail, and would not (as always happened in my favorite English novelist, Dickens) end up victorious and living happily ever after. *Wuthering Heights* retained the tradition of courtly love that is seen, for example, in *Ivanhoe* but without the adventure necessary to captivate the interest of a teenage boy, for whom romance is still more vested in valor than in love. It is my impression that teenage girls are likely to be more captivated with *Wuthering Heights,* often preferring it to *Jane Eyre*.

No better contrast between the romantic and the courtly traditions exists in literature than in the novel *Ivanhoe*. I am not sure that anyone except teenagers, the last of the romantics in our generation, still reads *Ivanhoe*. In this novel, first published in 1819, Sir Walter Scott recreates the age of chivalry, but casts it in terms of nineteenth-century sensibilities. It is a historical novel. It deals directly with twelfth-century traditions, the codes of chivalry, the Knights Templar, the princes and the courtiers. Yet in *Ivanhoe* one sees the forerunner of the great Victorian romances, which were to reach their heights—and perhaps their limits—in the Brontës and that peculiar twentieth-century vestige of nineteenth-century romanticism D. H. Lawrence.

Ivanhoe is the story of a Saxon knight, returning from the crusades with his lord, Richard the Lion-Hearted, to find England captive to the Norman barons, who are attempting to maintain Richard's evil brother John in power. It is also a love story in which the putative hero and heroine are Ivanhoe and the Saxon princess Rowena. Despite the presumed happy ending, in which Ivanhoe is united with his fair Rowena, true love still remains unrequited, for true love in this novel does not reside with Ivanhoe and Rowena. Scott, clinging to the spirit as well as the forms of the courtly, retains the concept of *fin' amors,* while fusing it with nineteenth-century sexual passion. In *Ivanhoe* nobody gets quite what he wants. There are at least three recognizable and profound passions. One is Ivanhoe's passion for the Jewess Rebecca (although he himself barely recognizes it); another is Rebecca's passion for Ivanhoe; and the third is the passion of the villainous Sir Brian de Bois-Guilbert for Rebecca.

It is not necessary to do an exegesis of this complicated plot to say that the heroine in this book is Rebecca and the hero in a peculiar way is Bois-Guilbert. Rowena is a convenient plot device, a plastic saint without any true passions. She is the pure symbol of the aspirations of the courtly lover. She is the earthly version of the Madonna, and the desire she generates is less sexual even than the theological passion aroused in clerics influenced by the Maryistic tradition. It is not just chance that when *Ivanhoe* is translated into movies, television, or theater, the woman star is cast in the role of Rebecca, not Rowena. It is Rebecca who comes to life and captivates the romantic in all of us.

And what of Ivanhoe? Even he seems, to use the popular word of our day, too much of a "wimp" to be a true hero—too goody-goody to fulfill the fleshed-out needs of our complicated time, in which good and evil must not be totally separable; too "anal" to supply the unpredictable quality we now demand of romantic heroes; and too simple-minded, too out-of-touch, to be believable in our psychological age. The fire, the impetuosity, the blood, the sexuality, and the ultimate nobility lie with the dastardly, devious Sir Brian. When he states after a particular moment of devilish intention, "Many a law, many a commandment have I broken, but my word, never," we believe him.

For those who are unfamiliar with the story, the dénouement involves a peculiar and ironic set of self-defeating maneuvers on Brian's part. In his intense passion for the Jewess Rebecca, for whom he is prepared to give up honor, titles, and privileges, he finds himself trapped into having to fight, not for her, but against her champion, who in this case, of course, will be, with the serendipity of fiction, Sir Wilfred of Ivanhoe. Sir Brian knows that if he wins the battle against Rebecca's champion it will, according to the courtly code of chivalry, "prove" the Jewess to be a sorceress and she will be burned at the stake. He is certain that he will win, and suggests the only means of saving her. At the eleventh hour he offers her, beyond life, his reputation and his Christian soul:

> "Rebecca, if I appear not in these lists I lose fame and rank—lose that which is the breath of my nostrils, the esteem, I mean, in which I am held by my brethren. . . .
>
> If I appear in the fatal lists, thou diest by a slow and cruel death, in pain such as they say is destined to the guilty hereafter. But if I appear not, then am I a degraded

and dishonoured knight, accused of witchcraft and of communion with infidels: the illustrious name which has grown yet more so under my wearing becomes a hissing and a reproach. I lose fame—I lose honour—I lose the prospect of such greatness as scarce emperors attain to; I sacrifice mighty ambition—I destroy schemes built as high as the mountains with which heathens say their heaven was once nearly scaled; and yet Rebecca . . . this greatness will I sacrifice—this fame will I renounce—this power will I forego, even now when it is half within my grasp if thou wilt say, 'Bois-Guilbert, I receive thee for my lover.' "[6]

Rebecca refuses to "barter"—the prototypical character trait attributed to the Jew by the anti-Semite—and demands of the Christian knight an act of pure charity, the essential ingredient of his presumed faith. Bois-Guilbert refuses. He is, after all, the product of a nineteenth-century sensibility, and the only passion for which he can commit such sacrifices is love. He describes for her the agonies of death at the stake and says to her, "It is not in woman to sustain this prospect."

"Rebecca answers with the pride of a modern feminist:

Bois-Guilbert . . . thou knowest not the heart of woman, or hast only conversed with those who are lost to her best feelings. I tell thee, proud Templar, that not in thy fiercest battles hast thou displayed more of thy vaunted courage than has been shown by woman when called upon to suffer by affection or duty. I am myself a woman, tenderly nurtured, naturally fearful of danger, and impatient of pain; yet, when we enter those fatal lists, thou to fight and I to suffer, I feel the strong assurance within me that my courage shall mount higher than thine."[7]

Eventually her champion appears. But Ivanhoe is in a desperate position, still not recovered from his wounds, which had been tenderly nursed by Rebecca through at least half of the book. Weary from his ride, barely astride his spent horse, he is no match for Bois-Guilbert. Yet Ivanhoe emerges the victor when Bois-Guilbert mysteriously falls dead. "Unscathed by the lance of his enemy, he had died a victim to the violence of his own contending passions."[8] Every reader of *Ivanhoe* assumes this to be a choice made by Sir Brian as the only means of liberating the woman he loved. It is, at its most romantic, a statement of the meaning of love.

And most readers will see the feeling that *Ivanhoe* has for Rowena as something less than the passion he felt for Rebecca. Scott intends us to believe this or he would not have ended his novel by telling us that Ivanhoe

> lived long and happily with Rowena, for they were at-
> tached to each other by the bonds of early affection, and
> they loved each other more from the recollection of the
> obstacles which had impeded their union. Yet it would be
> inquiring too curiously to ask whether the recollection of
> Rebecca's beauty and magnanimity did not recur to his
> mind more frequently than the fair descendent of Alfred
> might altogether have approved.[9]

In Sir Brian's sacrifice of his life for Rebecca, and in her eschewal of all future love since she cannot have Ivanhoe, we see the mark of true passion. But other forms of love are also present here. Surely in the final section quoted here, Scott offers a quieter relationship based on commitment, idealization, a shared past, and a dedicated future that meets the designation of love. There are other reasons for the contrasting images of the two loves: the blond Rowena and the dark Rebecca.

Ivanhoe is not intended to be a historical account or a study of the moral aspects of chivalry. It is a story, an act of creation, a romance by a man who was clearly a romantic. In every creation we learn something of the nature of the creator, and, if he is a true artist, something about the nature of all human sensibility. The Oedipal aspects of *Ivanhoe* are so transparent that it does not require any extensive psychoanalytic exegesis. We are offered two images of the loving woman. Rowena is pure but distant, gentle but unsensual. She is Ivanhoe's childhood ideal, she is a Saxon, of his blood, his lineage. She is the ward of his father and she is a distillation of Platonic beauty and goodness. She is the Madonna or the heavenly Aphrodite. And always she is compared in a confusing counterpoint of fevered dreams with the veiled and dark image of Rebecca, exotic, sensual, shadowy, mysterious, a creature half illusion and half reality.

The role of Rebecca in relationship to Ivanhoe is clearly marked. She is the giver of life. When the critically wounded Ivanhoe is left on the battlefield, abandoned by his father ("I have no son"), it is Rebecca who nurtures and nurses him and, with her "magic potions and herbs," brings him back to life. Rebecca is the nurse, the caretaker, the soothing, touching, caressing, healing, sensual, and forbidden mother. She bathes him and feeds him through prolonged and extended periods of helplessness. Rowena exists in the sunshine of public places, of banquet halls and tourneys. She is the princess—a figure of ritual and privilege. She is brightly lit and never revealed. Rebecca exists in the bedrooms and the private hidden spaces of the ghetto. She is a creature of darkness and dreams. She is always veiled and never hidden.

Most important of all, Rebecca is taboo. She is a Jewess, an infidel. She can never be seriously considered by Ivanhoe as a true love object. It is not just against class and convention, it is not just sacrilegious; such a union is literally unthinkable to him. Ivanhoe is never aware of his growing passion for Rebecca; only the reader and perhaps Rebecca are privy to his unconscious. He never allows himself the conscious perception of his love of her, let alone considering marriage to her. Certainly these are the two visions of the mother that every son possesses.

It is only the wild, tempestuous, and defiantly cynical Bois-Guilbert who is prepared to violate all taboos, to defy all convention and all authority. Guilbert is ready to sacrifice his worldly goods, his reputation, his salvation, and what is more important than all of them in an age of chivalry, his honor, for the sake of Rebecca. This is more than love. This is the fatal passion of Phaedra. He ignores that which ought not be ignored. Duty, obligation, religion, honor are not cheap goods to be cast aside. They too have claims on each of us as mighty in many ways as the claims of love. He is, as he was accused of being, bewitched. He represents the untrammeled and unfettered incestual impulse which exists, covert and denied, in the unconscious of each of us.

The incestual strain was not unfamiliar in the literature of chivalry nor in the classics before that. King Arthur's doom is fixed with his incestual relationship with his sister, just as the downfall of that other mighty king Oedipus was the price of his incestual relationship with his mother. Culpability existed in the action, independent of ignorance of the fact. A kind of knowing is always presumed. The power of the incestual drive is acknowledged in this literature by the destruction to which it must inevitably lead, and the irrelevance of all exculpating evidence of fate, predestination, or ignorance. Nothing can mitigate the action. Intent is irrelevant, because an unconscious intention is always assumed.

In that masterpiece of French literature *Phaedra* Racine cruelly juxtaposes the joy of Hippolytus' "entrapment" in pure love with the agony of the same, but incestually tainted, passion in his stepmother, Phaedra. The story is a retelling of the classic drama of the passion of a noble woman for her handsome stepson, and her revenge when he spurns her advances. Hippolytus, declaring his pure love for young Aricia, says:

> Since
> some six months past, ashamed and desperate,
> wearing where I go the arrow which
> has rent me, I engage in futile struggle
> against myself and you. Yes, where you are
> I flee; and where you are not, there I seek
> to find you; in the depths of woods your image
> is at my heels; the light of day, the dark
> of night—all trace again before my eyes
> the beauty I avoid—all things unite
> to render to your hands Hippolytus
> the rebel. I myself, as all the fruit
> of my inept precautions, search myself
> and find myself no longer.[10]

Hippolytus' "struggle" elicits no compassion, only affectionate recognition. He is a slave of love, a "slavery" to which we all aspire. He expresses the very essence of fusion. His identity has been handed over to another. Phaedra also inveighs against the gods in declaring her love. She too is the unwilling victim of the god of love, but our heart agonizes for her.

> Think not at the moment when
> I love you that I fail to feel my guilt,
> or that I like myself for loving you—
> nor deem my weak compliance nourishes
> the poison of this maddening love which so
> unseats my reason! I, unhappy victim
> of vengeful gods, abhor myself far more
> than you could possibly detest me. I

can call upon the Gods to witness that!—
those Gods who lit the fatal fire in
my body, burning in my veins—those Gods
whose cruel sport it is to lead astray
a feeble woman's heart![11]

The first object of desire, after the detachment of libidinal interest in the self, is the parent of the opposite sex, according to the psychoanalytic theory of sexual development. Freud, impressed by both his clinical experiences and the mythic preoccupation with incest, presumed a universal presence of incestual desire in all human development. The process of sexual maturation will demand that we detach ourselves from the powerful hold of the incestual object. Eventually all neuroses were to be viewed in Freudian theory as a failure in the resolution of the Oedipal conflict, which was the nuclear constellation of all mental disorder. Successful resolution does not, however, mean total abandonment of incestual desire (no aspect of infantile sexuality is ever completely lost) but merely its displacement and subservience to a nonincestual object.

The capacity to detach one's sexual interest from oneself and fuse in love with the parent is, however, a necessary first step toward real love. The bewildered mother who is hurt when the same prepubescent son who wanted to marry her a few short years ago refuses to kiss her ought see in this peculiar reversal the mark of her successful mothering. The residual traces of this incestual attachment are revealed in both the nature of the loved object we choose and in the way we relate to her. The lover looks for the shadow of the parent in the loved one and either embraces its presence or recoils from it, depending in great part on the success or failure of his resolution of his incestual interest.

I have said that the hallmark of true love, the necessary

and essential ingredient, is the fusion of self with person to a point where the other person's life, his happiness, become transcendent over one's own; the sacrifice of self at least in the dramatic world of romantic literature becomes the fulfillment of self. Roberto Unger, in his book *Passion,* stops somewhat short of this point but comes close enough for me to feel kinship with his ideas: "The experience of passion is located at the point where distinctions between desire (wanting something from the other person) and knowledge (viewing him and oneself in a certain way) collapse."[12]

Obviously loving and being loved can and should coexist in one relationship—there is no real conflict between the two. One may so dominate the psychological needs of an individual as to exclude the other, but they have a natural compatibility. When, however, we compare loving commitment with passion there is a question of true compatibility. Is sexual passion incompatible with commitment and authentic love? Is it destroyed by time and familiarity? If sexual passion cannot coexist with loving, then romantic love is an impossibility except as an evanescent and ephemeral phenomenon. Parental love requires only the capacity to give and receive love; what sexuality may exist must be repressed and denied. Parental love requires two of the essential ingredients—fusion plus the caring aspects. Romantic love demands the presence of sexual passion.

The various arguments about the two Aphrodites, the two conflicting aspects of love, that have extended over the centuries suggest an essential conflict. Personal experience would seem to support this, beyond any need for verification by empirical data. The first kiss is different from the thousandth, and the intensity of the passionate feeling of young or new love is different in some way from romantic love that has matured in time.

It is intriguing to see the psychologists, both within and

out of psychiatry, rediscovering love and in the process struggling with the same contradictions that the philosophers and aestheticians have dealt with in the last two thousand years. One author, Marion J. King, traces the natural life cycle of romantic love and states poetically:

> The third phase [of love] marks the completion of the romantic venture; at the same time it is a beginning. Part of this beginning is the gradual evaporation of that intoxicating spirit that pervaded the relationship before it was sealed into a lasting bond. Indeed, romantic love thrives on anticipation, on a measure of unfulfillment, and a longing for consummation. Where every form of separation—physical, social, and personal—is abolished in favor of the fullest intimacy possible, a change in the quality of the relationship is unavoidable. One cannot long for what one possesses, although one can deeply cherish it.[13]

One can find dozens of quotes out of the psychological literature approaching this same conflict between commitment and passion. According to one writer, J. L. Singer, romantic love is "built around potentiality, the touchstone of fantasy, not just what is given but what might be."[14]

The answer to the dilemma of the two Aphrodites may rest in our definition of passion. Young passion may be different from mature attachment, but different does not mean antithetic. We must not confuse appetite with passion. The equation of human passion with animal instinct seems absurd in this modern age of psychology. Yet it is done. And surprisingly, the same equation was made over two hundred years ago, and seemed equally absurd to that most prescient of students of human behavior Henry Fielding:

> In our last book we have been obliged to deal pretty much with the passion of love. . . . It may not, therefore, in this

place be improper to apply ourselves to the examination
of that modern doctrine which certain philosophers
among many other wonderful discoveries pretend to have
found out: that there is no such passion in the human
breast. . . .

To avoid, however, all contention if possible with these
philosophers . . . and to show our own disposition to
accommodate matters peaceably between us, we shall here
make them some concessions which may possibly put an
end to the dispute.

First, we will grant that many minds, and perhaps those
of the philosophers, are entirely free from the least traces
of such a passion.

Secondly, that which is commonly called love, namely,
the desire of satisfying a voracious appetite with a certain
quantity of delicate white human flesh, is by no means
that passion for which I here contend. This is indeed more
properly hunger; and as no glutton is ashamed to apply
the word *love* to his appetite, and to say he LOVES such
and such dishes, so may the lover of this kind with equal
propriety say he HUNGERS after such and such women.

Fielding concedes that the love for which he is an advo-
cate seeks gratification as avariciously as the grossest of all
appetites. Further he concedes that in the passion of real
love, there are elements of the hunger he describes, and that
it heightens the experience of love. He then plaintively in-
quires:

In return to all these concessions, I desire of the philosophers to grant that there is in some (I believe in many)
human breasts a kind and benevolent disposition, which
is gratified by contributing to the happiness of others.
That in this gratification alone, as in friendship, in parental and filial affection, and indeed in general philanthropy,
there is a great and exquisite delight. That if we will not
call such disposition love, we have no name for it. That
though the pleasures arising from such pure love may be
heightened and sweetened by the assistance of amorous

desires, yet the former can subsist alone, nor are they destroyed by the intervention of the latter. Lastly, that esteem and gratitude are the proper motives to love, as youth and beauty are to desire; and, therefore, though such desire may naturally cease when age or sickness overtake its object, yet these can have no effect on love, nor ever shake or remove from a good mind that sensation or passion which hath gratitude and esteem for its basis.[15]

Fielding identifies a passion, a feeling of "great and exquisite delight," quite independent of desire or lust. Lust is used with more frequency these days to describe that aspect of human nature which we share with the animals—a sexual drive which is turned on with a certain automaticity at the anticipation, viewing, or thought of another person in a sexual experience.

C. S. Lewis explains it perfectly:

Sexual desire, without Eros, wants *it*, the *thing in itself*; Eros wants the Beloved.

The *thing* is a sensory pleasure; that is, an event occurring within one's own body. We use a most unfortunate idiom when we say, of a lustful man prowling the streets, that he "wants a woman." Strictly speaking, a woman is just what he does not want. He wants a pleasure for which a woman happens to be the necessary piece of apparatus. . . . Now Eros makes a man really want, not a woman, but one particular woman. In some mysterious but quite indisputable fashion the lover desires the Beloved herself, not the pleasure she can give.[16]

Lust is the desire for the casual and anonymous sexual feeling: the erection that occurs without intention of necessary pursuit or even valuation of the object. It is what some women patients have occasionally described to me as a purely visceral phenomenon on seeing an attractive street laborer stripped to the waist in the summer. It is one that men describe all the time.

Unger's definition is a particularly attractive one: "Lust is sexual attraction untransformed by love, or generally, uninspired by the imagination of otherness."[17] Unger sees lust as attacking the most important connecting links between biology and culture. In lust, "sexuality rebels against its service to the reproduction of society and threatens to subvert the proprieties of kinship and domesticities. It turns into a free-floating and potentially disruptive force."[18]

It is not by chance that Unger uses Freud's term "free-floating"; the description of lust that he has offered, raw undirected energy untouched by human imagination, unconcerned with the sensibilities of its object, conforms to Freud's description of the primitive infantile libido.

Lust, or appetite, is a human feeling, but in the case of most of us it is never the exclusive determining force in driving sexual behavior. We are, as Freud understood, constrained by cultural institutions. There are laws. We do not rape the weak women, at least those of us who have consciences and sensibilities or even those of us who only fear punishment.

If lust, then, is accepted as the term for that which we share with the lower animals, passion is that which is uniquely human and can be experienced by no other species. It requires idealization and imagination; it exploits mystery and anticipation; and it demands, at least for a minimal period, the investment of time. Passion is the inevitable human transformation of lust that differentiates the sexual experience from the other pleasures inherent in satisfying other bodily hungers or needs. The pleasure of sexual gratification cannot be directly equated with the pleasure of emptying one's bladder or filling one's stomach.

Lust is heightened by newness, novelty, and adventure,

but passion can be maintained, albeit with difficulty, over long periods of time, indeed throughout the lifetime of an individual. It can be rediscovered and rekindled by various nonsexual but romantic aspects of loving. The romanticized and idealized elements of a love relationship—fantasy and memory—can sustain the passion beyond the impulse-driven period of early ecstasy.

In one of his most elegant poems, Wordsworth describes the maturation of love:

> She was a Phantom of delight
> When first she gleamed upon my sight;
> A lovely Apparition, sent
> To be a moment's ornament;
> Her eyes as stars of Twilight fair;
> But all things else about her drawn
> From May-time and the cheerful Dawn;
> A dancing shape, an Image gay,
> To haunt, to startle, and way-lay.
>
> I saw her upon nearer view,
> A Spirit, yet a Woman too!
> Her household motions light and free,
> And steps of virgin-liberty;
> A countenance in which did meet
> Sweet records, promises as sweet;
> A Creature not too bright or good
> For transient sorrows, simple wiles,
> Praise, blame, love, kisses, tears, and smiles.
>
> And now I see with eye serene
> The very pulse of the machine;
> A Being breathing thoughtful breath,
> A traveller between life and death;
> The reason firm, the temperate will,
> Endurance, foresight, strength, and skill;

> A perfect Woman, nobly planned,
> To warn, to comfort, and command;
> And yet a Spirit still, and bright
> With something of angelic light.[19]

Wordsworth recognizes the inherent magic in romantic love that allows for the transformation of the "moment's ornament" that is the infatuation of the "May-time" and "dawn" of love, into the mature love of a real woman "breathing thoughtful breath." Yet, even when viewed "with eye serene" she retains the magical quality of the original Apparition, she remains a "Spirit still."

It is not passion that is the antagonist of love, but only lust. Lust is often despoiled, minimized, or mitigated by the consideration of the other person as a human being. When one engages the other person as a person rather than a thing, lust becomes converted in part into human passion.

But lust, pure lust, is also a self-defeating phenomenon. The courtly lover of the Middle Ages intuitively understood that only through the frustration of the hunger could he maintain the intensity of his feeling for his loved one. Satisfaction is the death of appetite. Pure sexual hunger is a fragmentary temporal phenomenon, and like any of the biological hungers, it abates with the fulfillment of its desire. Pleasure is the goal of lusting, but the gratification of the drive reduces it. In that sense Freud was right and lusting is a form of sustained pain. With an instinctual theory of pleasure, the ejaculation or the orgasm is all; it relieves the pain of the impounded libido, fulfilling the definition of pleasure.

In this view, lust is equated with pure animal instinct, unmitigated, untransformed, and unchanged by relationship. Whereas love obviously demands idealization, lust does not. I, frankly, do not recognize the operation of such pure instinct in human affairs. Even lust is not uninformed by our past—nothing in the human being is totally liberated from the human imagination. When lust is indiscriminate it is less than human.

It is always treacherous to equate the complex, emotionally modulated drive of a human being with the simple, often mechanical drives of lower animals. A male dog is attracted to a bitch in heat because of an olfactory stimulus, a pheromone, that operates like a chemical switch, turning on a mechanism which is so impelling and powerful that the male animal is driven toward the consummation of a sexual act. I have had a dog all my life. Only two times have I been bitten by my own pet. Once was when my puppy was seriously injured by an automobile and frantic with pain. The second time was when I attempted to restrain my male dog in proximity to a female dog in heat surrounded by a pack of male dogs. Here the sexual drive potentiated by the competitive presence of the other male dogs overwhelmed him. A male dog is responding to an olfactory stimulus. He does not care whether the female dog is well-formed or mis-shapen, well-bred or a mongrel, black or white, one-tenth his size or five times as large, old or young, his daughter, his sister, his mother, or simply the dog next door. None of this makes any sense or is even conceivable as a model for human lust, let alone love. It *does* matter to us whether the object of our desire is our mother or the girl next door. Human sexuality not only operates according to different psychological rules than animal sexuality does, it is guided by different biological directives.

The sexual drive of men and women is independent of an estrus. It is also independent of a fertile life period. Postfertile men and women can feel true lust and desire. It is even independent of male and female sex hormones. The psychological component of sexuality can carry desire forward in a castrated adult. There is no acceptable comparison between the behavior of an animal in heat and the passion of a person in love, or more specifically a person falling in love. In every way passion conforms not just to the sexual drive but to an image constructed about the objects of our romantic pursuits that makes them different, special, superior to other people.

The sociobiologist E. O. Wilson sees all of these startling human sexual variations from traditional primate sexual behavior as serving love or bonding:

> Human beings are unique among the primates in the intensity and variety of their sexual activity. Among other higher mammals they are exceeded in sexual athleticism only by lions. The external genitalia of both men and women are exceptionally large and advertised by tufts of pubic hair. The breasts of women are enlarged beyond the size required to house the mammary glands, while the nipples are erotically sensitive and encircled by conspicuously colored areolas. In both sexes the ear lobes are fleshy and sensitive to touch. . . . Women remain sexually receptive, with little variation in the capacity to respond, throughout the menstrual cycle. . . . Unusually frequent sexual activity between males and females served as the principal device for cementing the pair bond. It also reduced aggression among the males. The erasure of estrus in early human beings reduced the potential for such competition and safeguarded the alliances of hunter males.[20]

Even at the level of pure sexuality, appetite not yet love, Wilson sees the operation of human imagination on the sexual drive:

> Human beings are connoisseurs of sexual pleasure. They indulge themselves by casual inspection of potential partners, by fantasy, poetry, and song, and in every delightful nuance of flirtation leading to foreplay and coition. This has little if anything to do with reproduction. It has everything to do with bonding.[21]

During that now historical period when the "good girl, bad girl" duality dominated teenage romance, a teenage boy, "in love" with his girlfriend, would copulate with "fast" girls, but the passionate excitement inspired by the good girl—the unavailability undoubtedly adding to the excitement—was unmatched. A glance or a note from the loved object would induce more passion than the sight of the nude body of the available girl. This passion was unrelated to any physiological stimulation or to any realistic comparison of the beauty of the two. The sexual excitement was a fusion of endocrinology and imagination. It always has an unanalyzable and mystical aspect. The response is more religious than reflexive:

> I cannot exist without you—I am forgetful of every thing but seeing you again—my Life seems to stop there—I see no further. You have absorb'd me. I have a sensation at the present moment as though I were dissolving. . . . I have been astonished that Men could die Martyrs for religion—I have shudder'd at it—I shudder no more—I could be martyr'd for my Religion—Love is my religion—I could die for that—I could die for you. My Creed is Love and you are its only tenet—You have ravish'd me away by a Power I cannot resist.[22]

This letter of John Keats to Fanny Brawne is more than a declaration of love. It has the urgency and energy of a sexual act in the same rhythmic and driving way as Molly Bloom's soliloquy at the end of Joyce's *Ulysses*.

It was Freud, with his wonderful inconsistency, who again laid the roots for an understanding of human passion as distinct from human sexuality. This distinction is elaborated in the concept of idealization of the loved object. This concept of "idealization" is as central to the experience of love as fusion is to the definition of love.

Freud sees human desire as arising in almost the opposite

direction from animal desire. The sexual scent of the female animal in heat triggers the sexual behavior of the male animal. In Freudian theory, the sexual appetite originates within ourselves and is then "invested" in the love object. The desire does not arise from the loved individual itself— the object does not release any pheromones—rather it is we who have "cathected" the individual with our own sexual energy. In so investing her we have enlarged her and created an idealized image. That to which we are passionately drawn is not the unadorned and uninvested sexual object but the sexual object we have created by investing her with attributes that we have supplied.

Pygmalion is the ideal figure to illustrate classical Freudian theory. Pygmalion could not have fallen in love with Galatea except for the fact that he had created her to his ideal image of womanhood. It is not the creation of another sculptor with which he falls in love. That would have been a different story, a lesser one, and inconsistent with the Freudian view of passion. Galatea must be the product of Pygmalion's artistic imagination.

Stendhal anticipated Freud's concept of idealization of the loved object by utilizing the imagery of crystallization:

> In the salt mines of Salzburg a bough stripped of its leaves by winter is thrown into the depths of the disused workings; two or three months later it is pulled out again, covered with brilliant crystals: even the tiniest twigs, no bigger than a tomtit's claw, are spangled with a vast number of shimmering, glittering diamonds, so that the original bough is no longer recognizable.
>
> I call crystallization that process of the mind which discovers fresh perfections in its beloved at every turn of events.[23]

Every person in love is a Pygmalion creating out of the raw materials—the clay, wood, marble—of actuality, a self-perceived image of perfection which he is prepared to see in the other person. We will not acknowledge these traits as products of our imagination—only as the actual stuff of the person. Helen, Beatrice, Hippolytus, and Romeo are ideals created in the minds and eyes of their beloveds. Here, again, we see in Freud the product of his training in German idealism, in which the actual world is secondary to the world of our perception.

This idealization is not randomly determined, but is shaped by our own culture and the unique aspects of our personal histories. These factors will insist that it does make a difference whether the loved object is fat, thin, black, white, passive, or aggressive. The basic ingredients will be necessitated by our personal psychodynamics. Once these are fulfilled, we may start the idealization process. After the original preconditions have been satisfied, we are free to supplement the actual attributes of the individual with those we want him to possess. We will endow him with the attributes we admire, independent of their roots in reality, and we will at the same time begin to romanticize whatever traits actually happen to come along with the package.

I am here extending Freud's concept of idealization into a two-step event. It is not just anyone we invest. We start with an ideal image conditioned by our past—perhaps our memories of our mother or our reactions to her—and even here it is not our mother as she was but as we perceived her. Then, given the minimal illusion necessary to start the process, we will begin to see in the loved one what we need in a woman ("She was everything to me"). We will begin the process of idealization.

In the young, and in those in the early stages of love, one sees passion at its most intense, and one usually also sees it almost intimately bound to sexual drive. With the maturation of a relationship, various forms of idealization will occur that are less contingent on pure sexual drive, to compensate for the normal diminution in sexual excitement. There is an intensity to the first touch that will be missing with familiarity, but there is a "knowing" quality about the familiar touch with its shared secrets and common experience that can serve and sustain the passion of a mature love.

The flight from mature love that we now see, the almost frantic pursuit of the adolescent forms of passion prevalent in our culture, may say more about the conditions of our culture—the fear of death, the worship of youth, the distorted emphasis on power and machismo (demanding of the aging man that he reassert his position among other males in the sexual world by seeking a younger mate)—than it does about the nature of passion.

What confusion there is about the various stages of passion in a committed relationship may well represent a nostalgia for the ephemeral but specifically human phenomenon of falling in love.

At the very beginning of a recent book, *Falling in Love,* Francesco Alberoni starts with the following question and answer: "What is falling in love? It is the nascent state of *a collective movement involving two individuals.*"[24] This rather opaque and complex statement is the presentation of a conclusion that is more readily understood at the end of the book than at the beginning. It is, in its insight, clever, original, and elegantly simple. Alberoni draws a distinction between "falling in love," which he describes as an act or an event, and "loving," which is a temporal phenomenon, a process, something that goes on.

Falling in love happens at a moment in time and is a unique experience with particular joys. Falling in love happens *to* us. It does not issue *from* us. Alberoni reserves the concept of falling in love for a "collective movement." Unfortunately, love does not have to be a "collective" event. When falling in love happens to both of us at the same time it is a glory; when only one party falls in love it can be agonizing.

I am intrigued by Alberoni's use of the word "nascent." I presume that the translator was true to the literal and specific meaning that "nascent state" has in English. "Nascent" means coming into being, being born. In chemistry the word has a specific, and in this case a particularly informative, meaning. A nascent element is an element that has just been released from a compound, and because it is newly created, it has unusual properties. The nascent chemical acts differently than the chemical it is about to become because the atoms of the element have not yet combined to form the molecules which will give the element its fixed characteristics. Nascent chlorine, at the moment of its release from the compound, will not behave like the product it is in the process of becoming. It is different in the nature of its behavior, in the predictability of its reactions (indeed, there is a certain unpredictability about nascent states), and in its essential character.

So, too, is falling in love different from love. The elements which will be integrated into the mature state of love still exist in an unstable association. All the elements of love are there, but the true character of the two is quite different. In a charming and poetic way, Alberoni approaches the subject of love itself at the end of his book by deciding that we identify love as the process of repeatedly "falling in love" with the same person. Love, he declares, involves prolonged periods when one takes the relationship for granted, even at times assuming a freedom from any bonding with the loved object: "Then it happens again. That indifferent face, that voice become unique; her absence becomes unbearable, her presence infinite joy. Everything about her moves us; everything about her brings nostalgia and satisfaction."[25]

In the end the author is prepared to conflate falling in love with love itself:

> Perhaps love, particularly the strongest love, presents itself to us in the same way: as falling in love, as falling in love again and again with the same person. A parent's love for his child takes this form too. For the mother, the child is there; he is present because he cries, because he needs something, because he may be in danger, because he is frustrated. But every so often during the day or at night or when she is far away or when she looks at him, he "appears" to her as an object that evokes desire, nostalgia, infinite tenderness, and self-fulfillment.

He concludes his discussion with what is perhaps the "message" of the book, a comment that is more of the nineteenth century than the twentieth, an affirmation of love and its central role in our lives:

> Everyone, even the poorest person, has been given this gift, which lays the foundation for the value of existence, an absolute foundation in something that has value in itself and is rediscovered. Those who lose the hope of rediscovering it die.[26]

While I find a certain delight in Alberoni's descriptions, I do not agree with his conclusion. I like his earlier insight in separating the nascent and the actual states, in recognizing the common elements in both, and in realizing that the differing combinations establish a different quality in loving and falling in love.

I am not sure, however, that all of us are capable of constantly falling in love in a pattern of renewal, although I recognize the necessity of renewal in loving. It is not dissimilar from the process of rediscovery in other aspects of life. Lost in the everydayness, in the actuality, of living, we tend to be numbed to the magic and mystery that is part of existence. And then in some moment we will reexamine the stars. We will notice, really notice, through the frame of a library window the arch of oaks that have stood there unattended for weeks or months or years. We will see our child approaching from a distance and actually perceive her. We will have a heightened awareness of our husband or wife in some casual moment, an awareness whose origins may be bound in mystery, but which nonetheless catches us at the heart. We will rediscover love.

One cannot always live at a fevered pitch. One learns to appreciate the passion and joy inherent in mature love which is distinguished from falling in love. Alberoni is correct in recognizing that falling in love remains in latent form in the stability of mature love, ready to be revived at unexpected and therefore delightful moments in its full, volatile nascent state. George Bernard Shaw, in another context, discussed the different intensities of living that can bring fulfillment. In *Back to Methuselah* a young and passionate man insists to his male companion that things are "in crisis." The elder replies: "My dear Burge, life is a disease; and the only difference between one man and another is the stage of the disease at which he lives. You are always at the crisis; I am always in the convalescent stage. I enjoy convalescence. It is the part that makes the illness worth while."[27]

There is excitement in the crisis. There is excitement in the new. And there is excitement in the dangerous. One need not deny the specific pleasures of the state of falling in love in order to espouse the pleasures of being in love. If we can have both at the same time, so much the better. The concept of passion need exclude neither infatuation nor commitment.

It is not unnatural for us, questing species that we are, always to overvalue what we do not have. It is not surprising that with age we romanticize youth; with mature love we long for the experience of falling in love. Loving is so much quieter; it is so much more difficult to appreciate a process than an event. As C. S. Lewis puts it, there is "no sudden, striking, and emotional transition [with love]. Like the warming of a room or the coming of daylight. When you first notice them they have already been going on for some time."[28]

Neither lust nor falling in love nor mature loving can be equated with animal instinct or animal bonding. They are all honorable components of the passion involved in those attachments we call romantic love. One cannot imagine the goose—which may be more faithful in its monogamy than the human being—ever "falling in love" or ever truly loving. Imagination is at the heart of human love, as it is at the basis of all our art and culture. Ovid, wisely and poetically, set imagination at the center of human uniqueness. In describing human creation he states that Prometheus mixed matter with fresh running water and molded us into the form of the all-controlling God: "And though all other animals are prone, and fixed their gaze upon the Earth, he gave to Man an uplifted face and bade him stand erect and turn his eyes to Heaven."[29]

Passion is a product of our capacity to look to the heavens; to discover meanings in life, not simply methods of survival. Passion is a uniquely human experience. The warmth and light of the glowing embers that characterize its late stages are as fundamental a part of the pleasure as the incendiary flare when the fire is first ignited. The drama of the new-lit fire explodes into consciousness, commanding our attention. The warmth and light of a constant love, ultimately more nourishing, may exist as so much a part of our environment that it escapes our notice and is undervalued, until it is lost. C. S. Lewis, astonished at the multiple ways he is capable of missing his dead wife, says: "Grief is like a long valley, a winding valley where any bend may reveal a totally new landscape." He found himself one day enjoying the kind of ramble that had made him happy in his bachelor days, and felt summoned to a past kind of happiness that existed before his marriage:

> But the invitation seemed to me horrible. The happiness into which it invited me was insipid. I find that I don't want to go back again and be happy in *that* way. It frightens me to think that a mere going back should even be possible. For this fate would seem to me the worst of all; to reach a state in which my years of love and marriage should appear in retrospect a charming episode—like a holiday—that had briefly interrupted my interminable life and returned me to normal, unchanged. And then it would come to seem unreal—something so foreign to the usual texture of my history that I could almost believe it had happened to someone else. . . .
>
> Did you ever know, dear, how much you took away with you when you left? You have stripped me even of my past, even of the things we never shared.[30]

The loss of love is often the most graphic and sometimes the only way many of us experience, and therefore really know, the nature of love and the concept of fusion.

6 ❧ THE LOSS OF LOVE

It was astonishing to me—
and at first inadmissible—when I began to recognize how
seldom I thought of my parents, how emotionally irrelevant
they had become to me during my adult life. I had been
raised in a close-knit, protected, somewhat provincial family, bound even closer by the restrictions on travel and independent pursuits imposed by the Great Depression. During
childhood much of my social and emotional life was involved with extended groups of uncles and aunts, cousins
and kinfolk, some of whose exact blood relationships I never
completely understood.

Yet, once married and involved with my own children,
away from my extended Ohio family, I rarely thought of
even my own parents. My wife would remind me of birth-
days and anniversaries; it was she who would prompt me to
the telephone once a week for my casual hellos; it was she
who would write the letters. At that time I could never have
acknowledged the degree of my dissociation from them.
When I was reminded, I thought of them with love and
affection. It was with the death of my parents, and the
contrasting degree to which they have occupied my thoughts
since then, that I became aware of this strange interlude of
detachment.

Friends tell me that I must have been extraordinarily close

to my father, since I mention him so frequently. These are my current friends; I suspect that the friends I knew between the ages of twenty-one (my marriage) and thirty-four (my age at the time of my father's death) would not have heard frequent allusions to him. He was not, it would have seemed (falsely of course), any longer an operational part of my life as he had been during the period of his authority and responsibility for me in my childhood and teens.

I assumed without thinking much about it that I loved him. I never analyzed that love. Had I done so at that time, in my scientific, objective, analytic way I might have come to the painful (and false) conclusion that I did not love him. I was not aware of any *feelings* of love. I was aware of my respect for him; I knew I would have happily fulfilled all the moral duties and responsibilities I owed him. I would have ascribed this to a sense of decency or to a pattern of behavior to which I had been conditioned in great part by *his* profound sense of responsibility. I might even have recognized the kinship of my behavior to his; I might have defined our relationship as one of respect, affection, duty, and "love" in an ill-defined way, but I did not live with the feeling of loving him.

Despite evidence to the contrary, he was always perceived in my mind as strong, independent, and enduring. I assumed that when he needed me I would be there, that I would comfort him in his declining years. I had no test of my commitment or my attachment. There were no declining years. He simply died in his fifty-eighth year. It was only with his loss that I became aware of the intensity of my love.

My unconscious knew better. During that period I had come to New York, away from all friends and family, and was struggling to survive in this strange and hostile environment. Still in residency training, with two children under eighteen months, nowhere a helping hand, no one to spell my wife or me, and no money to buy the comfort and surcease that is so freely given by family, like some latter-day pilgrims we faced our first Thanksgiving away from home. I had just started my training analysis when I had my first dream: during psychoanalysis I looked down and noticed that my tie had been cut.

That was it. So undramatic, so unromantic. I was disappointed and was prepared to dismiss it and wait for a second more elegant and literary product with which to start my journey into my unconscious. My analyst had me devote an entire week to that dream.

In the process of analyzing that dream, I first recognized its relationship to the upcoming holidays. We were alone, on our own; the ties had indeed been cut. Very specifically, though, the dream related to my father. He was a collector of ties, racks and racks of ties were hung in his closet. It was his only self-indulgence. The tie that was cut was my tie with my father. But my analyst pressed me for further associations. From somewhere in my unconscious emerged an association with the ritual of cutting a black ribbon worn by a mourner at a funeral. From this the denied feelings of depression emerged. I was mourning the loss of my father. More precisely, I was mourning the death of my childhood. For now, in this strange place, there was no father to turn to for support. I was the father. And I was feeling unsure with little self-confidence. Since my psychoanalyst was a good old-fashioned European orthodox Freudian, the tie was finally interpreted as a phallic symbol, and my feelings of helplessness were defined as a sense of impotence, thus linking it to the universal concept of castration anxiety. That dream brought me into contact with my unconscious, my fears, my male competition, but peculiarly, not with my love for my father. Love was not a topic one dealt with in analysis—except the pain of its absence or loss.

When my father later died I did not experience what I thought was a proper grief reaction. It was certainly not the spontaneous, emotional, exhaustive wrenching I felt on hearing of my mother's death fifteen years later. Even allowing for the difference in my age, the changed person I had become from the person I once was, and the differing conditions of the two deaths, I am convinced that the response to the death of my mother was conditioned and facilitated by my father's.

The emotion that I recognized at the time of my father's death was a sense of injustice and resentment. With the detachment of distance and the application of more sophisticated psychoanalytic reasoning, I now realize a part of the anger I felt must have been directed toward him. At the time, though, his death seemed an assault on my sense of the rightness of things. This decent, good, and hard-working man had been deprived of the rewards of his labor, the capacity to enjoy the leisure of a later life, the opportunity to bask in the pleasure of the company of his grandchildren. And with it all, I felt my children's deprivation in not having the opportunity to know him, except obliquely through anecdote and other people's memories. Was this perhaps a disguised projection of my own feelings of deprivation? I do not know. Had he been alive but separated physically from me by necessity I would not have been feeling deprived. This seemingly contradictory set of statements indicates that the fusion that occurs with loving is so complete that it often evades detection. We are not aware of our attachment to the other person because we are not merely attached but fused. The actual presence of the person may be unnecessary, since he is always present. It is a seamless union of a part of the self with a part of the other, until the unredeemable loss of the other exposes the raw and ragged line of juncture.

It is also true that with parents the "denial" of love—the

extinction of love from consciousness—must be part of that inevitable movement toward independence and maturation necessary to establish a primary identity as a parent rather than as a child. The good parent prepares the child to be able to separate. Perhaps in death my love for my father no longer challenged my central identity as a parent and husband, no longer threatened to revive the dormant boy within the man, and was therefore permitted once again to erupt into conscious awareness.

It may be that between father and son so little time is allowed, so little affection countenanced within the strangling rules of masculinity in our culture, that only with death or its impending presence can love be recognized. The silent aspects of love are beautifully realized in a scene between Rufus and his father in James Agee's novel *A Death in the Family:*

> He knew that each of them knew of the other's well-being, and of the reasons for it, and knew how each depended on the other, how each meant more to the other, in this most important of all ways, than anyone or anything else in the world; and that the best of this well-being lay in this mutual knowledge, which was neither concealed nor revealed. He knew these things very distinctly, but not, of course, in any such way as we have of suggesting them in words. There were no words, or even ideas, or formed emotions, of the kind that have been suggested here, no more in the man than in the boy child. . . . Rufus felt his father's hand settle, without groping or clumsiness, on the top of his bare head: it took his forehead and smoothed it, and pushed the hair backward from his forehead, and held the back of his head while Rufus pressed his head backward against the firm hand . . . and [he] drew Rufus' head quietly and strongly against the sharp cloth that covered his father's body, through which Rufus could feel the breathing ribs."[1]

It is through the loss of love in all of its various forms that one becomes exposed most nakedly to both the need for and the meaning of love. The literature of separation is exhaustive. I have examined in great detail in other places[2] the role of separation in the establishment of an independent sense of oneself. One builds one's identity through a series of separations and rejoinings, starting with the original separation from the mother and culminating with the capacity for the joining that is essential to mature love. Each separation involves a mixture of anxiety and self-confidence. Premature or unexpected separation is inevitably a dreadfully painful experience.

Separation anxiety is the primary fear of childhood. To the child, separation represents not just the loss of a source of pleasure but the loss of his exclusive means of survival. The aware child in the first year of life is most profoundly cognizant of his own helplessness. Of all the creatures that occupy his world, he is the only one incapable of surviving on his own. He cannot run from danger; he cannot attack an aggressor. But he quickly learns he can survive by clinging, by dependency. And just as quickly he learns that to ensure that dependency he must ensnare the powerful parents into a loving union with him. He ingratiates, he cajoles, he tests limits, but he is keenly aware of the need for approval and the need for love. In the conscious mind of the child and therefore inevitably in the unconscious mind of the adult, loss of love is equated with loss of life.

The closest that the child can come to a visualization of death has to be separation from the parents. For the child, with her distorted and limited sense of time and space, even brief separation can produce an almost total sense of terror. Visualize for a moment the image on the face of a child temporarily separated from her parent in a department store, on a beach, or in any crowded area. The panic is instantly recognizable.

The same panic may appear on the face of the parent if he has lost sight of the child in a crowd. Even though the panic may seem the same, there are different roots. The parent is concerned with the reality of the situation and his role as a primary caretaker. The water at the beach is a potential hazard. In every crowd there may be an abductor. Even when the danger is exaggerated by the insecurity of the parent or the paranoia of the times, the parent is responding to the potential event wrapped up with the separation. The child is responding to the separation itself. For her the separation is the symbolic death without a need to visualize, or capacity to conceptualize, any specific instrumentation of her destruction. The separation is not something leading up to a destructive event. It is the event. To the child, proximity to the parent is the equivalent of what the umbilical cord was to her as a fetus or what the respirator cord may become at the end of her life. All three represent our total and absolute dependence on something external from ourselves for our own survival.

With maturation there comes a sense of time and proportionality, and for most of us a recognition of some command over the events that shape our fate. Nonetheless, the residuals of the childhood experience survive and continue to influence our behavior. The perception of death is rarely in terms of our own nonexistence. How does the self perceive a world without that perceiving self? I have a feeling that the nonexistent self—like antimatter—is a concept that eludes most of us. What is often substituted in both dreams and in free association is the nonexistence of everyone else. That is, to be dead is to be an isolated self but still to be. This view of death underlies the fantasies about being witness to one's own death that are common among people attempting suicide. It also explains the pervasive anxiety of both children and adults about the unlikely possibility of being buried alive. We are incapable of visualizing our own death, so we visualize a living death, a "death" of irrevocable isolation. The power of this fantasy and its endurance is exemplified by a straight-faced nineteenth century advertisement for a coffin conveniently equipped with a periscope and bell to facilitate a call for help should one find oneself inadvertently buried alive.

Except in phobic states, separation anxiety in the adult is usually reserved as a response to real abandonment or its symbolic counterpart in death. Rejection in love can be one of the most awesomely painful of all experiences. In this abandonment some will experience a blow to their self-confidence which only after the fact may be recognized as not being true self-confidence but a confidence in the-self-united-with-the-other. They will regress, remembering only too well the basic lesson of childhood: we survive not through our own efforts but through the protection of adults. In all of us, rejection is likely to be perceived as an assault on our pride and self-esteem.

In early childhood we know that the support of our parents is assured because of their love and involvement with us. This love is not received as a magical and wondrous blessing; it is accepted as a part of the natural environment. We do nothing to generate it, and it seems as automatic a part of the environment as the food which comes with each scream of hunger in infancy. We are loved because of what we are rather than what we do; in the first year of life we do very little.

In too brief a time we are banished from this Garden of Eden. We will experience the wrath and disappointment of the gods as well as their love. We will learn that love is not ubiquitous and inexhaustible but is contingent on our behavior. At first the alternations of parental anger and affection may be perceived as random and unpredictable, but only too soon we will relate the bestowing and withdrawal of love to what we do or fail to do. Whether we are good or bad will be indicated by the ebb and flow of parental approval. This is not intended as an argument for infinite patience and affection. Parents are not intended to be all-suffering martyrs. The parental approval mechanisms serve a useful purpose. These emotional responses of the parent begin to shape the moral world of the child and will be part of an indoctrination of values that bind the ethics of the child to the ethics of his parents. It would be good if the child were capable of understanding that love is constant and independent of mood and anger, but that is a sophisticated lesson only learned in time, and then, unfortunately, by a minority of us.

The parents' love, therefore, is both an instrument for survival and a reflection of our lovability and our worth. To be rejected by a lover is to feel unsafe as well as unworthy. The danger lies in a general extension of these two feelings. The bankruptcy of our sense of self-confidence and self-esteem can lead to the state of hopelessness and helplessness that constitutes clinical depression.

Early abandonment or severe deprivation of affectionate bonds can produce a flaw in the self-esteem apparatus which will never wholly be healed. A vast and convincing literature[3] has adequately demonstrated that if a child is denied the opportunities for loving and caring human contact he will never feel lovable, and in addition he may be seriously flawed in his capacity to love. Bowlby's study of English children separated from their parents in the Blitz of World War II and Spitz's study of institutionalized children showed that human care in early childhood—touching, stroking, cooing—are essential for the development of a capacity for loving. We share this trait even with the higher apes. Researchers have shown how early deprivation from its own kind leads to the development of a monkey incapable of socialization, incapable of attachments, incapable of sexual activity, and, if the deprivation is severe enough, incapable of fending for its own survival.

Death is probably always felt as a form of abandonment. But if the death of the parent occurs early in life the surviving parent or surrogates can adequately supply the affection necessary for emotional maturation. The full effects of extreme deprivation are usually seen only in children abandoned to the most isolated and primitive institutions. Surprisingly little warm human contact is necessary to initiate the processes that build the kind of self-respect and self-confidence that allow the development of a loving adult. The infant is so dependent on the presence of this adult caring that nature seems to have allowed for a wide margin of safety to ensure the development of this response.

Death, nonetheless, always leaves a dynamic imprint. The effects of the death of a parent on very young children have been well researched. What is less obvious is the different dynamic mechanism that may be initiated by the death of a parent during the teen years. Within the course of a five-year experience I was exposed to two male patients who, as teenagers, had lost their mothers. It is not necessary to discuss the specific dynamics of these individuals nor the details of their life situations. They were raised in different traditions, had different backgrounds, and lost their mothers at different ages, yet they were left with the same configuration which I have since found a common feature in men who have lost their mothers during their teens. Both of these men formed long-lasting relationships with women toward whom they offered an understanding that is not common for men in our culture. Both had total inability to leave their wives even when, for different reasons, the two marriages seemed exhausted, but both seemed determined to provoke their wives into leaving them. When the wives responded, there was a frantic overvaluation of the marriage with desperate attempts to reconstitute it. Both had a profound sense of guilt in their primary relationships. Both of these men, ironically, seemed to fulfill their need to receive love not only through individual attachments but through the approval of large masses of people. Both were performing artists with great esteem and recognition—they were the adored children of massive populations of parent surrogates.

At this point it would be best to separate the two case studies, since they are not Bobbsey twins and the diversity between them is greater than the similarity. Let me focus on one. This patient was married relatively young and established a relationship of respect and affection with his wife. She was a woman of intelligence and charm who managed a successful independent career while establishing the home which was so important to him. By choice, they had no children. The marriage quickly became an essentially asexual union, although neither was inclined to admit it. Since neither was the sort that could have endorsed the idea of an open marriage, self-deception became the means for each to think the other was faithful. He assumed his wife's fidelity but was intrigued by the thoughts of her potential involvements.

In a sense he had established something akin to the relationship of an adolescent boy to a seductive mother. When he thought of leaving his wife, which was often, the constraints were cast in terms of who would take care of him, his possessions, his home. The loss was always visualized in respect to her services rather than herself, a characteristic that is typical of the teenager. He was always "falling in love" but never had the courage to commit himself to another woman. In this one relationship with his wife he had extended his commitments as far as he dared. He thought often of his wife's death and felt he could tolerate that more readily than leaving her or being left by her. He was too guilty to leave and too frightened to allow her to abandon him. Death, being independent of his action, could alleviate both guilt and fear. His extramarital attachments were so superficial that their severing left no bleeding edges. He had found a kind of partial relationship and commitment which he could tolerate. He had trusted one woman sufficiently to love her fully, and she had betrayed that trust by dying. He would trust no other.

To have a mother die during the defiant period of adolescence, when one is still desperately seeking to disengage, and before one has reached the mature time of life when one can express through acts of generosity and love one's gratitude for the sacrifice of a loving parent, is to feel an overwhelming incompleteness and a profound residual guilt. Somehow or other one has committed some awful and ill-defined act of treachery toward the mother. Perhaps this was even instrumental in her death. During the immediate bereavement period and for some years after, this feeling that one's ingratitude or wretchedness or indifference destroyed the mother will often lead to a displacement of one's own guilt to someone else. Again in an interesting parallel, both of these men went through a period of intense hostility toward their fathers, seeing either their cheapness, their indifference, their neglect, or their lack of serious attention to the medical condition of the mother as being the "cause" of her death.

The fact that when confronted with death we so often seek a causal agent is in part a testament to the general guilt we all are likely to feel when a loved one dies. "Perhaps it was my fault" leads to the protective displacement represented by asking: "Whose fault is it?" A doctor, an indifferent institution, and the surviving spouse are likely and convenient targets. We also pursue a causal agent because it is painful to accept that something so awesome and absolute as death can arrive quixotically and indifferently. The cruelest reality is the awareness of the role of a random and therefore unjust tide in human affairs.

The readiness to assume responsibility for the loss of a loved object is not reserved for situations of bereavement. Any leaving of a beloved can be narcissistically interpreted as a sign that one has not been worthy of the love or, worse, that one has been responsible for the loss through acts of malice or ingratitude. This is clearly reflected in an early memory of my own. I must have been between ten and eleven, certainly no older. It was the heart of the depression and we had living with us what now would be called an au pair girl, but then was simply referred to as live-in help. I have no idea of her age. In retrospect I realize she could not have been more than twenty-two or three. She was known to me only as Julie. She was, at least in my memory, beautiful, and while her features are indistinct I visualize her always with the clearest of blue eyes and long, shining clean ash-blond hair braided into a halo around her face. She was patient and gentle, and in my mind a wondrous and talented artist. She taught me how to draw, helped me with my homework, and I am sure, although I have never reconstituted these memories, was a fantasy object in my sexual life. And I, I was an unappreciative, selfish, and cruel monster.

One wintry morning she had prepared my breakfast, as was usual, and because of the cold day had made hot cereal, which I did not like. I was angry and upset and said she did it on purpose because she knew I did not like it and I refused the cereal. She attempted to cajole me, but I would not make up and left for school angry. I do not remember anything more of that incident. I do know that my mother informed me that very same evening that Julie would be leaving. I was horrified. My mother might not know the reason she was leaving, but I did. It was that I had finally tested the limits of her endurance, had treated her unspeakably, and she would stay no longer. While she was too loyal and I was too frightened to admit the cause of her departure, the two of us "knew." I was the instrument of my own destruction. I had lost something I cherished, someone I loved, because of my selfishness and arrogance.

Never mind that Julie was young and had a boyfriend she was about to marry. All of that for some reason was unknown to me or repressed by me. Never mind that my parents—being aware how much we children would miss her—had discussed with Julie how soon before her leaving we ought be told. For years afterward I was convinced that had I only eaten the oatmeal or whatever that hot sticky mush was, Julie would never have left me. I had not lost my mother, my father was still there, and a continuity of love existed, but nonetheless I began to understand the obligations of love through that "abandonment." When the abandonment is severe, as in the loss of an actual mother, the capacity to trust oneself, let alone some other, can be seriously impaired. When one of the men I previously described was offered a surrogate mother, a friend of his mother's whom the father later married, he would not allow a relationship to develop. Despite all evidence of her being a loving person with no children of her own, desperate for his love, he never accepted her love or offered any in return.

Since trust generally comes with some difficulty, trust betrayed is a particular outrage. Since there is always some lingering anxiety about our own self-worth in the most secure of us, complete trust, placing one's fate in so tender and fragile a vessel as a human relationship, is an act of faith.

When that faith is betrayed, the anxiety caused by the sense of diminished self-worth is reinforced by a profound rage. The less the relationship was one of true love and mutual interdependence and fusion and the more it was a narcissistic "love," an attachment of dependency and a form of reassurance, the greater the sense of betrayal.

When one reads in the paper of a body being discovered with forty knife wounds in it, the knowledgeable reader rightly assumes a sexual motive implicit in the attack. In men these so-called "crimes of passion" are generally not crimes of passion as we know them but crimes of humiliation. When the withdrawal or rejection of love is interpreted as a public statement of inadequacy, when it is viewed as an announcement of unworthiness in a way that is an attack on the rejected suitor's manhood (the gender here is not by accident), and when the humiliation is perceived through the heightened sensibilities of a paranoid individual, the conditions for a "crime of passion" are all in place. Here I do think there is a gender difference.

Women who kill "for love" seem different from men who kill "for love." Love has traditionally played the same central role in women's pride system as power has in men's. When women grieve over lost love, it is the love which they mourn, amplified by the feeling that in losing their loved one, they are losing their security, their status, and their self-worth. The reality factors are often greater here. With men one feels the humiliation is primary and the loss often only a vehicle for the announcement of the humiliation.

Still, most women do not react like Medea or Phaedra when rejected. When a woman responds with murderous rage, she too must experience a dimension of humiliation in her loss. One widely publicized case which clearly demonstrated this combination of lost love and humiliation was that of Jean Harris. One had the feeling that Mrs. Harris truly loved Dr. Tarnower and the rage was the product of a trust deceived. Mrs. Harris seems to exemplify the fury— that hell hath not—of the traditional woman scorned. How different it was in two male cases of crimes of passion (one reported in a book, one not) to which I devoted major research effort.

In the unreported case the crime of passion involved the brutal murder of a girl who was not even known by the criminal, yet I would classify it as a crime of passion in every sense equivalent to that which was presumed to have been done for love. In this case a teenage boy, an adopted child of restrictive fundamentalist Protestant parents, stabbed to death an eight-year-old girl. The child had come to see Santa Claus in a department store where the young man was working as a stockboy. He lured her into a back room, made her take off her clothes, and attempted to masturbate while looking at her nude body. Despite an erection he was incapable of an ejaculation, and with a sense of "betrayal somehow" (his words to me) and a fusion of fear and humiliation, he picked up a knife and repeatedly stabbed the child. He was found not guilty by reason of insanity, but this being Canada, he was in effect given a lifetime sentence instead of the five or so years he would have served in prison as a convicted adolescent. I had interviewed this man extensively while he was in prison. He was eager for me to write his story—at that time he felt hopelessly entrapped in the prison situation and conceived of publicity as his only way out (he was in his late twenties). For complicated reasons I was hesitant to pursue the project.

Over ten years later another crime of passion attracted my attention—but this time for different reasons. I was deeply concerned about the extension of the insanity defense, disturbed that psychoanalytic exculpation was destroying a sense of responsibility under law, and distressed by the extraordinary way in which victims of crimes are forgotten and the compassion and sympathy which are their due are preempted by the very criminals who robbed them of their lives. I decided to publish this case.[4]

Richard Herrin, using a claw hammer, had battered to death his "beloved," Bonnie Garland, while she lay sleeping in her own bed in her parents' home. My interest in the case began when I read a newspaper interview with Richard on the day of the murder. Bonnie had survived the night and was found gasping, drowning in her own blood. Richard was informed by the priest to whom he had turned himself in that Bonnie was alive. Richard responded, "She can't be alive. When I hit her, her head burst open like a ripe watermelon." What kind of a person says a thing like that? What kind of a person even thinks that way?

I do not want to pursue the details of this case but rather to point out that in Richard's defense his lawyer made great issue out of the fact that this was a tragic example of love betrayed. Richard had never loved before; in losing Bonnie he was losing the only love of his life. It is my conviction, however, that Richard never "loved" Bonnie—not in the sense of fusion or attachment which is the necessary condition of love. What Bonnie betrayed was not Richard's love but his sense of manhood. He felt humiliated more than bereft. He saw Bonnie's rejection as exposing to a mocking world his own self-image of inadequacy. Bonnie was not only Richard's evidence of his lovability, but a bulwark of his own shaky and vulnerable sense of potency, both sexual and other.

The death of a truly loved one will also often be accompanied by a preliminary sense of betrayal, but here it is one small aspect of a complex of emotions of fear, anger, hurt, and deprivation—all mitigated by the protective power of the unabated love.

In the same Agee novel previously cited in this chapter we see the strengths that must be mobilized after death:

> When grief and shock surpass endurance there occur phases of exhaustion, of anesthesia in which relatively little is felt and one has the illusion of recognizing, and understanding, a good deal. Throughout these days Mary had, during these breathing spells, drawn a kind of solace from the recurrent thought: at least I am enduring it. I am aware of what has happened, I am meeting it face to face, I am living through it. There had been, even, a kind of pride, a desolate kind of pleasure, in the feeling: I am carrying a heavier weight than I could have dreamed it possible for a human being to carry, yet I am living through it. . . . She thought that she had never before had a chance to realize the strength that human beings have to endure; she loved and revered all those who had ever suffered, even those who had failed to endure. . . . She thought that now for the first time she began to know herself, and she gained extraordinary hope in this beginning of knowledge. She thought that she had grown up almost overnight, and when at length the time came to put on her veil, leave the bedroom she had shared with her husband, leave their home, and go down to see him for the first time since his death and to see the long day through, which would cover him out of sight for the duration of this world, she thought that she was firm and ready.[5]

Whatever the cause, whether death or abandonment, when that other person has been seen as the instrument of our survival rather than the source of our pleasure—when the loved one has been endowed with too large a portion of our self-esteem—a sense of loss may be extended into a depression. With dramatic frequency this tends to occur more with women than men. This is not due merely to a different biological capacity for love (which it is now being suggested may exist), nor to the different cultural roles assigned to men and women in terms of loving (which I know exist). The different responses to a loss of love are directly related to the different metaphoric meanings that being loved have for men and women in our culture. We have trained generations of women to identify their self-worth in terms of their attachments, as we have conditioned men to vest their pride in work and mastery.

This has been expressed chillingly and brilliantly in a quotation I have used in the past. Kierkegaard says in *The Sickness unto Death:*

> Despair is never ultimately over the external object but always over ourselves. A girl loses her sweetheart and she despairs. It is not over the lost sweetheart but over herself-without-the-sweetheart. And so it is with all cases of loss whether it be money, power, or social rank. The unbearable loss is not really in itself unbearable. What we cannot bear is in being stripped of the external object, we stand denuded and see the intolerable abyss of ourselves.[6]

It is not the loss of the other but the depletion of the sense of self from which we suffer in despair. Women have suffered more from loss of love partly because they have truly loved more and better, but also because their symbolic sense of worth—as well as their actual financial and social security—has more frequently been vested in the partner than in the self.

The presumption exists that a person with a ripe capacity for love finds the loss of even a true love a survivable phenomenon. With the liberty of comic fiction, Jorge Amado pays tribute to the survivability of his heroine, Dona Flor:

> Sleepless in her iron bed, forsaken and alone, Dona Flor embarked on the route of the past, harbors of happiness, tempest-tossed sea. She evoked scattered memories, words, the brief sound of a melody, reconstructed the calendar. What she wanted was to break the fetters of this

twilight, go beyond the day's work, the night's rest, live again. Not this colorless eking out an existence, not this vegetating in a smothering swamp of mud, this life without Vadinhol. How could she break through this circle of death, cross the narrow door of this time devoid of meaning? Without him she did not know how to live.[7]

But Dona Flor is the essence of life, she will not despair, and, the reader is neither surprised nor offended that barely a month after her husband had died,

the expression of suicidal suffering no longer stamped her face. It was still sad, but not despairing nor expressionless . . .

She had buried certain emotions and certain feelings—desire, love, matters of bed and heart, for she was a widow and respectable one. She was alive, however, and could feel the light of the sun and the gentle breeze, could laugh and find joy, acceptance.[8]

There is one special kind of bereavement that demands attention. It is the intense bereavement over the loss of a child. A study issued by the Institute of Medicine[9] found that the loss of a child compared with the loss of a parent or spouse, "revealed more intense grief reactions of somatic types, greater depression, as well as anger and guilt with accompanying feelings of despair."[10] "Parents seemed totally vulnerable, as if they had just suffered a physical blow that left them with no strength or will to fight."[11] Participants in a support group for bereaved parents showed that " 'bizarre' responses, regressive behavior, and suicidal thoughts were common."[12] One researcher compared various groups of depressed patients and was surprised to find what a high proportion of depressed people had experienced the death of a child in the previous six months, supporting her view that the "death of a child is the most significant and traumatic death of a family member."[13]

But in addition to the devastation of the response there is the unrelenting length of bereavement. Almost anyone who has professionally or even personally dealt with bereavement would agree with the conclusion of one researcher: "The most distressing and long-lasting of all griefs is that of the loss of a grown child."[14]

Many studies have also shown that the loss of a child is not mitigated, as one might logically think, by the presence of other children or by a supportive and loving spouse. Peter De Vries writes:

> A neighbor had been robbed by the Fates of a nine-year-old boy whom I will unabashedly describe as hyacinthine-haired, and a year later was still inconsolable to the point of unfitness for human society. I reminded him sharply that he had three other children, and he turned on me with clenched fists. "There aren't enough children in the world to make a dent in grief for one," he said. I had little suspicion then that I would be crying foul myself, under terms more final than his own.[15]

In many ways a young parent's life is more disrupted by the loss of a spouse in a loving marriage than by the loss of a child: the shattering of basic life patterns, the absence of a husband or wife to share in the labor and responsibility of child care, the financial duress and sociological imbalances that must be accommodated—all would seem to suggest that the death of a spouse would produce a more devastating bereavement. Yet subjective experience, as well as statistical studies, seems to confirm the profundity and durability of the grief over a child. What then is to explain the intensity of our feeling about the loss of a child?

When approaching this question on an individual and personal level with patients the answer will inevitably be in terms of the "unnaturalness" of the event. The small number of my patients who have lost a child have retained the grief in latent but readily revivable form during an entire lifetime. What can this special response to the death of a child reveal to us about the nature and meaning of love? I do not think that one must draw the conclusion that parental love is a stronger or more enduring love than romantic love. A comparison is difficult. I have no idea how one would control the variables and even if one makes such a supposition, how in the world could you "prove" its correctness. When approached from a historical point of view it is apparent that even a beloved spouse is more replaceable, although at time of death this will certainly not seem to be the case. Traditionally, the surviving spouse of a good marriage, after having overcome the grief response, has been seen as a better bet for remarriage than the abandoned person in a divorce. It may be that a capacity for identification, fusion, and love has been proved in one good marriage and therefore is a natural predictor of future events.

I have seen cases in which the death of a spouse has left the survivor with a sense of painful loss that lasted a lifetime, but I have never, except in cases of clinical depression, seen the persistence of true mourning and grief that almost routinely occurs with the death of a child. It may be that the answer is to be found in the intuitive response routinely given by laymen—that such a death is unnatural, and the unnatural offends our sense of moral order and rightness, frightening us with its implication of a disordered and unjust universe.

These days religious belief, if held at all, is likely to be characterized by less conviction than in the past. It is more likely to be pantheistic than fundamentalist. Many of us have lost the assurance of either a "meaning" to death ("God works His will in mysterious ways") or a reunion with the dead in the afterworld. Having given up our sense of some sort of afterlife in heaven we suffer a doubly agonizing loss with the death of a child. The loss is irrevocable and forever. We will never be reunited with the child in a heaven that does not exist. But as cruelly, those of us who acknowledge no immortality through a heavenly extension of this earthly life take comfort in a different form of immortality. We see our immortality as residing in the flesh of our flesh and in the spirit of our spirit, in the physical and psychological extensions of ourselves that are our children. For those of us who have no religion at all, the loss of the child is the loss of the only immortality we recognize—the continuation of our genes through our children into future generations, but beyond that, the extension of our principles, our ideals, our personality, and our values through the introjection and incorporation of ourselves by our children in a process that extends through generations and centuries. I see in my grandchildren the characteristic traits, values, and foibles of my parents, whom they never knew.

In losing our children, then, we not only suffer the loss of the part of ourselves that comes with the loss of any loved one, but we lose our future selves. In so doing we lose whatever mystical meaning survives in an existential philosophy. Our children represent the ultimate in fusion. It is not just that they are forged into our identities and that we are incorporated into theirs; they are the instruments which will carry our identities into the future that we will never know and will now never know us. In an ironic way our sense of self is more vested in them than in ourselves.

If the loss of a child is the unbearable burden, the loss of love in whatever form is an agony of giant proportions. Death is almost more tolerable than rejection. We can still curse the fates. We can still see the dead love as the primary victim, mitigating our desire to indulge in self-pity. She has lost her life; I have only lost what is seen as the meaning for my survival. In rejection, the separation from the loved one was not forced by some unrelenting fate. Much crueler is the knowledge that the absence was by choice! And even more unbearable is the awareness that it was the choice of the one we idealized and cherished most.

If even death may be perceived as rejection or betrayal, how much more intense are the feelings of self-diminution when we are dealing with actual rejection. It is in many ways the opposite of the exhilaration and experience of falling in love. Rather than the delight of imminent and expected passionate fusion there occurs an unexpected mutilation: the unanticipated cleavage of the self. A part of one's own personhood has been ripped away, resulting in a disintegration of stability. We are left in a transient period of confusion of identity. We are still in the shock-like state of not recognizing our own "self," not knowing who we are without that other person who had been woven into our own fabric of identity.

The entire scenario of bereavement can be played out with any abandonment. Differences do occur. The rage that is so humiliating in mourning can be supportive and cleansing in rejection. The passion of hatred rivals that of love. Any passion sustains a sense of self, and at the core of all abandonment is the wounded and incomplete self.

In the following scene from George Eliot's novel *Middlemarch* we see both the despair of an assumed loss of love and the pain of a rejection. Will is frantic. He has been seen by Dorothea (Mrs. Casaubon), whom he loves, in a scene of apparent intimacy with Rosamond. Rosamond had arrogantly and foolishly assumed Will returned her passionate interest in him. To Will's mind she has now destroyed any possibility of his winning Dorothea. Rosamond, recognizing finally the true state of affairs, addresses his all too apparent distress:

In flute-like tones of sarcasm she said,

"You can easily go after Mrs. Casaubon and explain your preference."

"Go after her!" he burst out, with a sharp edge in his voice. "Do you think she would turn to look at me, or value any word I ever uttered to her again as more than a dirty feather?—Explain! . . .

"Explain! Tell a man to explain how he dropped into hell! Explain my preference! I never had a *preference* for her, any more than I have a preference for breathing. No other woman exists by the side of her. I would rather touch her hand if it were dead, than I would touch any other woman's living."

Rosamond, while these poisoned weapons were being hurled at her, was almost losing the sense of her identity, and seemed to be waking into some new terrible existence. She had no sense of chill resolute repulsion, of reticent self-justification such as she had known under Lydgate's most stormy displeasure: all her sensibility was turned into a bewildering novelty of pain; she felt a new terrified recoil under a lash never experienced before. What another nature felt in opposition to her own was being burnt and bitten into her consciousness. . . .

The poor thing had no force to fling out any passion in return; the terrible collapse of the illusion towards which all her hope had been strained was a stroke which had too thoroughly shaken her: her little world was in ruins, and she felt herself tottering in the midst as a lonely bewildered consciousness.[16]

Rejection in love is devastating. It is not just a pronouncement of our unworthiness, it is a public announcement. Beyond that, all of the less-than-heroic events preceding the rejection that would have been mitigated by success seem enlarged in failure. Shame and humiliation compound the lowering of self-esteem. In Turgenev's *Spring Torrents*, Dimitry Sanin is trying not to remember his rejection by Madame Polozov:

When he came to the moment when he had turned im-
ploringly to Madame Polozov, when he had so far abased
himself, when he had thrown himself at her feet, when his
enslavement had begun—then he turned aside from the
images which he had conjured up; he did not wish to
remember more. Not that his recollection was unclear—
oh no! He knew, he knew all too well everything that had
happened after that moment, but shame stifled him, even
then, so many years later. He was afraid of the feeling of
self-contempt which he knew he could not conquer, and
which he knew beyond doubt would wash over him, and,
like a tidal wave, drown all other sensations, as soon as he
allowed his memory to speak. But try as he might to turn
away from the mental images which welled up inside him,
he was powerless to obliterate them all.[17]

Yet statistics are indicating that with increased divorce,
delayed marriage, and prolonged longevity more and more
of us are going to face rejection, loneliness, and a loveless
life. We have learned in the past how to survive many things
that are antithetical to our biology; it is our strength that we
can create new institutions that allow us to flourish when
the old institutions, which at one time had been seen as
necessary for survival, prove maladaptive under evolving
conditions. As civilization advances, it becomes progressively more difficult to define that which is necessary for the
fulfillment of our nature, since we are constantly changing
our nature to accommodate to the strange cultures we continue to create. It is reasonably safe to assume that love and
loving are ultimate qualities for the survival of our species,
for if survival were possible without these, the creature that
survived would no longer be human.

One comfort in the discussion of love is that there exists
an essential element in loving that cuts across all forms of its
expression. The potential for passion exists in the world of
nature, religion, friendship, ideas, and the caring for other

people. Nothing can refute the particularly crucial role that romantic attachments to members of the opposite sex play in the panorama of our existence. The person alone need not be loveless even though he may inevitably have to suffer from loneliness. If love is recognized as an active rather than a passive phenomenon, then the instrumentation for loving is within the self. Rather than waiting for love to come to one, one must begin to freely distribute the love one possesses, in the hope that it may bring love in return but in the recognition that even if it does not, the act of loving is its own special reward.

The problem is that the single person is likely to see himself as in a position of deprivation. Aware of his unfulfilled hungers for love, he makes the illogical assumption that love is a scarce commodity that must be husbanded and protected. Freudian theory saw love as a "closed hydraulic system," a zero-sum game, to use today's terminology, in which anything spent in one area would not be available in another. Love is not like a fixed sum of money or a filled tank of gasoline. Love operates, to paraphrase Dr. Johnson, not like a cistern but like a well. It does not simply collect and store. It is a generative phenomenon, and even here, the metaphor is inexact. Since the more spent the more there is, love is a regenerative phenomenon. It is a regenerative phenomenon that tends to feed upon itself. Love must never be hoarded or conserved. It is the spending, not saving, of love that increases the quantity.

I am not underestimating the intense pain of loneliness. It is an awkward, deeply frustrating, and irrational condition for so communal an animal as *Homo sapiens*. But we live in times when the fear of loneliness usurps the proper role of loving. We may marry not for what we hope it will bring us, but to escape that from which it saves us. Take the case of novelist Philip Roth's David Kepesh. After three years de-

voted to "doubting-hoping-wanting-and-fearing," David
Kepesh decides to marry Helen Baird:

> I marry Helen when the weight of experience required to
> reach the monumental decision to give her up for good
> turns out to be so enormous and so moving that I cannot
> possibly imagine life without her. Only when I finally
> know *for sure* that *this must end now*, do I discover how
> deeply wed I already am by my thousand days of indeci-
> sion, by all the scrutinizing appraisal of possibilities that
> has somehow made an affair of three years' duration seem
> as dense with human event as a marriage half a century
> long. I marry Helen then—and she marries me—at the
> moment of impasse and exhaustion that must finally come
> to all those who spend years and years and years in these
> clearly demarcated and maze-like arrangements that in-
> volve separate apartments and joint vacations, assump-
> tions of devotion and designated nights apart, affairs
> terminated with relief every five or six months, and hap-
> pily forgotten for seventy-two hours, and then resumed,
> oftentimes with a delicious, if effervescent, sexual frenzy,
> following a half-fortuitous meeting at the local supermar-
> ket; or begun anew after an evening phone call intended
> solely to apprise the relinquished companion of a note-
> worthy documentary to be rerun on television at ten; or
> following attendance at a dinner party to which the cou-
> ple had committed themselves so long ago it would have
> been unseemly not to go ahead and, together, meet this
> last mutual social obligation.[18]

We do not have much faith in the survivability of this
marriage. Loving is a defense against loneliness, but it must
be more than that. Marriage, to survive these days, requires
more than love and good intentions. It requires courage,
commitment, and a bit of luck, among other things. And all
marriages should not survive. One is allowed to make a
mistake without having to suffer with it until death. There
will be those who, having married as a protection against a

lonely and loveless life, will encounter the loneliness of a loveless marriage. The pain is often greater with the illusion of companionship. Divorce will offer relief from this pain and opportunity for something better. Sometimes the dream will be fulfilled, but often the options will be lost for sociological or psychological reasons.

The current statistics of divorce and the patterns of remarriage suggest the possibility that a considerable percentage of women in our culture will be excluded from the options of marriage and romantic love.[19] There must be some solutions, but they will inevitably necessitate the abandonment of old gender stereotypes and the institution of new symbols of prestige and desirability beyond the worship of the youthful body that seems the sickness of our times.

The natural persistence of the sexual appetite in women well beyond the age of fertility and into old age is a unique attribute of our species and ought to be honored by some socially acceptable means of gratification. We have tried separating sex from romance or love, and what seems to have evolved is a deterioration and denigration of both. Living alone is antithetical to the whole principle of the biology of the species. We need a newer and more rational sexual revolution that reveres constancy, respects maturity, restores mystery over mastery, and rediscovers romance.

Many women support their husbands through their early careers, only to be abandoned in their forties and fifties when the husband, in an attempt to deny his own aging or in an effort to impede a growing awareness of an impending decline in power, feels the urgent need to establish a relationship with a younger woman. A sense of betrayal is almost always a part of the response, but interestingly, the more self-pride, the more self-respect, the more self-esteem the woman has, the less her sense of betrayal. When the all in "I have given you all and you have rejected it" is seen as a thing of value, the sense of betrayal is less. In the course of treatment of such individuals it is precisely at the time when the patient values herself that she will overcome the sense of betrayal and be prepared to seek new love and new commitments.

Our current social biases are cruelly unfair to the middle-aged and unattached woman. Some have found in caring alliances with their own group some protection—the salvage of some dignity—from the humiliations our culture has forced on them. In the long run we must change our culture to be more equitable and more respectful of the aging process. But the worship of youth is difficult to exorcise, particularly when the power given to men in our culture permits them to "buy" youth even in their decline. Power is an aphrodisiac, a young woman told me, in explaining her attraction to a man forty years her senior.

The only protection for the single person short of a new revolution in values is in the recognition of the self-enhancing aspects of the loving mechanism. The alone and lonely person must enter new communities and new activities not with any expectation of finding love (being loved) but with the reassurance that the energy and force of loving can be used to exercise its restorative magic on the user. It is the wonder of love that in spending it we become enriched.

It is a difficult charge to give the lonely person. The fear that inevitably accompanies isolation tends to mitigate against assertion and activity. The lonely and isolated individual must, further, fight against the value judgments of our society, which has devalued the unattached person, particularly the woman, and has made the state of loneliness a stigma. The cultural stigmatization, when joined with the biologically induced fear of abandonment (with its implications about worth and love), may be interpreted by the lonely person as the ultimate and primal proof of her unlovability and unworthiness. This must not be allowed to happen.

We may be forced to live a life isolated from *romantic* love, but it need not be a life separated from passion. Keeping the distinction clear between being loved and loving will help. Having an ability to love freely, generously, and courageously is another matter.

7 ⬧ THE CAPACITY
TO LOVE

"The human being, alone among creatures, is born incomplete, with the capacity to share with his Creator in his own design." The human species contains within it the potential, and beyond that, a genetic directive, for loving. Yet not all people are capable of loving, and certainly not to the same degree. The capacity to love, to both give and receive love, will be modified by conditions of our common culture or the facts of our unique historical development. The ability to love can be totally eradicated in some people by severe deprivations or abuses in childhood. It will be inevitably diminished or enhanced by the nature of our individual experience. In addition, there remains the unresolved and crucial question of whether there is a gender difference in both the capacity for and experience of love.

Freud certainly saw a major difference between the biological capacities of men and women. For this he has been attacked by feminist writers. Now that the feminist movement has won its battle for respectability and recognition, and has seen its arguments accepted, if not in practice at least in theory by a large part of the intellectual community, it may be time for generosity of spirit and a reevaluation of Freud. While he, like Aristotle, committed the transgression of reducing women to lesser intellectual and creative crea-

183

tures, in areas of sex and love he was an egalitarian; he acknowledged feminine sexual entitlements and supported their aspirations for sexual pleasure. While he cast his model of love almost exclusively in terms of the development of the male child, he extended his conclusions to women and in so doing may be considered one of the parents of feminism.

In defiance of the Victorian culture of which he was a part and in the face of the hypocrisy which denied the normal claims of sexuality, he affirmed that sexuality was the function, the privilege, the right, the natural endowment of all: the bourgeoisie as well as the proletariat; the infant as well as the adult; woman as well as man. It is within the context, and only within the context, of the Freudian revolution, with its dramatic reexaminations of the role of sexual desire, the nature of sexuality and the universality of this urge, that feminism could have emerged.

Freud's influence is so powerful in the 1980s that one is inclined to forget that the roots of these ideas were established in the 1880s. Freud was a product of nineteenth-century Viennese culture. His attitudes were framed by the thinkers who were prominent and influential at that time. In recent years as those outside the field of analysis began to examine Freud (philosophers and sociologists like Paul Recoeur, Herbert Marcuse, Philip Rieff, and Norman O. Brown), the nature of his indebtedness to certain philosophical positions became clear. He was greatly indebted to the philosopher David Hume, although one is not sure to what degree this was a direct influence or simply an indirect or coincidental arrival at similar conclusions.

The philosopher who is more and more perceived as Freud's intellectual mentor is, as previously mentioned, Schopenhauer. Freud's attitude toward culture as expressed in *The Future of an Illusion* and to a lesser extent in *Civilization and Its Discontents* reveals the influence of

Schopenhauer: the fundamental pessimism, the central role of conflict in human affairs, and the power of the sexual instinct in influencing areas once deemed nonsexual.

Freud was patronizing and demeaning in his attitudes toward women, sharing prejudices that were common to his culture and his time. Perhaps he felt reassured in his biases by Schopenhauer's extraordinary hatred of and contempt for women. Schopenhauer was a notorious misogynist. Reading *Of Women*[1] one encounters not simply disdain for women, but actual physical revulsion and disgust.

Freud's psychology of women[2] is not vituperative, like Schopenhauer, but is nonetheless an embarrassment for those of us who revere his creative imagination. One might well be back at the banquet table with Socrates, Plato, Aristophanes, and the boys. Rationality, intellect, all matters of the mind, are deemed predominantly masculine. Worse, Freud attributed the gender differences to biological distinctions. But this man, himself a biologist, surely must have been aware that even if there were differing genetic influences operating on men and women, they would be of a limited magnitude and could be readily modified by environmental adjustment. The overarching similarity between genders exists in their sharing the extraordinary characteristics unique to our species: intelligence, imagination, and a mutable nature.

Even if there were a weighted directive toward aggression in men and domesticity in women, toward hunting in one and child-caring in the other, the weakness of biological determinants in shaping human behavior ought to have been apparent to Freud from his clinical observations and his studies of the past. People "today" (and the today could be 1880, Vienna) do not behave the way people behaved "yesterday," whenever that yesterday was. Yet our biological directives are identical. In role playing it is almost always culture that dominates.

I mention these factors here because as a Freudian who is about to discuss the potential importance of biological differences between men and women, I wish to acknowledge the legitimacy of the complaints of modern writers about the bias Freud introduced into psychoanalytic theory. Still, if placed in the proper context and compared with others as in Philip Rieff's comparison of Freud and Jung—Freud does not fare too badly. Jung writes: "How is a man to write about woman his exact opposite? . . . for woman stands just where man's shadow falls."[3]

During the period of struggle for justice for a disadvantaged group, it may be necessary to assume or to insist that there are no distinctions or cultural variations between black and white, homosexual and heterosexual, man and woman. Justice demands the erasure of all social and political distinctions in the treatment and consideration of the groups. Therefore it may seem mischievous and impolitic to point out the considerable differences that may actually exist between the culturally observed behaviors of the privileged and of the abused populations. The differences might well be used politically and punitively. It is only after there is some security in the political area that one can begin to approach the fact that black culture is different from white culture; that homosexual object choice and homosexual love serve different dynamics than do heterosexual object choice and heterosexual love; and that women and men may operate with a different set of biological influences. This can be safely done only in a climate that will not automatically equate "different" with "inferior."

Because of political considerations, genetics and biology remain the underexplored areas of research in human behavior. We have the tools and understanding to explore these areas. The difficulties are enormous, but the multiplicity of variables in understanding human behavior exist regardless which frame of reference one utilizes. The developments in child psychology, neonatology, social psychology, pediatrics, education, genetics, and child psychiatry came at a time when it was politically important to emphasize the essential sameness of rather than the differences between the sexes. While the data we have today are pathetically incomplete, they suggest that future study will reveal that the sexes have different attitudes toward attachment and caring, and ultimately different attitudes toward romantic love.

Pediatricians have known for years that boys and girls develop at different rates. Cognitive skills and verbal abilities, on average, mature much earlier in girls than in boys. The level of motor skills, large muscle capabilities, and motor power at any given preschool age is preponderantly more developed in boys. In recent years we have begun to see fundamental questions raised about whether the primary motivators that underlie and organize behavior may not be different between the sexes.

Observation of play patterns among boys suggests a different set of underlying values than that which operates with girls,[4] and while one must be careful to avoid drawing hasty biological distinctions, the research suggests that there is an essential difference. To watch a group of boys playing as quiet and noncontact a sport as baseball is to expect a riot at any moment. Accusations, imprecations, curses, threats, rage, and ranting form the background music that accompanies every game. But the game goes on. Even the threat of mayhem does not disturb the continuation of the game to its appointed number of innings. If there is occasional bloodshed—a bloody nose from a rough tag, a badly scraped knee in a slide—the game goes on.

Girls, on the other hand, are more likely to play with words of support and encouragement, and when conflict arises will discontinue the game rather than risk tension within the group. This differing behavior pattern suggests that in the play of boys the *game*—the competitive aspect— is of fundamental importance and the relationships are secondary. The group is only instrumental to the game. With girls the relationship is the primary concern, the game being simply a convenience of that group.

Certainly it is logical to assume that there would have to be a difference in the distribution between the sexes of the attributes of both aggressiveness and nurturing.[5] It is impossible that direct aggression could be as biologically encouraged in women as it is in men. Being physically smaller and slighter, women were inevitably dependent on men for their survival in precultural times. A direct conflict with a man utilizing physical force, not augmented by such technological tools as a gun or some other weapon, could be suicidal. Checks on direct expression of aggression built into the organism must reflect this obvious differential. Similarly, since the mother must be encouraged to nurture and nurse her child during the first years of life there must be powerful reinforcement in women of the normal caring and protective tendencies that I believe are inherent in both sexes.

Psychologist Margaret Harlow assumes that there is a difference in male and female protectiveness and parentalism toward the young. Nonetheless she feels that the difference is vastly less than among the higher apes. She points out that in most subhuman primates the paternal male's role is confined to protecting and comforting all young within the group, not just his own specific young. The mother and her infants, for which she takes primary responsibility, cluster about the male leader or leaders. The male leaders take primary responsibility for the horde, the mothers being specifically custodial in relationship to their own children. Harlow notes that adult males tend to be tolerant of all infants, occasionally "mothering" abandoned older infants. They will also protect the small young from some bullying by the stronger. She insists that in the human being the variation is somewhat less marked: "The paternal affectional system is stronger in human males, doubtless enhanced by culture." She then goes on to suggest that paternal caring behavior may significantly differ from the maternal because of the underlying endrocrinal changes that accompany birth in the female; this endocrine surge, she feels, helps strengthen and shape maternal behavior. Despite the gender differences, genetic and hormonal, she emphasizes the necessity of proper early conditioning to allow the biological traits to mature to expressiveness: "The paternal system, like the maternal one, depends on the prior establishment of the affectional ties to others of the species."[6]

Conventional wisdom, across cultures and times, has generally vested the compassionate and caring attributes in women and the aggressiveness in men. No gender has a monopoly on either, and life experience can tune one in and the other out of either or both sexes. What is clear is that "modern" (if one is free to call the entire period of recorded history in our culture modern) concepts of "femininity" and "masculinity" have established gender stereotypes that allow women to feel more comfortable with their affectionate and loving aspects, and guilty and confused about their aggressive and ambitious traits.

It may not be as evident that men, too, pay a considerable price for such gender stereotyping. To be denied the pleasures of caring and loving, to be made to feel ashamed of one's own sensitivity and sensuality, to feel guilty for dependency desires—this is to court the obsessive and sterile world of power that is currently considered the proper goal of masculine endeavor. It is tragic to deny either gender access to the pleasure of either loving or mastery.

Thomas Mann saw himself as a creature torn between the diverse natures of his intellectual, obsessive Prussian father and his sensuous, creative, artistic Bavarian mother. He associated the hard-driving ambitious aspects of his personality with masculinity and the north, and the sensuality and artistic feeling with femininity and the south. Nowhere is this better expressed than in that elegant and obviously autobiographical story "Tonio Kröger":

> He surrendered utterly to the power that to him seemed the highest on earth, to whose service he felt called, which promised him elevation and honours: the power of intellect, the power of the Word, that lords it with a smile over the unconscious and inarticulate. To this power he surrendered with all the passion of youth, and it rewarded him with all it had to give, taking from him inexorably, in return, all that it is wont to take . . .
>
> And then, with knowledge, its torment and its arrogance, came solitude; because he could not endure the blithe and innocent with their darkened understanding, while they in turn were troubled by the sign on his brow. But his love of the word kept growing sweeter and sweeter, and his love of form; for he used to say (and had already said it in writing) that knowledge of the soul would unfailingly make us melancholy if the pleasures of expression did not keep us alert and of good cheer.
>
> He lived in large cities and in the south, promising himself a luxuriant ripening of his art by southern suns; perhaps it was the blood of his mother's race that drew him thither. But his heart being dead and loveless, he fell into adventures of the flesh, descended into the depths of lust and searing sin, and suffering unspeakably thereby. It might have been his father in him, that tall, thoughtful, fastidiously dressed man with the wild flower in his buttonhole, that made him suffer so down there in the south; now and again he would feel a faint, yearning memory of

a certain joy that was of the soul; once it had been his own, but now, in all his joys, he could not find it again.[7]

Throughout his writings Mann alludes to the conflicts between "icy intellect" and "scorching sense" ascribing the former to the masculine aspect of his personality and the latter to the feminine. It should be obvious to any thinking person that no gender has a monopoly on either rationality or passion and that the balance between the call or commitment to either may differ within the sexes. To elucidate different biologically determined gender propensities between the two genders is not to bind one to those biological factors, but to free one from them.

Biological indices of behavior may, at their limits, tell us how far we can culturally deviate from them before we endanger the species, but there is a vast expanse that may be traversed; the boundaries for acceptable variability are wide. Biological differences may also be illuminated to show us ways to mitigate or even ignore our biological directives (we do fly without wings, and travel underwater without gills), when such biology is inconvenient to our culture, our values, or our aspirations.

In *On Human Nature*, Edward O. Wilson states:

> The genes hold culture on a leash. The leash is very long, but inevitably values will be constrained in accordance with their effects on the human gene pool. . . . Human behavior—like the deepest capacities for emotional response which drive and guide it—is the circuitous technique by which human genetic material has been and will be kept intact.[8]

Independent of the fact that Wilson is absolutely correct in saying that our genes set the ultimate limits to our behavior, those of us trained in the psychological field are aware of just how long that leash can be and how far we can extend it. Genetic determinism, for example, demands that the human infant be provided with a primary caretaker; it does not necessitate that the caretaker be a woman rather than a man. Culture has the capacity to change our character and custom beyond the recognition of our fellow creatures with whom we share the same biology. The Aztecs could not at first conceive that the mounted Spanish warriors that devastated their lands could really be their fellow creatures.

The artistic device of inventing alien creatures (from Swift to Spielberg) to illuminate the foolishness that culture is capable of imposing on character is extraordinarily effective. When, as in the movie *The Gods Must Be Crazy*,[9] the "alien creature" is someone who shares our time and our biology, a "cousin" separated only by culture, the effect is even more convincing. Culture is, as the sociologists as well as so many of our great biologists[10] have affirmed, the preeminent power in changing the natures of human beings.

A famous quote, attributed to Freud, states that all in life is *Arbeit und Liebe*. If the terms are used broadly enough I think most of us can agree that work and love are all. By "work" Freud must mean all forms of mastery; by "love," all relationships and attachments. Life is doing, feeling, and relating. Biological and genetic research suggests that women have been handed a primary drive for attachments while men have been oriented toward work and mastery. But no one in these sophisticated times denies the importance of both for feelings of fulfillment in both genders. It is not nature but modern culture that seems to have insisted on imposing an arbitrary exclusivity to gender roles.

What western culture seems to have done is pervert a biological differential which may exist and create an absolute and artificial division. It tore apart the two foundations of human pleasure—*Liebe* and *Arbeit*—and assigned work to men and love to women and in the process corrupted the pleasure in both. No one ought be limited to one major pleasure source. In addition to the deprivation of the excluded pleasure area, the demands placed on the one acceptable area will tax even its potential for pleasure and nurture. Work cannot be all nor can love; nor should they have to be. While women have been deprived of the "joy"—more accurately the position and power—of the workplace in our modern capitalist society, men have been deprived of the joy in loving. I am not sure which deprivation is greater. In terms of political power, of course, women have suffered more. But in terms of the very meaning of human existence, to be deprived of a sense of the importance of, and capacity for, love is at least as egregious an injury. As a psychoanalyst intimately involved with the truest and most honest expression of people's feelings, I am distressed to discover how few male patients have a sense of love. One begins to wonder if they have the capacity for love. This does not mean that a man cannot value his wife or value his child, but I am beginning to question whether the real fusion that I have identified as the seminal component of love exists in most men.

This cleavage of work and love influences the way both sexes conceive of love in addition to altering the innate capacities for love. I am convinced that most men only vaguely know the meaning of love. By contrast many women, forced to vest their entire pride and security in love, can extend their need to a point beyond the possibility of fulfillment even by a fully loving creature, let alone that love-cripple who is the typical man. The difference is painfully and exquisitely expressed by Flaubert in the contrasting attitudes of the two lovers, Emma Bovary and Rodolphe:

But when she saw herself in the glass she wondered at her face. Never had her eyes been so large, so black, of so profound a depth. Something subtle about her being transfigured her. She repeated, "I have a lover! a lover!" delighting at the idea as if a second puberty had come to her. So at last she was to know those joys of love, that fever of happiness of which she had despaired! She was entering upon marvels where all would be passion, ecstasy, delirium. An azure infinity encompassed her, the heights of sentiment sparkled under her thought, and ordinary existence appeared only afar off, down below in the shade, through the interspaces of these heights.[11]

Contrast this with Rodolphe's response to Emma's words of adoration to him, "You are my king, my idol!":

He had so often heard these things said that they did not strike him as original. Emma was like all his mistresses; and the charm of novelty, gradually falling away like a garment, laid bare the eternal monotony of passion, that has always the same form and the same language. He did not distinguish, this man of so much experience, the difference of sentiment beneath the sameness of expression. Because lips libertine and venal had murmured such words to him, he believed but little in the candour of hers; as if the fullness of the soul did not sometimes overflow in the emptiest metaphors, since no one can ever give the exact measure of his needs, nor of his conceptions, nor of his sorrows; and since human speech is like a cracked tin kettle, on which we hammer out tunes to make bears dance when we long to move the stars.[12]

Early in my clinical experience I observed that men rarely committed suicide over the loss of a loved one, whereas this was the preponderant reason for women's suicide.[13] Men commit suicide over the loss of their business or other representations of position or power. This does not mean that men *value* their business over their wife or their child. If given the choice in advance I have no doubt that the typical man would save his child over his business. But in suicide we are dealing with an internal reality in which the symbol transcends the actuality. With the loss of a loved one, a woman will often see the loss of her capacity for survival. Women are likely to vest their pride, their confidence, and their identity in their attachments; men are more likely to vest these same things in their achievements and their position.

Nowhere in literature is that tragedy of confused expectations and impossible aspirations better expressed than in *Anna Karenina*. Vronsky offers what he honorably believes to be love. If it is not, it is what passes for love in most men and is accepted as such by most women. Anna wants a love to meet her needs, needs that surpass what most women of her time expect, and no man could give.

> Anna turned that glaring light in which she was seeing everything on to her relations with him, which she had hitherto avoided thinking about. "What was it he sought in me? Not love so much as the satisfaction of vanity." ... "Yes, there was the triumph of success in him. Of course there was love too, but the chief element was the pride of success. He boasted of me. Now that's over. There's nothing to be proud of. Nothing to be proud of, only to be ashamed of. He has taken from me all he could, and now I am no use to him. He is weary of me and is trying not to be dishonorable in his behavior toward me ... He loves me, but how? The zest is gone, as the English say .... Yes, there's not the same flavor about me for him now. If I go away from him, at the bottom of his heart he will be glad.
>
> "My love keeps growing more passionate and selfish, while his is dying, and that's why we're drifting apart. ... And there's nothing I can do. He is everything to me, and I want him more and more to give himself up to me entirely. And he wants more and more to get away from me. ... He tells me I'm insanely jealous; but it's not true.

I'm not jealous, but I'm unsatisfied. . . . If I could be anything but a mistress, passionately caring for nothing but his caresses; but I can't and I don't care to be anything else. And by that desire I rouse aversion in him, and he rouses fury in me, and it cannot be different. Don't I know that he wouldn't deceive me, that he has no schemes about Princess Sorokina, that he's not in love with Kitty, that he won't desert me! I know all that, but it makes it no easier for me. If without loving me, from *duty* he'll be good and kind to me, without what I want, that's a thousand times worse than unkindness! That's—hell!''

Duty, goodness, kindness, fidelity, will not satisfy Anna. Vronsky must "give himself up entirely" to her. And he cannot. The seeming insatiability of her love deters him. And as Anna muses, she extends her personal feelings to the human condition in general.

"I don't know these streets at all. Hills it seems, and still houses, and houses . . . And in the houses always people and people . . . How many of them, no end, and all hating each other! . . . We are drawn apart by life, and I make his unhappiness and he mine, and there's no changing him or me. Every attempt has been made, but the screw has lost its thread.''[14]

Tolstoy homes in on Anna's depression like a skilled modern-day psychiatric diagnostician. The hopelessness, the helplessness, the shame, the bankruptcy of self-respect and self-esteem, and finally the projection of her own despair to the generalized world about her are the marks of depression. "The screw has lost its thread,'' and with that statement we can anticipate Anna's suicide before she herself is aware of her resolve.

Other indications of sharp gender differences have emerged from investigations into an altogether different mental illness. It had been known that the delusions of paranoid men tended to be predominantly homosexual. The voices heard in male paranoia were mocking accusations of homosexuality. So constant was this association that Freud originally postulated that paranoia was a protection, a defensive maneuver against recognizing one's latent and unconscious homosexuality. Rather than fulfill his homosexual desires, the patient represses, denies, and finally projects them (the defensive maneuver that characterizes paranoia) onto others. It is not I who desire him; it is he who desires me. By this theory, homosexuality is the alternative or the opposite of paranoia. Experience indicates that while latent homosexuality may play a part in some paranoia, it is hardly the central or exclusive mechanism. They are obviously not the antithesis of each other. There are paranoid homosexuals and there are latent homosexuals who have no propensity for paranoia.

The dominant theme in all paranoia is the fear of social humiliation. In a male-dominant society, therefore, the ultimate symbol of reduction is the loss of phallic power. If one examines this association between male paranoia and homosexual delusions it reveals more about the social role of men than about the disease. It confirms that the ultimate degradation represented in paranoia will be visualized by the typical heterosexual man in our society as the loss of his male role, his abandoning the sexual dominance of maleness and his being relegated via homosexuality to the subjugated role of a woman.[15]

The error in Freud's reasoning was based on the fact that the three major cases of paranoia on which he built his theory were all men. Women paranoid patients never heard accusatory voices proclaiming their lesbianism. The monotonously common message of their delusions was the accusation of harlotry. To a woman in this culture the most humiliating accusation was that she could fulfill her sexual role, that she could actually enjoy sex, that she could be an active participant in it, that she was, in other words, what her culture defined as a whore. I have a strong conviction that with the liberation of women from the stigmatization that formerly went with indulging in sexual pleasures, the delusion of being called a whore will give way to more "masculine" delusions, relating to power and humiliation, perhaps even to the elaboration of homosexual delusions. If male homosexuality were to become as culturally acceptable as most pretend it is now, I would expect a decline in such fantasies or delusions of homosexuality in paranoid men. I am much more confident of the change in women.

Homosexuality is different in nature, not just in object choice, from heterosexuality. It is not just that the homosexual selects a partner of the same sex; the mythology, the culture, and the dynamics of homosexuality differ greatly from those of heterosexuality. What is of more interest in the context of this discussion of gender difference in love is the vast difference between male and female homosexuality; they are so different that they are almost antithetical.

Through studying male homosexuality and female homosexuality we may see as through a magnifying lens something about the nature of the gender roles assigned to men and women in our heterosexual world. The sociology and culture of the two express it clearly. While all generalizations are precarious in such mixed populations as I will describe, the statistical facts are preponderantly as follows (allowing for the exceptions at the edges of all bell-shaped curves):

Male homosexuality is *sexually* oriented, and the promiscuity, the sexual athleticism of the male homosexual is astonishing in the heterosexual world. The emphasis on phallic size, youth, beauty, power, and dominance and submission makes male homosexuality seem a kind of hyperbolic extension of the masculine role as it is defined in our society. Female homosexuality, with its emphasis on caring and attachment, tends to minimize the sexual role. It tends to be extraordinarily devoted and monogamous, with warm and tender attachments prevailing over sexual needs. Aging seems to intrude less on it, and the idealization of form and figure, the narcissistic element so dominant in male homosexuality, seems of minor importance in female homosexuality. Indeed, prestige and power seem less a factor here than in the heterosexual world.

With the feminist revolution women are beginning to find their way into the world of power and mastery. One hopes they will not, in grasping for the privileges of power inherent in the masculine role, find themselves trapped in the lovelessness that has characterized that role. Women at least know where the power is; it is in the world of work and money. But men seem unsure how to enter the world of love. Where in this world is that marketplace? There are no law-school or medical-school equivalents in the world of relationship to lubricate the transfer from one role to another.

Ready access to sexuality for all may have eased the burdens for some adolescent men, but it seems to have created confusion for others. In the days when "good girls" didn't "do it," frustration prevailed. And even that was not inevitable; for the enterprising there was always some access to "bad girls." The very frustration allowed for an idealization of that "special girl," and this, while not yet love, was at least an approximation of it. That idealization no longer exists. The heavenly Aphrodite is extinct. The young man of a previous generation could have said "I want a girl just like the girl that married dear old dad," but that "girl" does not exist, and if by chance she appeared she would be offended by the appellation "girl." In the process of being deprived of their exclusive place in the world of power and having already been deprived of a special prerogative in the world of sexuality, men now seem bewildered as to how to compensate, since they have not yet discovered the joy of romance and romantic attachments.

Since the world of human biology is so readily modifiable by culture, we ought take a look at the cultures themselves. If cultural directives can influence the capacity to give and receive love between genders can they not also influence the general capacity for love in the entire population? In other words are certain cultures productive of loving, while others are inhibiting of the capacity to give and receive love?

If the genetic evaluation is difficult, the cultural and developmental influences are even more complex. One complicating factor is the tendency to confuse demonstrativeness, a capacity to show or display affection, with a capacity to feel affection. We know that cultures differ markedly in their tolerance for public displays of emotion on the part of adults, particularly display of something so "private" as love and affection.

One notices the difference between Stockholm and Naples not just by the language and climate or the nature of the architecture, but by the noise level—by the amount of talking that goes on, by the animation, by the facial expressiveness. An English middle-class lounge in Sidmouth, with its separate tables and its quiet coffee bar, is simply not the same as an equivalent establishment in Tel Aviv, if there even is an equivalent establishment.

Cultures also differ in their encouragement of affectionate displays even in private—touching, fondling, hugging, kissing—between parents and children. The average bourgeois American, at least this average bourgeois American, reads with astonishment of the upper class English environment in which for example Winston Churchill described himself as growing up with his parental contact limited to formal occasions and meetings; children were sent away from home surprisingly early. At the other extreme there are simple tribal cultures in which children are nursed or allowed access to the breast until three, four, and even older, or in which children in the first years of life are carried in close bodily intimacy by the mother throughout her activities. It is difficult to visualize a British aristocrat of the Edwardian day carrying her child swaddled to her body for an hour, let alone a year. These differences in what a culture defines as proper parental behavior influence not just the public and private behavior of the parents, but the kind of character traits that will be encouraged in the children.

In a similar manner a culture may encourage displays of aggression and hostility and discourage shows of compassion, tenderness, or affection. Recent literature has focused attention on two such extreme examples, the Icks[16] and Yanomamos.[17] The Icks, the "Mountain people," have elevated cruelty to a virtue, while the Yanomamo Indians of South America boast of their aggressive and mean (by our standards) treatment of their wives and children. Most of us, however, are not interested in the extremes but are concerned with the variations among more typical western cultures, or the differences over time within the same culture. We are concerned because our children often fail to conform to certain values we respect and we are unaware of what, if anything, in our culture or our individual behavior has brought this to pass. The key question, at any rate, is whether there is any necessary connection between the capacity to show and display emotion and the capacity to feel it. And here one must be careful.

To honor the dead, the traditions in northern Protestant countries demand that one contain oneself, that one show respect for the dead by not crying in public, by not "making a scene," by acting with courage and dignity. To do otherwise would be self-indulgent, a dishonoring of the dead, a selfish display. This reserve would be viewed with horror in warmer Mediterranean cultures or in the Jewish or Muslim traditions. The lack of emotional display would be seen as a mark of the limits of the experienced emotions. Grief, in these more expressive cultures, is felt and communicated to the group; the mourner is encouraged to catharsis, often goaded on by the rabbi or imam; the tears, wails, breast-beating, and rending of clothes are seen as honoring the dead by marking the intensity of the loss in a public gesture. The absence of such demonstrations in an Anglo-Saxon group must seem to them a sign of coldness as well as custom, for such grief as they experience is uncontrollable, beyond human restraint.

There is no way to calibrate emotions or to quantify grief. I am quite sure that in this case, the death of a child, the quiet grief-stricken Welsh, Swedish, or English mother will be experiencing the same intensity of loss, pain, and anguish as the inconsolable Sicilian or Lebanese mother. Nonetheless, we cannot be totally sanguine about what we do when we discourage shows of affection and displays of emotion.

The coercive impact of cultural determinants on behavior is irresistible to most trapped within the boundaries of that culture. The power of cultural indoctrination has the consistency of a biological determinant. Our culture has created an exaggerated form of masculine identity and feminine identity which for all practical purposes has dictated the aspirations and life-styles of the men and women under its influence.

The cultural or psychological values of the parents will always be transmitted as mandates to their children. We know that one of the most powerful stimuli for the development of warm, affectionate, and loving natures is receiving love and affection in childhood. We also know that severe deprivation in early life can destroy the capacity, not just for love, but for human attachments in general; and beyond that for the compassion, empathy, and identification associated with the mechanisms of conscience and all moral behavior. Further—novelists, poets, and moviemakers—those most sensitive interpreters of culture, suggest that the differences observed between cultures are a matter not simply of form but of substance. The absence of display may be tantamount to the absence of the feeling.

Compare the works of Ingmar Bergman with those of Federico Fellini. Running like scarlet threads through the fabric of all of Fellini's work is passion and its problems, sensuality in all its grief and glory, love with all of its joys and all of its frustrations. He is not alone in this involvement with love—it is a characteristic theme of the great Italian filmmakers. When Bergman deals with love at all, it is almost inevitably secondary to the sense of isolation and detachment that is the hallmark of his work. If there is any passion, it is involved with death and its meanings, but even death seems merely an extension or an epitome of the isolation of normal living. From *Wild Strawberries* through *The Seventh Seal* to *Cries and Whispers,* one senses only the loneliness and despair, the isolated heart desperate for resonance, for the nourishment that comes from being caressed and touched and held by others. There is no fusion here.

There is comedy in all of Fellini's tragedy because there is real passion. Fellini is the apotheosis of feeling. I cannot recall laughing in a Bergman movie, even laughter through tears, for he is the poet of isolation. So much of twentieth-century art deals with the tragedy of the isolated individual, trapped in a life that keeps him from his kind and keeps him from pleasure, or tragedy compounded by the horrifying existential assumption that it is the only life that he will ever

experience. Sartre, in *No Exit,* wisely places his hell right
here on earth in an ordinary hotel room where three neurotic people are doomed to spend eternity together and yet
alone.

Yet, all generalizations about cultures are only of statistical value. The variations within cultures are as enormous
as those between them. So generalizations about culture
must not be used to pass any judgment on the behavior of
any individual within the culture. We live, as Freud instructed us, in a continuum. All of us possess within us at
least fractional elements identical to those which seem to
dominate our neighbors, regardless of how different the external expression may seem. The saint and the sinner, the
hero and the coward, are built of the same stuff, combined
in different proportions to create the appearance of uniquely
different entities.

No modern culture is purely homogeneous. Family struc-
tures within it will modify the amalgam of the dominant
culture. Subcultures that exist within every complex western
culture will also mitigate the influence of the dominant culture.

The relationship between display of affection and the capacity to feel love, while not a direct one, may not be negligible. This is important to recognize because of the power
of culture in shaping the nature of our species now and in
the future. If, as I believe, our culture is diminishing our
capacity for love and its components: sympathy, empathy,
compassion, identification, fusion, and commitment, this is
a dangerous direction which ought to be reversed. Cultures
can encourage the elements of their own destruction. In a
time like the present where technology has (while not yet
reducing us to a single culture) connected us in our different
cultures to one common fate, we are capable of annihilating
our species.

To summarize, the capacity to love varies according to genetic potentials, the mandates of culture, and variations of individual experience. Genetics seem to operate in at least two ways. There may be an inherent *gender* difference in both the priority and the quality of loving. If this directive does exist, it is a soft one and, unlike the genetic determinant for eye color, is readily mutable by personal experience and cultural pressures operating through the labels "masculine" and "feminine." Secondly, there exists, at its most extreme, a genetically determined pathological condition called autism which makes not just loving but all relationships with others difficult or impossible. Whether there is, beyond the pathological, a normal variation in genetic capacity for loving is impossible to determine with our current research capacities. All evidence seems to suggest that whatever variation may occur would be negligible when exposed to developmental conditioning. Cultural variability and its power to modify normal genetic traits have been emphasized. Now what about the developmental experiences?

I have already suggested my bias for the power of developmental factors in childhood in determining the character of adult behavior and perceptions. Probably the most significant elements in determining any individual's capacity to love can be located in individual development. It lies within the psychological history, as shaped by the multiple family dynamics that make each individual different even from a sibling. The child's self-perception, perception of others, sense of commitment, and sense of purpose all impinge on the ability to give and receive love. The directives built into the child by the parents, operating on the child's constitutional endowments or limitations, will determine the grown-up child's character traits in the area of loving as in all other areas. This is a simple restatement of the dynamic and developmental principle that evolved from Freud's libido theory. To a Freudian the child is always father to the man.

All current behavior is a product of forces and counterforces whose roots extend into our past. Despite all of the shortcomings of the libido theory—its overemphasis on genetic determinism, its relegation of the emotions to a secondary role in human experience, its simple-minded and wrong concept of human energy as a limited and confined resource, its failure to appreciate the transforming power of the human imagination—it has since its inception held a grip on the imagination of psychologists and creative artists.

The strength of the libido theory lies in its building a *developmental* and *dynamic* model of the interplay between nature and nurture that, in one scheme, explains pathological and normal behavior, character and personality traits, culture and its institutions, and conscience and the nature of morality. It is because I am Freudian that even while I reject Freud's instinctual theory, I turn to individual development in childhood to find the main roots for the adult's capacity for love.

The need to analyze the effect of environment on the character of our children and their children is hardly theoretical these days. The survivability of our species may depend on the character traits we encourage or suppress. In great part we can be what we choose to be. If we desire our children to be leaner, stronger, more generous, less competitive, more courageous, less narcissistic, less gender-stereotyped, more empathic, more giving, more loving, more caring, more committed, less hedonistic, more imaginative, more honest, less self-deceptive, more sensitive, more decent, wittier, and more spontaneous (to indicate a few of my biases), there are ways to encourage those traits. I am not saying those are the only traits that ought to be encouraged. You may have an alternative or even opposing list. You may

have the same list and define the same terms differently. We
need not argue about the nature of the list, since this is not
a philosophical book on morality. We only have to acknowledge here that such character traits as the ability to love are
shaped by the directives that emerge from the value systems
of the general culture, and these are further modified by the
specific conditions of the individual's personal history, the
biases of the family, or even the fact that there was no
family.

I would like to first discuss—if only to acknowledge and
dismiss—some extreme pathological states that formerly had
been viewed as faults of upbringing but at present seem to
be so biologically determined that they develop independent
of and seemingly immune to environmental modification.
These fortunately rare conditions are important to this discussion because it is vital that parents and others involved
with the nurturing of children with severe pathological states
free themselves from a lifetime of guilt and self-rebuke, and
recognize the degree to which these children are biochemi-
cally and genetically flawed.

There are certain individuals who cannot love and beyond that cannot relate at all: autistic children and severe
schizophrenics. I recall with pain and horror a training clinic
in which a young psychiatric resident was interviewing the
mother of an autistic five-year-old boy. It was the first such
case I had ever seen and an image that will never leave me.
The young psychiatrist conducting the interview (who was
later criticized for his question by the senior child psychiatrist teaching the class) asked the mother whether she had
ever held, embraced, fondled, or otherwise offered her child
love in his first year or two of life. The mother, angry, hurt,
and defensive, answered: "Have you ever tried to embrace
an icicle?"

There are some children and adults so seriously flawed by

nature that they are capable of only the most primitive and dependent attachments. Well before modern concepts of narcissism, before even the modern distinction between neurosis and psychosis, Freud labeled all illnesses of the mind "neuroses"—literally, nerve diseases. Those neuroses which had their origin in psychological, as distinguished from organic, conditions were labeled "psychoneuroses" (a redundancy we have since dropped). Some of Freud's patients were what we today would call schizophrenics. These patients, whether catatonic or hebephrenic or chaotically delusional, were totally intractable to what Freud then called his "talking cure" and would now be called "psychoanalysis." He labeled this group of refractory and incurable conditions the "narcissistic neuroses."

Even in those early days, psychoanalysis recognized that engaging the patient emotionally was a fundamental step in curing him. Freud postulated that these patients were too narcissistically involved with themselves—they seemed to reside in an inaccessible world of their own creation—to form a relationship with the therapist. The analysis of the transference, then as now, was seen as a central element in treatment. These "narcissistic neuroses" are now labeled "psychoses" and they are still by and large resistant to psychoanalysis.

"Schizophrenia," like "cancer," is a broad term that covers a multitude of conditions varying dramatically in malignancy and treatability. At their most extreme, severe schizophrenics are incapable of feeling for other individuals and are often incapable of feeling any form of pleasure, a condition referred to as anhedonia. Beyond that there are those pathetic creatures who seem incapable of any feeling, good or bad. The self-infliction of pain through cigarette burns or razor lacerations is described by certain schizophrenics as a protection from the awful feeling of feeling nothing. One not involved in this state can only barely imagine the horrors of a condition in which the pain of self-mutilation is a relief.

There is one other group outside the broad range of normal variation that must be considered—the psychopathic personality. Here there may also be a genetic factor at play. Even though psychopaths are defined psychologically as "abnormal," they are not defined as "sick." This seeming contradiction, abnormal but not sick, reflects the social implications of sickness and health. Psychopaths do not suffer from their developmental abnormalities; they make those about them suffer. The psychopath, whether he is a result of constitutional determinants, as some theories would have it, or a product of massive and severe deprivation in early life, seems to have no capacity for guilt, empathy, love, or conscience. He also has an impaired capacity for foreseeing the consequences of his acts or anticipating a future wherein he will be forced to pay for his transgressions. His behavior is viewed as criminal, not sick. Most cultures will not allow amoral, exploitative, cruel and conscienceless behavior to be excused by labeling it sickness. Psychopaths are recognized by most psychiatrists as untreatable, and are generally held to be beyond the purview of psychiatry. Psychopaths represent a large percentage of the criminal caste.

Only time and the aging process seem to mitigate the behavior of the true psychopath. It is with the diminution of passion in general and the ascendance of fear over rage that the antisocial behavior diminishes. The lost generation of psychopaths that tyrannize our public spaces may invoke our sympathy, but we can best acknowledge this sympathy by devoting our energy to the prevention of psychopathic conditions rather than uselessly insisting that they need treatment. They are immune to treatment.

Again I want to caution that everyone who transgresses

the law is not a psychopath, and that many psychopaths operate successfully within the law.

Modern studies offer an alternative to the genetic determination assumed as the cause for the so-called "constitutional psychopath." This pathway to psychopathy has been amply traced to the severe neglect in very early childhood previously described, both by observation of this neglected population and by relating the results to the pioneering works connecting primate behavior with human development.[18]

A child must have physical contact with adults during the first year of life; the physical contact must be more than mechanical feeding and protection from the elements. The human baby is born incomplete. If he is deprived of light in the first weeks of life, vision will not develop. If he is deprived of stroking, handling, cooing, and general communication with adults, the capacity to relate and to be loving will never develop. Let me caution that I mean *severe* deprivation. This condition, an artifact of neglect and ignorance, is fortunately rare.

Beyond these extremes there exists a whole range of conditions in childhood that will enhance or reduce the capacity to give and receive love. Some conditions will inhibit one ability more than the other, although there is likely to be a linkage between the two.

Having acknowledged the presence of these severely aberrant and still mystifying groups, the autistic and the psychopathic, I can proceed to the wide range of individuals who differ in their capacity to love, yet all fit within Freud's wide and generous boundaries of normalcy.

The capacity for all intimacy with our fellow creatures, including romantic love, while part of our natural endowment, is dependent for its fruition on environmental factors operating on us during our developmental years. The potential for attachment is achieved by the child's passing through predictable and necessary stages to reach a point of maturity whereby he can give up the self-involvement and primary narcissism that is normal to the child and engage in the mutual loving that is a desirable normal attribute of the adult.

In the process of arriving at that stage of mature mutual love, the traces and shadows of all the previous immature drives will persist but will now be joined under the dominant drive for heterosexual union. Freud saw all of this in terms of sexual drive and sexual gratification. Love was neglected, presumed to be an ancillary phenomenon. Nonetheless, the Freudian concept of a developmental scheme for the sexual instinct is equally applicable for love, affection, and identity beyond the sexual role.

One of the few psychoanalysts who has remained within the classic language and tradition of psychoanalysis but has imaginatively and courageously extended the original Freudian model of human behavior beyond considerations of the sexual instinct and its "vicissitudes" to include narcissism, affect, and love has been Dr. Otto Kernberg. He states: "Only relatively normal people have the capacity for falling in love and developing such a passionate attachment into a stable love relationship."[19] Freud would have been more severe. He would have dropped the word "relatively." To Freud the touchstone of maturity was the capacity to abandon a narcissistic involvement with the self and learn to relate to a person of the opposite sex—other than one's parents.

Pathologically persistent preoccupations with the self have been studied and classified as states of narcissism. The layman must guard against confusion about what the term "narcissism" means in psychoanalysis. Just as "depression" has an entirely different meaning in clinical psychiatry than it does in everyday language, "narcissism" has a clinical meaning. It is a serious misunderstanding to consider either Freud's earliest formulations or these later elaborations of narcissism as representing an extension of self-love. There is no love in narcissism—only anxiety; there is no self-love—only self-involvement.

In mythology, Narcissus was a youth of great beauty who was so infatuated and occupied by his own image reflected in a pond that he rejected the offers of love from an enamored wood nymph. Her punishment was to convert him into a flower, doomed to isolation and examination of his reflection in the waters of the pond. The myth of Narcissus involves self-love. The current misunderstanding about the nature of narcissism stems both from the recognition of the myth that inspired Freud and from the early use of the term in the libido theory. The early phases of childhood development were called "autoerotic" but were also referred to as narcissistic. Current advanced use of the concept of narcissism refers to self-involvement, not self-love.

The best indication that the narcissist is not involved in self-love is Freud's primary test for love: idealization of the loved object. The narcissist has not an enhanced sense of himself but a terribly diminished sense of self. His involvement with self is nothing like infatuation. If he looks constantly in the mirror it may seem that it is to admire the reflected image, but it is really a fearful need to reassure himself of his attractiveness. Narcissism holds the same relationship to self-esteem that narcissistic pleasure bears to true pleasure. Both narcissistic pleasure and narcissism serve the primitive and fundamental need of reassurance.

The narcissist is concerned with his safety and survival, and like a child he vests his security in others. Central to that purpose is the need for constant reassurance from all that he is approved and lovable. For the narcissist popularity and adoration are not luxuries—nor true pleasures; they are insurance policies and safety measures. Unfortunately, narcissistic reassurance, like narcissistic pleasure, is only a quick fix. Neither truly nourishes. Like a cocaine high or an alcoholic binge they create an illusion of well-being and safety that is quickly diminished and more often than not will lead to a rebound reaction of despair and dread, driving the poor approval addict for yet another and another quick fix.

A Don Juan may be seen as a kind of love junky who never gets the reassurance of real love. He has no idea what fusion means; he is always separating himself from the very thing he so desperately needs, a loving partner. Women are simply objects to be used as instruments for reassurance. He treats them as mirrors on the wall from whom he is insistently demanding to be told that he is "the loveliest of them all." All he will ever get is a temporary and illusory reassurance, and he will be driven to making the same demand to a thousand different mirrors at a thousand succeeding moments in time. When he asks to be told that he is the most lovable and deserving of everything, he is really asking whether he is worthy of anything at all. Narcissism is a vessel that cannot be filled. If the difference between loving and being loved is the difference between the well and the cistern, the narcissist is a cistern with a leaky bottom or no bottom at all.

All of us possess a certain degree of narcissism. It is the magnificence of Freudian theory that it sees in the normal person the pathological trait transformed and mitigated through its integration into and domination by mature and constructive ends. We all contain narcissistic elements within our personalities, but we contain them in different degrees. We also seek, through methods that Freud would have called sublimation, means of gratifying these narcissistic needs that are creative and adaptive. To become an actor rather than a laboratory scientist is an intelligent and healthy maneuver to gratify one's narcissistic needs through a constructive, socially useful, and rewarding occupation. The narcissist receives the great gratifications inherent in the performing arts, and every performance allows him the attention of a thousand adoring fans. After each performance, unlike the surgeon, architect, or salesman, he is treated to applause. Thundering and resonating from all those clapping hands he hears: "I love you, I love you, I love you."

This in no way mitigates the talents or the joy of the actor in his art. Psychoanalytic "explanations" of behavior are not deeper explanations but alternative explanations. There are equally intriguing dynamic explanations of why one becomes a banker, an editor, or a psychoanalyst. The performing artist can take pride in his work with no concern about what unconscious motivations may underlie his choice in the same way as a minister or social worker can. All of them represent healthy incorporations of unconscious needs into socially worthwhile and personally gratifying occupations. Then too, some performing artists may not be particularly narcissistic at all, simply blessed with a talent that demands an audience for its ultimate fulfillment.

So it is not merely the quantity of the narcissistic elements that survives from our childhood but the way we can or cannot sublimate, transform, and utilize them. If they are sufficiently overwhelming because of either a genetic predisposition, as Freud would say, or the unhappy results of dynamic factors in our development, we may be doomed to a narcissistic preoccupation so severe that it precludes loving others. There is not enough energy left to endow an object other than ourselves. There is not enough security there to make the trust and commitment that are so essential a part of true loving.

Fortunately, most early experience is not quite so crippling. We may be able to love, but the nature of our loving will be conditioned by the degree of our insecurities. We may require of our loved one a bonus beyond loving commitment, some socially enhancing aspect—beauty, wealth, power—that supports our own insufficient self-esteem. The nature of this will be determined by our values and the status symbols in our culture.

Stendhal referred to this reassurative aspect of love as "vanity-love." Today we are likely to dump these needs into the increasingly inflated category called narcissism.

> The great majority of men, especially in France, desire and possess a fashionable woman as they would possess a fine horse, as a necessary luxury for a young man. Their vanity, more or less flattered and more or less stimulated, gives rise to rapture. Sometimes sensual love is present also, but not always; often there is not even sensual pleasure. The duchess de Chaulnes used to say that a duchess is never more than thirty years old to a snob.[20]

For purposes of simplification I have tended to discuss individual limitations in the capacity for loving under the rubric of narcissistic behavior. This term (not used by Freud in this way) is simply a restatement of Freud's assumption that sexual incapacities are arrested developments. Incapacities of loving may also be seen as arrested developments. But what causes arrests in development?

Freud postulated that genetic predispositions were a primary cause, which is difficult to affirm or deny. Nonetheless he acknowledged their modifiability by "accidental" or environmental factors. These factors can be divided into two broad categories with an inexhaustible variety of individual modifications. First would be the absence of clear and accessible models. A boy or a girl who does not have a clear model with which to identify may have great difficulty in defining a sexual sense of self. Our ability to relate to others is contingent on some constant sense of a self who will be doing the relating. The second broad category is the intrusion of fear or rage into the sexual-pleasure apparatus.

Love unfortunately is not all. Survival, at least during childhood, takes precedence. Ironically, after a capacity for loving is established it may well preempt the primary role of survival. Some of us will sacrifice our lives for those we love, but first we must be secure enough to arrive at that point. The mechanisms whereby fear and rage are introduced into the sexual arena have been explained using many different languages and metaphors. The classical Freudian one is probably as good as most. It groups these problems around the central constellation of the Oedipal struggle. The degree to which the child is capable of resolving his Oedipal problems will determine the ease or difficulty of future relationships. What does this mean?

The growing child in attempting to move from self-involvement (autoerotism) to object love will take as its first object the parent of the opposite sex. This is fraught with danger. An indifferent, frightening, rejecting, or absent parent will make this progression difficult if not impossible. An overly seductive parent will make the attachment equally frightening as the child matures and confronts the incest dread which Freud presumed to be a genetic endowment in all of us. To complicate the equation there is the other actor in the triangle, the parent of the same sex. To love the father is seemingly to bring one in competition with the mother, who is also seen as an essential agent in our survival.

The attitudes of the parents toward the emerging sexual

and affectionate behavior will determine the attitudes of the child. To take a simple and common phenomenon, if there is more tolerance and encouragement of tenderness on the parts of our daughters than of our sons, we will develop a generation in which women are more capable than men of expressing tenderness. If gentleness in our boys is viewed as a dreaded symptom of potential homosexuality, we can effectively destroy all capacity for gentleness in our men. If performance is rewarded and affection repelled in boys, if seductiveness is the most effective device for girls to gain their ends with us, we will encourage precisely those traits, thereby creating gender differences, which we may then wrongly assume to be genetic and inevitable.

There are differing family attitudes toward all aspects of sexuality, affection, friendship, and love. Both the attitudes encouraged and the models observed will shape the eventual behavior of the emerging adult. If the child's love and confidence in the parent is betrayed by rejection or indifference, then love and confidence in all others will come with greater difficulty.

When summarized like this it all sounds so complicated, so difficult, but the fact is that most of us retain some potential for loving in adulthood. Somehow we muddle and struggle through. Family differences produce different behaviors, but different may be just fine. Heterogeneity is the strength, if also the despair, of our species. We do not have the predictability of the bug or the baboon, but we have a flexibility that serves survival.

Now once again we must return to culture, for while families vary, the boundaries of that variation are sharply delineated by cultural definitions. Families vary within every culture, but always within culturally determined limits of normalcy. Bushmen families vary as dramatically as American families, I imagine, but the limits of variability in each group will be determined by an implicit if not defined concept of normal parental behavior which differs between the two cultures. Cultures will rise and fall on the nature and the adaptability of their definitions of normalcy.

The question arises over and over again whether ours is a more narcissistic time than others. It is a difficult question to answer. As soon as a theoretical construct like narcissism becomes fashionable, everyone wants to join the club; everything becomes narcissism. And once everything falls within the same rubric, that heading ceases to have any useful distinguishing purpose. Ours may simply be the age that has discovered the term "narcissism," and therefore uses this new definition to reclassify old problems. I know that the original concept of narcissism has been so twisted and distorted as to allow it to encompass every wrong in our society. Nonetheless, we do know that times differ, and there is a growing sense that there is something in our time that encourages narcissistic self-involvement at the expense of commitment.

Many social commentators assume that the process by which we fall in love is changing. According to one, "There is no hard evidence on the matter, but a number of cues suggest that the conditions of modern living have altered the process in the following ways: the first phase—falling in love—does not reach the peak of excitement that it used to exhibit; the second phase—being in love—is shorter; and the third [commitment] more rarely reaches its full fruition."[21]

The psychological literature is always contradictory as it gropes its way—with limited empirical data, different life experiences, and different professional biases—to some consensus. There is nothing even approaching agreement in the current psychological literature as to how romantic love is faring with the younger generation. One writer argues that certain cultural trends, "including the disinclination for adolescents to postpone gratification, the trend towards convergence of sexual roles, and the increasing emphasis on communal rather than dyadic relationships," have diminished "the intensity, mystery and excitement of romantic love."[22] But in the same publication another argues that "adolescents are now more interested and capable of intimacy than they were a generation ago; that they are more open, honest, and caring in their relationships; and that shifts in the direction of individual self-discovery and self-expression have resulted in an increased emphasis on meaningful relationships."[23]

Margaret Mead is quoted as saying that children in the seventies suffered a "crisis of commitment,"[24] yet other experts see potential good in today's prolonged adolescence, arguing that "consolidation of identity which used to occur in late adolescence is delayed, perhaps indefinitely. The longer time available means that the individual does not need to make his or her defects in construction part of the character structure but can begin to discover in himself or herself new potentials."[25]

We know that the culture makes a difference in psychological and moral attitudes toward sex and love. The experts cannot even agree on what the differences are, let alone what caused the presumed changes in our sexual attitudes, or whether the changes are for the better or worse. This is part of the confusion of living during an ongoing revolution. We had not had sufficient time to completely adjust to the Freudian revolution demanding a recognition of the true nature of sexuality when we were precipitated into the equally powerful gender revolution by the demand of the feminist movement that as we reevaluate the nature of the sexual experience, we also reexamine the nature of love, the nature of work, and the different roles assigned to men and women in each of these.

For love to flourish, the following seem essential: the courage to risk being hurt; the capacity for identification; the ability to trust; the willingness for commitment; and the necessity for all of us to relinquish the hunger for instant and superficial gratification in order to experience and appreciate the more profound but delayed gratifications that are involved in utilizing and giving oneself in mature love. True loving is worth the risk.

As Stendhal eloquently phrased it: "Love is an exquisite flower, but one must have the courage to go and gather it on the brink of a dreadful precipice. Apart from ridicule, love is always haunted by the despair of being abandoned by the beloved and of being left nothing but a *dead blank* for the remainder of life."[26]

The problem is not just with loving. In many areas we see that ours is not an age that has honored any concept of community, even the community of two. This has been the age of the individual, the glorious and isolated self. There are few hosannas heard these days for commitment, duty, responsibility, and dedication to purpose. It would be surprising if love were not a victim of these trends.

Commitment must be part of any definition of mature love. There is, if not hard evidence, at least reasonable indication that there has been a failure of commitment in our time: a serious decrease in our confidence in relationships; a sense of increasing isolation and existential angst; and a doubt about the nature and purpose of life which is compounded by an erosion of our trust in the traditional institutions (marriage, religion, government) that no longer seem to serve our purposes.

If even commitment is difficult, then certainly the fusion that I demand in my definition of love would seem too much to ask of our frightened young. And yet the case for loving is an urgent and powerful one and must be made. If our culture is eroding those conditions in which love flourishes, we must change the conditions of our culture. The binding force of love is the only force—with the possible exception of the binding force of terror—strong enough to support the weighty burdens of our complex modern community.

8 ❧ THE CASE FOR LOVING: BEYOND PLEASURE

I have earlier defined plea-
sure as the feeling of joy resulting from an enlarged sense of
self. The great pleasures expand the sense of self beyond the
muscle and sinew, the appetites and urgencies of survival
and the ordinary. With the possible exception of religious
ecstasy, which seems reserved for an increasingly smaller
part of the population, love is its ultimate expression. In
"losing" oneself in love or "surrendering" oneself to love
we create a larger self. What we sacrifice is the isolated
half-creature of Aristophanes. What we recover is a multiplicity of fused identities with those we love that will leave
us an enlarged and fuller self even after separation. Even
after death, the lost person will remain a part of our experience, our consciousness, our sense of self and our sense of
purpose.

Love is also something beyond pleasure. Love describes a
state of existence, a tacit set of contracts, a moral arrangement, a changed sensibility, an altered identity. As distinguished from infatuation or falling in love, it is a process,
not an event. Love inevitably necessitates two conditions
which often tend to be conflated: trust and commitment. It

is important to see not just how they are similar, but how they differ.

To fuse one's common fate with that of another demands the strength and courage of a confident self, and a trust in the other of the highest order. Trust is also an emotional experience. Trust, to quote the dictionary, demands a "firm belief or confidence in the honesty, integrity, reliability and justice, of another person." It is an act of faith; it is love's testament.

Commitment, on the other hand, is an act of will and a statement of intent. It is a promissory note to love. When we commit something to another we in a sense entrust it to them. To quote the dictionary again, by committing we "give in charge or trust." When the commitment is to love, what we are giving in charge or trust to the other person is nothing less than ourselves. Commitment comes hard these days, as Francine du Plessix Gray indicates:

> "But I'm terrified, Stephanie, don't you see, terrified of becoming too attached to you, and then disillusioned." This is what we mostly talk about, *his* fear of all attachment, I can seldom get in a word edgewise about *my* fear of it. "What if you were Cinderella, what if I'd found in you the only woman who can wear the slipper? Just think, what an awesome notion: the notion that there is one single person in the world who suits us better than any other human, that we have finally found the other half of the primal being Plato writes about. What happens if something goes wrong *then?* The whole universe collapses!"[1]

Commitment is in this sense the deliverance of our destiny to another for safekeeping. But commitment means more than that. It also means a "pledge or a promise to do something."

At one time the act of marriage was for a large part of our population an irrevocable and inviolable commitment to a shared fate and a shared experience. Most of us in our marriage ceremonies did "solemnly swear" to love, honor, cherish, obey, trust, or any combination of the above. And most of us swore—knowing it was anachronistic—to do so "till death do us part."

With the rise of individualism and its emphasis on the existential rather than the divine, with its concomitant elevation of pleasure over purpose, of fulfillment over duty, of right over responsibility, it was inevitable that *nothing* was likely to exist till death do us part. The dissolution of the bonds of marriage became a possibility not just for the elite, for whom it had always been an option, but for the mass of humanity, who, while sharing in theory the bounty of the democratic promise, had only in very recent years been allowed to share it in practice. It is one of the few egalitarian promises that have been fully realized. Marriage just isn't what it used to be. To which many would add, "Thank God!"

In his defense of the institution of marriage, psychologist Ned Gaylin has said:

> In the present period of rapid social change, there is much conjecture about the viability of the institution of marriage. Figures abound to highlight the plight of the modern marriage: two out of every five marriages end in divorce; illegitimate births have nearly tripled since 1960; fifteen per cent of American children live in single parent homes (double that of 25 years ago) etc. However the other half of the story might well lead to some different conclusions. Of the forty per cent of divorced individuals, over three-fourths remarry. Furthermore, two-thirds of our population who marry for life stay married far longer due to the increase in our life span. Despite what recently appeared to be a declining marriage rate (but which ac-

tually proved to be a delayed marriage trend) America is still the most marrying country in the world.[2]

The negative statistics have accelerated in the few years since the publication of that article. In Ned Gaylin's article he refers to marriage as the "civilizing of sexuality." I would have preferred the use of the word "passion," for certainly more than just sexuality is implied in the contract and commitment of marriage. But I think the word "civilizing" is carefully and well chosen. It is not the word most people would use. The critics of marriage, who see an inherent antagonism between passion and long-term commitment, prefer to speak of the domestication of sexuality.

While "domestication" literally means "to accustom to home life, to make domestic," it carries the secondary and powerful meaning of "tame." One current dictionary defines it as follows: "To tame [wild animals] and breed for the many purposes of man; to adapt for home cultivation." Some feminist writers would say that is precisely what marriage actually has done, not to wild animals, but to women. Other current critics of marriage go beyond this indictment and see marriage as an instrument for the containment and domestication of passion itself. To them marriage is more than a disservice to women. It is a disservice to passion.

"Civilize" has none of the reductive and pejorative aspects of "domesticate." Civilization is the process of civilizing or becoming civilized, which includes "social organization of a high order." To civilize something, whether passion or sexuality, is to "bring or come out of a primitive or savage condition and into a state of civilization." It is to "elevate" something, to "improve" it, to "refine" it. The civilization of sexuality is the bringing of sexuality and the passions in general out of the sexual wilderness and into fusion with concepts of trust and service, justice and compassion, altruism and responsibility. Marriage involves the fusions of the aspirations of two human beings and the acceptance of the necessity for a collective consummation of their dreams and desires. Love is the underlying fusion of identities which makes that common fate a possibility.

Despite the lowered estate of marriage in our current culture, it is still generally regarded with respect and awe. Marriages are not entered into lightly, and while most may not endure, the termination is usually enacted in pain and disappointment. With most couples about to marry, despite the statistics, there is the assumption, perhaps a self-deluding one, that this is to be a permanent affair. Divorce, for all of its frequency, has a residual stigma even in a society that has embraced it; on an individual level it is almost always viewed as a betrayal, a failure, or both. For the bulk of the people in our culture, marriage is a central life goal, and the marital state is part of their projected self-image of the future.

Recently, however, marriage has come under attack from a theoretical point of view. Derek Parfit, the distinguished British philosopher, attacks marriage as an essentially immoral action.[3] The basic argument is that it is a promise extended over such a length of time as to make the promise unbelievable and implausible. Since only short-term promises can be kept, Parfit asserts only short-term promises should be made. They alone carry moral weight. Thus, Parfit is attacking the very morality of marriage. Since marriage was designed in great part to serve the moral order, this is a stab at the heart.

In a direct response to this argument, another British philosopher, Susan Mendess, answers with logic, wit, and a lacing of good common sense. She exposes the absurdity of the concept of a trial marriage by saying: "It is bizarre to respond to: 'Wilt thou love her, comfort her, and keep her?' with: 'Well, I'll try.' "[4]

She concludes by saying that the claim that "the marriage vow is either impossible or improper is false. It is possible to commit oneself unconditionally because commitment is analogous to a statement of intention, not to a prediction or a piece of clairvoyance."[5] Further, she points out that we are not helpless in circumstances when we sense our commitment wavering. The very fact of the commitment determines what we are prepared to see as the possible solutions. When presented with a quandary as to how to handle a difficult five-year-old, we do not consider, as one alternative, abandonment of the child. We are committed to her care, and we do not conceive of "divorce" as an alternative to this commitment. Obviously the contractual moral responsibility we make to our children is beyond that which most of us are prepared to grant to marriage. The inviolate marriage can be a nightmare; however, the trivialization of marriage is not the only alternative.

Ironically, the most powerful defense of marriage may be found not in the logic of philosophers but in the language of our poets. The great poet of marriage, the great defender of the faith in our time, is none other than that much maligned romantic D. H. Lawrence. In his afterword to *Lady Chatterley's Lover,* he makes a case for marriage that would do justice to a canon lawyer.

Lawrence starts by acknowledging that "we are just in the throes of the great revolt against marriage, a passionate revolt against its ties and restrictions. . . . there are few married people today, and few unmarried, who have not felt an intense and vivid hatred against marriage itself, marriage as an institution and imposition upon human life."[6] He proceeds with his argument in defense of marriage by comparing Christian society with Roman society. Marriage as a religious sacrament was offered as an alternative instrument to the institutions of government for the protection of the child. He is saying, in effect, that if you abandon the family you will find as your only alternative the overwhelming power of the state.

In offering this argument, Lawrence presciently anticipated events that are now occurring in courts of law in the United States in areas that he could not possibly have imagined. The family is being attacked under the rubric of a rights crusade. Current movements have altered the language of rights. Rights originally were defined in the old-fashioned sense of autonomous rights—what Justice Brandeis in his Olmstead decision called the most precious right of all, the right to be left alone.[7] Rights meant that there were certain things, certain decisions, certain areas of one's life that were none of the state's business; what you wore (unless you chose to wear nothing), what you felt, what political ideas you espoused, etc. Initially the rights defined your autonomous privilege against government interference. Basic-rights movements like the civil-rights movement and the feminist movement were in a sense requests to be let alone, to be declassified as a special agency or group. Those active in the movements asked to be treated with independent respect as everyone else is treated. They wanted blackness or gender to be irrelevant to personhood and autonomy.

More recently, a new language of rights has come into use. Rights are seen as claims against the government. This is best illustrated by such movements as those for the rights of the mentally retarded, the rights of infants, the rights of fetuses. Because of the original meaning of "rights," many assume that what is being championed is the autonomy of these vulnerable communities, but that is not what it means. There is no way that a fetus can get up in a court of law and declare its intention and its autonomy. There is no moral way a mentally retarded child could be allowed to sign a contract that gives away all his earthly possessions. These are the autonomous rights of a competent adult. What is actually desired by those who espouse the rights of the fetus or the rights of the infant or the rights of anyone who is physically or emotionally incapable of exercising autonomous rights is a reallocation of power.

When people are incapable of exercising their rights of self-determination, we have traditionally vested that power in their next of kin. In other words, acknowledging the kinship and ties of family, we have allowed a spouse or a parent to speak for the individual who cannot speak for himself. It is assumed, without so labeling it, that the fusion of identity that exists between a parent and child, for example, will allow the mother to best represent the closest and truest interests of her child. In the new language of rights, what is really being requested is withdrawing the power that has been vested in the family and bestowing it on those loveless institutions—the State, the courts, and legislative bodies.

D. H. Lawrence recognized this tension between family and state:

> The marriage tie, the marriage bond, take it which way you like, is the fundamental connecting link in Christian society. Break it, and you will have to go back to the overwhelming dominance of the State which existed before the Christian era. The Roman State was all-powerful, the Roman fathers represented the State, the Roman family was the father's estate, held more or less in fee for the State itself.

He is here defending marriage. He continues:

> It is marriage, perhaps, which has given man the best of his freedom, given him his little kingdom of his own within the big kingdom of the State, given him his foothold of

independence on which to stand and resist an unjust State.
Man and wife, a king and queen with one or two subjects,
and a few square yards of territory of their own, this
really, is marriage. It is a true freedom. Because it is a true
fulfillment.[8]

One can either accept Lawrence's logic or not, but it is in
his passion that he is most convincing. Unfortunately many
of us today find his prose so florid it is difficult to tolerate.
Had he rearranged the ideas and language into stanzas appropriate to poetry we might have been more sympathetic
to his ripe romanticism. Yet I find something touching and
finally convincing in the very mysticism of his defense of
marriage:

> Augustine said that God created the Universe new every-
> day: and to the living, emotional soul, this is true. . . . So
> a man and woman are new to one another throughout a
> lifetime, in the rhythm of marriage that matches the
> rhythm of the year.
>   Sex is the balance of male and female in the Universe,
> the attraction, the repulsion, the transit of neutrality, the
> new attraction, the new repulsion, always different, al-
> ways new. The long neuter spell of Lent, when the blood
> is low, and the delight of the Easter kiss, the sexual revel
> of spring, the passion of mid-summer, the slow recoil,
> revolt, and grief of autumn, greyness again, then the sharp
> stimulus of winter of the long nights. Sex goes to the
> rhythm of the year, in man and woman, ceaselessly
> changing: the rhythm of the sun and his relationship to
> the earth. Oh, what a catastrophe for man when he cuts
> himself off from the rhythm of the year, from his unison
> with the sun and the earth. Oh, what a catastrophe, what
> a maiming of love when it was made a personal, merely
> personal feeling, taken away from the rising and setting of
> the sun, and cut off from the magic connection of the
> solstice and equinox! This is what is the matter with us.
> We are bleeding at the roots, because we are cut off from

the earth and sun and stars, and love is a grinning mockery, because, poor blossom, we plucked it from its stem on the tree of Life, and expected it to keep on blooming in our civilized vase on the table.[9]

And what does Lawrence see as the salvation of this mockery? Marriage. "Marriage is the clue to human life. . . . is not a man different, utterly different, at dawn from what he is at sunset? And woman too? And does not the changing harmony and discord of their variations make the secret music of life?"[10]

D. H. Lawrence then goes on to amplify his argument in a defense of the durability, through change, of passion. Men and women differ at thirty, forty, fifty, sixty, seventy, he acknowledges, but he finds some "strange conjunction in their differences":

Some peculiar harmony through youth, the period of childbirth, the period of fluorescence in young children, the period of the woman's change of life . . . the period of waning passion but mellowing delight of affection, the dim, unequal period of the approach of death, when the man and woman look at one another with a dim apprehension of separation that is not really a separation: is there not, throughout it all, some unseen, some unknown interplay of balance, harmony, competition, like some soundless symphony which moves with a rhythm from phase to phase, so different, so very different in the various movements and yet one symphony, made out of the sound of singing, of two strange and incompatible lives, a man and a woman's?[11]

I know of no more impassioned an encomium for marriage (as distinguished from love) than this from a man who has been maligned and misunderstood as an apostle of sexuality. And he places it as an afterword to what has been considered the most notorious twentieth-century novel of adultery! In defending marriage, Lawrence is the antithesis of the lusting defender of individual gratification. He recognizes the collective nature of loving. He recognizes that pleasure is more than just fun; that passion is more than mere appetite; that loving is more than simply being loved.

Individual fulfillment is achieved through relationship. The deterioration of the concept of pleasure and the corruption of loving are products of the larger tendency in our society to glorify that artifact of modern misunderstanding, the isolated self. We have seen, particularly in America, an extraordinary overemphasis on the individual. The question of the collective good versus individual gratification is only very recently beginning to reemerge in moral argument. I am confident we will rediscover the biological meaning of community if we have the time, and if the damage of an overextended individualism allows for the privilege of return. We are just beginning to see some cautionary anxiety about whether we have not taken our individualism too far.

Along with our bloated concept of individualism came packaged certain contingent attitudes, some good, some bad. Originally, of course, there was the optimism—a scientific technocracy would solve all material problems of our world—and the optimism then led to grandiosity—the good and free life would inherently follow from the creation of this material Eden—and then with the failure to attain the unattainable, we began sinking into an unwarranted and premature despair. We have lost our sense of the fundamental purpose of romance, illusion, and fantasy. Unattainable dreams also serve a purpose. We forgot that, and decided instead to settle for less. Love, true love, was a nineteenth-century myth; we settled for a sexual accommodation. Passion is difficult to sustain; we settled for titillation. Relationships are potentially painful; we rediscovered the onanistic self.

We take comfort in the strangest things: "Sexually, the current uncertainties about AIDS have at least one 'silver lining,' that is, the opportunity to increase one's sexual behavioral repertoire, to go beyond the standard intercourse and discover the many means of giving sexual pleasure without depending solely upon intercourse." This incredible comment was part of the statement of a distinguished medical group.[12]

One would think that one emergent and agonizing conclusion to be drawn from the AIDS tragedy is the danger of thinking in such terms as a "sexual behavioral repertoire"; that the problem may have been one of an already over-expanded "repertoire." But never mind. More important is that we find ourselves reduced to settling for such tarnished silver linings. Christopher Lasch in defining our culture as the culture of narcissism subtitled his book *American Life in an Age of Diminishing Expectations,*[13] thereby implying his understanding that the current self-involvement we call narcissism really represents a retreat from aspiration into despair.

Our diminishing expectations are directly traceable to the abandonment of certain dreams. Cynicism and pessimism are nourished by the death of hope. We cannot afford to abandon our grand dreams. To unshackle the bound Prometheus that is modern man we must—to quote that most romantic of nineteenth-century poets, Shelley—"Hope till hope creates from its own wreck the thing it contemplates." Faithful to my professional biases, I look to the past to start the process of liberating the present.

Modern America was born at the turn of the century, the issue of two powerful forces: nineteenth-century individualism; and a scientific revolution that seemed to make all things possible, all things within human grasp. The nineteenth century in America, like the twentieth, has been described as an age of rampant individualism. There was a difference. In opposition to the economic buccaneers, the Horatio Algers, and the survival-of-the-fittest mentalities of that earlier time were conflicting claims of other powerful institutions beyond the glorified self. Religion still had a fundamental meaning in most people's lives. While in earthly matters we might idealize material success, there was still a large proportion of the population that saw our life on earth as merely a transition to a better afterlife and knew it was easier for a camel to go through the eye of a needle than for a rich man to enter into the Kingdom of God.

The true freedom and autonomy suggested by laissez-faire philosophies at the turn of the century in reality only applied to the upper classes. The absolute dependence on work for basic survival left little time for philosophy for the masses. The laborer who was a "slave" to his job was not free to make significant choices. The woman and children who were dependent on his earnings were not free to change any fundamental conditions of their lives. They were equally captive to an arrangement of survival. To claim that the average person, man or woman, in the nineteenth century was autonomous or even perceived himself as autonomous in the way that we do in the twentieth century is to ignore the everyday reality of economics. Only in the psychological world which we now occupy are we beginning to appreciate that coercion is a complicated concept, and the free act and the free agent even more elusive to define. Certainly the agreement to work in a coal mine, even understanding the risks, is a different sense of contract than the agreement to fly on a space shuttle. A job was a survival need, but it was also a prison. The same can be said of marriage, for the woman with children. Freedom was at best a limited resource.

Notwithstanding the fact that economic coercion is still a

relatively important factor for the average person, a major change did occur after the First World War. For white America at least, the working class gradually became dissolved into the bourgeoisie. The future is a luxury of the middle class. The poor are too trapped in the present to acknowledge the future. Where true needs are large, dreams are usually small. Pleasure, self-fulfillment, self-actualization, finding one's true self, are unlikely topics in a manual of survival. With the expansion of our middle class, the ideal of a free and aspiring individual entered into the bread and butter world of the average man.

At the same time we were creating in America what has to be considered the most open and upwardly mobile society of modern times. I am well aware of the limitations placed on minorities; the reality is not quite as advertised. Nonetheless class distinctions were erased in America in a way that still has not occurred in England or France. Even a worker's son or, as we well know, one who was born in a log cabin could aspire to the presidency. There was an inherent and ebullient optimism in the assumption that every man, and perhaps finally every woman, could be president.

Simultaneously the rise of the technological state further enhanced the optimism and individualism of our political world. We could tolerate the death of God because we no longer needed Him. Man elevated himself into the central position in the order of things. We created our current anthropocentric universe. All problems were now solvable, and we would use our technology to solve them. With modern medicine, biology, mathematics, physics, and chemistry, we would master the forces of nature, contain the elements, conquer disease, and create a heaven on earth to replace the celestial one that we had abandoned.

Sigmund Freud, the prophet of this new individual and this new time, had already completed much of his major theoretical work before the end of the nineteenth century, although he had yet to be discovered and would not have his full impact until the mid-twentieth century. It is not incidental that Freud's influence in American life has been vastly greater than his influence in other western cultures.

The American intellectual community embraced Freud early, certainly by the 1920s, and utilized Freudian principles to shape the American dream. Philip Rieff has said:

> Three character ideals have successively dominated Western civilization: first, the ideal of the political man, formed and handed down to us from classical antiquity; second, the ideal of the religious man, formed and handed down to us from Judaism through Christianity, and dominant in the civilization of authority that preceded the Enlightenment; third, the ideal of the economic man, the very model of our liberal civilization, formed and handed down to us from the Enlightenment. This last has turned out to be a transitional type, with the shortest life expectancy of all; out of his tenure has emerged the psychological man of the twentieth century, a child not of nature but of technology. . . . we will recognize in the case history of psychological man the nervous habits of his father, economic man: he is antiheroic, shrewd, carefully counting his satisfactions and dissatisfactions, studying unprofitable commitments as the sins most to be avoided.[14]

In using the terms "economic man" and "psychological man" Rieff is referring to the dominant cultural view of ourselves that sustains our existence and shapes our expectations. "Religious man" saw himself as an instrument of a divine purpose. Life was a means to an end whose purpose might not be fathomable, but whose assumption gave comfort and direction. "Psychological man" as defined by Freud is the major concept to which I have attended in this book. It is the Freudian idea that has shaped our sense of ourself: we see our life as part of a dynamic process in which we are an active player; we see defeat as well as success as self-determined. We see internal conflict as a great source of our despair; we see the real world as less important than the perceived world; we see pleasure here on earth as an acceptable—perhaps the only acceptable—motive for behavior, since we for the most part have abandoned a belief in the hereafter; we accept the sexual basis of much of our behavior, and we justify the fullest expression of our sexual drives; we glorify self-fulfillment, whatever that may mean. Rieff was shrewd in recognizing the antiheroic (what I have alluded to as the antiromantic) implications of Freudian theory. And he was almost alone among Freudian scholars in recognizing that this persistent image would eventually lead to a self-serving philosophy which would weaken such concepts as responsibility and commitment.

The Freudian emphasis on the instinctual nature of the human being changed another fundamental aspect of our self-image. He brought *Homo sapiens* back into a continuity with other animal forms, in contrast to the religious vision, which had us, alone, created in God's image. Consonant with Freud, Charles Darwin offered the first logical alternative to fundamentalist religious explanations of the human being's place and purpose in the natural order of things. In one way this reduced us; we were no longer in God's image. In another way it inflated our role. Darwinian evolution and Freudian psychology liberated us from seeing ourselves as part of Someone Else's calculation. While we had been born by chance, we had evolved into a creature that through its unique intelligence and technology had the power to mitigate the forces of chance and evolution. We could travel as far as our vision might take us, perhaps even someday to the moon.

With the concept that success was possible for everyone and that success was a product of our own efforts came the distressing corollary that failure must also be acknowledged as of our own design. Failure is more dreadful when it is a self-inflicted humiliation, when it is seen as an indictment of self-worth.

The theoretical roots for a competitive society in which success was the prime support of self-esteem had been laid. Competitive pressures would logically increase, and with the higher stakes, trust in another would become increasingly dangerous. Anxiety is the logical physiological response to danger. With new opportunities came new risks. It was ultimately the mounting anxiety of ever greater expectations that eroded our self-confidence. The fulfillment of the promise seemed so much more elusive in practice than in theory. We became wary watchers of our own performance. Frightened of failure, especially when success was presumed to be so available, we began to seek everywhere for reassurance of our worth. The conditions for narcissistic self-concern were set.

Eventually we sacrificed our aspirations to appease our anxiety. Rather than stretching ourselves and risking failure, we would attempt only the easy and attainable. To avoid failure, we would abandon the large dream. The stage was further set for a trivialization of purpose and pleasure. If what we desired, whether romantic love or true passion, required an effort of will and risked the pain and humiliation of rejection and defeat, we reached instead for that which was readily attainable—the casual sexual encounter. To salvage our self-respect in this process, we cynically denied the existence of the true love whose quest we abandoned. We labeled it "realism" rather than fear of failure. Since the quick fix is not acceptable to our judging superego that knows better, we must add the self-deception of defining the counterfeit pleasure as the real thing.

Liebe was obviously in for a hard time. What about that

other prop of self-esteem, *Arbeit?* While not romanticizing what preindustrial work was like in rural societies, with industrialization the worker was reduced to an approximation of the machine. Very few of us in modern times finish anything that we start in the course of our work. We do parts and pieces of things and in that process are deprived of the gratification of mastery. We are also reduced to a monotonous and unending repetition of small tasks, which if divorced from the total scheme—and how can one avoid this isolation?—will be seen as meaningless and useless drudgery. That is what assembly-line work has come to be.

For the average man, work could not be a source of pleasure. Therefore we redefined work as the price one paid for the pleasure. We work to earn money, which in turn will be exchangeable for pleasures. Money can buy surcease from the agonies of poverty, but the "pleasures" it buys are generally trivial and narcissistic. There is no way that the degradation of work, which may occupy forty to eighty hours of time per week, can produce the means to purchase sufficient pleasure in the remaining hours to represent an even exchange. Work will not fill the gap left by an abandonment of love. Work in modern society has its own dreadful problems, producing yet another frightening hemorrhage to our pride and self-esteem.

The nascent elements of narcissism were being liberated from many changing institutions in our culture. We were cutting off attachments from many sources, further driving us into the corner of the isolated self. Americanization was the ideal and the goal for the average immigrants. The connections that inevitably bound them to their pasts were ruthlessly cut. There was contempt for the culture and tradition that had been abandoned and shame for the parents who might be identified with that culture and tradition. In cutting themselves off from the authority and control of our histories, we also psychologically destroyed the authority of parents. This again elevated the only things left: the individual and the present.

The generation of immigrants to America in the early twentieth century was collaborator in its own collapse. The children of the immigrant had contempt for their fathers because the fathers maintained such contempt for themselves. In the nineteenth-century Europe from which they had emigrated, the baker's son could only become a baker and a father of bakers. Under these conditions the son aspired to but never quite achieved the status of his father, whose bread was nostalgically perceived as somewhat better. It was not just that the modern child did not want to follow the immigrant father; more important, the father did not want the son to end up where he had. "Do you want to end up like me?" is the statement of a father urging his son, and later his daughter, on to future education in an upwardly mobile society. In so doing the father was inevitably setting himself up as a symbol of failure, forcing the child to invest his admiration in himself.

There is also a different sense of time and space now. We literally are moving faster; distances are shorter. When space is condensed, so is time. The leisurely journey from London to Bath described in the Georgian novels of Jane Austen took more time than it now takes to circumnavigate the globe. And because it took more time, the length of a pleasurable holiday with relatives was measured not in weekends but in weeks and even months. Pleasure was a relaxed process that involved spending time at a rate which by current standards would be squandering. Our current sense of time demands that pleasures be quickly realized and that they be immediately at hand.

Quick and immediate they are, facilitated by another grand transformation of modern life. We no longer have to go far to get much of anything. Everything comes to us. One must appreciate the passivity which has entered our lives, facilitated by our technological advances. At one time we were forced to work to bring heat and water to our homes. Logs were split and water fetched, where now we adjust thermostats and turn taps. Similarly, we had to travel to town meetings to exercise our political voice. We went to churches not just to pray to our God but to commune with our neighbors, to get "the news." The news now comes to us either delivered to our doors in the morning or on television at night, along with the evangelical preachers.

We do not make pilgrimages to the Chautauquas of the nineteenth century. The Chautauqua, with its lectures, concerts, amusements, and entertainments, comes to us over a television set that may be adjusted by a remote-control device clutched in the hand of a modern-day Oblomov who need not stir from the comfort of his isolated bed. All of these forces, and many more, shaped the identity of a modern individual psychologically driven, existing in the here and now, motivated by pleasure defined at its most animal and simplest terms, increasingly passive and progressively detached from traditional concepts of community, but still reasonably optimistic about his capacity to overcome existential anxiety and the problems of the technological world. As long as there was a lingering sense of a triumphant self, we seemed determined to avoid commitment. We were prepared to submit to the tides that drove us onto the shores of individualism.

Then a crucial element shifted the balance. As each solution we have found for our problems in the past twenty-five or thirty years capriciously and invidiously seemed to produce new problems of equal or even more threatening magnitude, we began to exhaust our supply of residual optimism.

The dropping of the atomic bomb announced that we are

all bound together in a security mechanism that would make one person's suffering or one country's suffering inevitably contagious. It also announced a new common destiny. War could now go beyond suffering and statistics to the annihilation of the human species. It is a frightening and new possibility.

The ecology movement, stimulated in great part by Rachel Carson's *Silent Spring*,[15] made us all aware of how truly limited our space was. We were now capable of contaminating the very waters that nurture our land and sustain our lives. We are capable of polluting the air which is essential for the very breath of life. The ecology movement established a direct relationship between what I do and what you do. There can be no absolute libertarianism that allows me to pollute the waters, even those which traverse *my* properties. Acid rain crosses political borders and in that crossing dissolves them. We are aware that we are bound by an environment which is more fluid than we had thought and will eventually allow the detritus of one culture to contaminate the nutrients of another. We have discovered that we have run out of—of all things—"out." We used to throw our garbage out. There is no more out. Out is where our neighbors grow their food; out is where other people's children play.

We began running out of crucial things. Not just fossil fuels. The final blow was to find that there must be limits to health care. In a peculiarly painful paradox we are now discovering that we cannot afford all the health care we need precisely at a time when medicine in fact has finally become a life-saving endeavor. We will not continue to sell livers to save the lives of children like luxury commodities for the rich. Shortage and distress are forcing us once again to think collectively. Paradoxically, our failures may yet save us. These problems that resist our individual solutions are beginning to force an awareness of the limits of individualism and the rediscovery of community.

The discovery of community, like the discovery of love, is often most poignant when one senses its loss. We have in our pursuit of individual liberties allowed for the destruction of the common space. People are concerned with the mounting crime in the streets and are offended by the fact that there are booby-trapped areas of major cities which the police dare not patrol and which are now off-limits. Ironically, it is often the poor confined to the prison that is called a ghetto that have demanded attention to law and order, while it is the affluent intellectuals who have pressed the concept of individual liberties. The language of rights is insufficient to deal with the moral problems of community. And the language of duties and responsibilities seems archaic and frighteningly conservative to some in our community. Perhaps the philosophy of justice, spurred by the work of John Rawls,[16] may compromise these conflicting moral claims; justice is by definition a communal concept.

I am convinced that we have reached the limits of individualism and our survival depends on rediscovering our need for community. In that process we have the opportunity to rediscover love.

Our overvaluation of the individual need not lead to self-reproach. Our concept of the individual has been the glory of the western liberal democracies and has distinguished us from the brutality and barbarism of the radical right and left. There is no sane person who *knows* the difference who would prefer to live in Communist Russia or Communist China rather than the United States of America or England or France. No, we need not apologize. The errors in overvaluing the individual are certainly less than those in overvaluing of the state. But we have moved too far and we must begin giving something back to the commonweal. We must reexamine such concepts as duty and responsibility. In so doing we may find the joy in serving others. The children of the upper middle class in the United States have been deprived of nothing except the privilege of being self-sacrificing, of being unselfish, of being caring. In depriving them of these attitudes we have diminished their sense of self, and have deprived them of the transcendent experience of love and service. At the turn of the century the great Russian philosopher Vladimir Solovyov said: "The meaning of human love is the *justification* and *deliverance* of individuality through the sacrifice of egoism."[17]

Freud is often cited in defense of the proposition that all is selfishness. This is a gross misreading, but it is understandable. When the only motivation for human behavior is the instinctual drive for sexual gratification, then everything, regardless of how self-sacrificing it may seem, is simply a permutation of that self-serving instinct. Freud derived all civilizing qualities as reaction formations and sublimations of sexual desire. However, this is a theoretical explanation of human character development, not a moral treatise. Of course, Freud knew that there were good and bad things in life, but he was interested in curing disease, not saving souls. The disciples of Freud must be blamed for the excess of evangelical zeal that converted a psychology into a *Weltanschauung*. The denial of altruism is a wearisome semantic game loved by college sophomores. If all is selfishness, one still can distinguish the good in "selfishness" from the bad. Hume had the answer for that. If one insists all is selfish, Hume says: "I esteem the man whose self-love, by whatever means, is so directed as to give him a concern for others, and render him serviceable to society, as I hate or despise him, who has no regard to any thing beyond his own gratifications and enjoyments."[18]

Self-involvement is not really self-love. The self-centered

person is alert and focused on the vulnerable and impover-
ished self. He demonstrates the wariness of the insecure. He
husbands his affections, because he is operating from a psychology of deprivation. Loving requires sufficient security,
self-confidence, and self-respect to trust in others. Loving
involves the courage of a commitment that risks the pains of
abandonment or rejection. The risk must be taken.

Freud had hoped that insight, analysis, and cognition
could solve the mysteries of the human spirit and ease the
burdens of existence. His insight has helped us along that
path, but his methodology precluded an understanding of
human love. Love is a romantic concept that Freud with his
contempt for romanticism could not embrace. He therefore
chose to ignore it. I use the word "chose" with the freedom
of a Freudian who is granted by Freud the privilege to im-
pute motives to people on the basis of their behavior.

When Freud did deal with love directly—I am aware that
by indirection he did deal with it sensitively—he tended to
introduce a note of contempt. If one scans the titles of
Freudian literature, looking for love, one is most likely to
first approach a series of short papers titled "Contributions
to the Psychology of Love."[19] Astonishingly, they are
actually essays on male impotence. Yet they say something
about Freud, particularly about his revolt against romanticism.

The papers focus on something which has been called the
"madonna-prostitute complex." In these papers Freud pos-
tulates that certain forms of male impotence are due to the
dread of incestual involvement. The understanding of the
madonna-prostitute complex has been turned topsy-turvy in
modern times. The current explanation is that the man is
impotent with a "good girl" because she reminds him of his
mother. He can establish affectionate bonds with the good
girl, but must reserve his sexual potency and desire for the

bad girl. In actuality Freud meant precisely the opposite. By involving herself sexually with the father, the mother betrayed the idealized and pure image of her that the son originally possessed. In seeking the prostitute, Freud suggested, this quasi-impotent man was seeking the mother. In either case the madonna-prostitute complex is Freud's way of reducing love to a simple resolution of an inappropriate choice of a love object.

But love is more than that, and failure in love is more than failure in potency. The relationship of sexuality and romantic love is complicated and encompasses many variables, as Milan Kundera understood. His characters Jan and Edwige are lying in bed. They have been discussing in intellectual terms the distinctions between masculine and feminine expectations from sex without any real understanding on Jan's part of feminine sensibilities:

> During the silence that had set in, Edwige's face began to acquire the blissful look that meant it was getting late, coming close to the time when Jan would set the empty reel spinning on her body.
>
> "Besides," she added after some thought, "making love is not that important."
>
> "You don't think making love is that important?" he asked, just to be sure he had heard properly.
>
> "No," she said, smiling at him tenderly, "making love is not that important."
>
> In an instant, he completely forgot what they had been discussing. He had made a crucial discovery: Edwige saw physical love as a sign, a symbolic act, a confirmation of friendship.
>
> That was the first night he ever dared to say he was tired. He lay down next to her like a chaste friend and let the reel be. And as he gently stroked her hair, he saw a reassuring rainbow of peace arching over their future together.[20]

It may be that the nature of love is so subjective that it is beyond knowledge and analysis. The fact that at its base it is undefinable is not a reflection of its insufficiency but rather the opposite. It is not a sign that it does not exist, but a sign that it exists in such an exalted state as to be approachable only through experience.

Finally even Freud, almost despite himself, would succumb to love. In that masterpiece of his declining years *Civilization and Its Discontents,* in many ways the apotheosis of his entire creative efforts, Freud contemplates the existential condition of the human being. If there is no heaven or hell, if there is no future life that is not an illusion, if it is all just here and now, and if it all involves so much suffering, what is there to justify human existence?

In the end this man who dealt with love so little in his theoretical work suggested embracing the concept of love. Only through loving can life make sense. Freud is sensitive to the fact, however, that through loving, and the extended self that results from identification, our vulnerability will be increased. For now, it is not only ourselves and the events surrounding our lives which can cause us grief but the vulnerability of all those whom we love and to whom we have bound ourselves in emotional identity:

> The weak side of this way of living is clearly evident; and were it not for this, no human being would ever have thought of abandoning this path to happiness in favour of any other. We are never so defenseless against suffering as when we love, never so forlornly unhappy as when we have lost our love-object or its love.[21]

The risks are not inconsiderable. A blow to a loved one can be perceived with an agony beyond personal pain. A blow from a loved one can elicit humiliation and despair beyond the power of any stranger's assault. And still we must take the risk. There is nothing else to give meaning to an existential life.

Love, beyond pleasure, is a dedication of the self through trust and commitment to an expanded experience. Because it is a willing and conscious utilization of all our capacities for generosity, altruism, empathy, service, self-sacrifice, and devotion—transcending a narrow concern for self and survival—love defines the humanity that sets us as a species apart from all others.

In our willingness to sacrifice pleasure for service and obligation to others we will be rewarded. We will discover a form of pleasure beyond comfort or vanity. In an examination of the human feeling of "being used" I have said that in certain loving conditions, being used should be a prideful experience.[22] But even being used in the crassest and most exploitative sense is not nearly so debilitating as the paranoid stance necessary to protect oneself against being used. To find oneself taken advantage of occasionally is not the worst thing. Far worse is to feel that each request for a favor is an affront; to view each approach as a potential exploitation; to measure meanly the give and take of relationships; to withdraw into the private and paranoid agony of the ever-vigilant. If to be used, to be humiliated, even to be exploited, is part of the risk-taking of commitment, then it is a price worth paying. It is an essential and necessary price that we must pay.

Roberto Unger concludes his book *Passion* (which in many ways might more aptly be entitled *Commitment*) with the following statement, which I suspect may have had its inspiration in *Civilization and Its Discontents:*

> A time comes when a person begins to stagger under the weight of his own selfhood. The torn and tenacious heart swings between the unresisting body and the uncompromising mind. At last, he stumbles and cries out. Will he

give up hope of being both together with other people and apart from them, and of having a character that is his very own and yet incomplete and transformable? Or will he subject himself, again and again, to experiments in vulnerability to hurt by others and to the risks of deliberate action? Experiments that empower the will and imagination and renew the life of relationship and identity. In the practice of science, as in the ordeal of the self, there is no rescue by immunity. Salvation through the acceptance of vulnerability is the only kind of salvation there really is.[23]

Hume rested the entire moral life on the capacity for identification—not his words, of course—or sympathy with our fellows. He saw moral philosophy as being bound in the relationships of care and love, of compassion and sympathy among people. Without the resonant heart responding in sympathy to those of our kind there can be neither joy nor goodness. William James reiterated his commitment to community as being at the heart of our moral life when he said:

Were all other things, Gods and men and starry heavens, blotted out from the universe, and were there left but one rock with two loving souls upon it, that rock would have as thoroughly moral a constitution as any possible world in which the eternities and immensities could harbor. . . . There would be real good things and real bad things in the universe; there would be obligations, claims and expectations; obediences, refusals and disappointments; compunctions and longings for harmony to come again, and inward peace of conscience when it was restored; there would, in short, be a moral life whose active energy would have no limit but the intensity of interest in each other with which the hero and heroine might be endowed.[24]

William James made a distinction between "knowledge of" and "knowing about." Cognition and analysis will make their contributions to an understanding of the experience of love, but will always be only contingent in their usefulness to having *had* the experience. Too many of our fellow human beings have been denied the capacity for experiencing love because of the confusion and contradictions in our understanding of the nature of love. They have been deprived of one of the few aspects of human existence that can truly be considered essential.

In contrast with James's two ways of knowing, Solovyov has described three kinds of knowing. The three sources of knowledge are experience, reason, and intuition ("The mystical realm")—to which correspond three kinds of knowledge, empirical, rational, and faith.[25]

In approaching love I have attempted to use what empirical knowledge is available through the psychological, psychiatric, and psychoanalytic literature. I have drawn inferences and deductions from my own personal experience. I have utilized the accumulated experiences of those who by practicing psychoanalysis are privileged to share the intimacy of "strangers." Still, the case for loving is incomplete. As Solovyov indicates, to complete a brief for love requires entering "the mystical realm," an unfashionable area in the modern community of ideas. Since love does not come easily, and is only knowable after the dangerous commitment has been made, it inevitably demands an act of faith.

Loving demands, beyond trust and commitment, an abandonment of self, an abdication of autonomy, a painful fusion with another vulnerable person or many other persons. Such heroic requirements cannot be motivated by logic and sensibility alone but must be driven by the romantic elements of our nature. Mature love will always straddle the romantic and realistic realms of human imagination. Only the human mind, which can understand so much, can understand its own limitations. When we recognize the limits of knowledge, we will reach beyond the knowable and embrace the mysterious and magical. The fusion that exists in loving must encompass both reason and faith.

I have faith in the concept of love, along with the intellectual conviction that it is a necessary central component of the human experience. It sustains the community on which our very survival depends, and it gives a special grace to the individual's brief and confusing tenure in this world. Beyond that, for the nonreligious, it offers the only defense against the apparent absurdity of an existential world. For those of us not blessed with the capacity to believe in a God or an afterlife, it provides a special kind of immortality through the extension of our traits, our values, our very identity beyond our limited time of biological existence. Through the power of love and identification, our finite self is extended by commingling with the many selves of those we love, and will be apportioned by them to those whom they love, spinning fine connecting lines in all directions down through generations, creating a tangled and mysterious web of immortality.

NOTES

INTRODUCTION

1. M. C. D'Arcy, *The Mind and Heart of Love* (New York: Meridian, 1956), pp. 235–236.

2. C. S. Lewis, *The Four Loves* (New York: Harcourt Brace Jovanovich, 1960), p. 63.

3. Walt Whitman, "When I Heard the Learned Astronomer," *The Complete Poems* (New York: Penguin Books, 1975), p. 298.

CHAPTER 1

1. D. H. Lawrence, *A Propos of Lady Chatterley's Lover* (New York: Bantam Books, 1983), p. 339.

2. D. H. Lawrence, *The Rainbow* (New York: Penguin Books, 1976), p. 138.

3. Johann Wolfgang von Goethe, *Faust,* translated by Alice Raphael (New York: Holt, Rinehart & Winston, 1955), p. 8.

4. Ivan Turgenev, *Spring Torrents,* translated by Leonard Schapiro (New York: Penguin Books, 1980), p. 100.

5. Mark Helprin, *Winter's Tale* (New York: Pocket Books, 1983), pp. 129–131.

6. D. H. Lawrence, *The Rainbow,* op. cit., p. 176.

7. Bernard of Clairvaux, St., Quoted in Irving Singer, *The Nature of Love* (Chicago: University of Chicago Press, 1984), vol. I, pp. 220–221.

8. I. Singer, *The Nature of Love,* vol. II, pp. 6–7.

9. George Bernard Shaw, *Androcles and the Lion,* Act II (New York: Brentano's, 1916), pp. 40–41.

CHAPTER 2

1. Here I refer not only to such distinguished figures as Darwin, Freud, William James, Julian Huxley, René Dubos, and the like, whose names are recognizable to the general public, but also to modern masters of biology such as Theodosius Dobzhansky, Adolf Portmann, Walter Cannon, and Ernst Mayr, who have looked beyond the limits of their special interests to speculate on the nature of the human animal.

2. I draw here on an earlier research of mine done on the nature of human dependency and attachments. Those interested in a more detailed argument elaborating on the need for love and the caring nature of our species are referred to Willard Gaylin, *Caring* (New York: Alfred A. Knopf, 1976).

3. W. Gaylin, "What's So Special About Being Human?" in *The Manipulation of Life,* Robert Esbjornson, ed. (New York: Harper & Row, 1984), p. 51.

4. Genesis 1:27–28.

5. Theodosius Dobzhansky, *Mankind Evolving* (New Haven, Conn.: Yale University Press, 1965), pp. 346–347.

6. B. F. Skinner, *Beyond Freedom and Dignity* (New York: Alfred A. Knopf, 1971).

7. W. Gaylin, "The Frankenstein Factor," *New England Journal of Medicine,* vol. 297, Sept. 22, 1977, p. 665.

8. Pico della Mirandola, "Oration on the Dignity of Man," in Ernst Cassirer et al., *The Renaissance Philosophy of Man* (Chicago: University of Chicago Press, 1956), p. 224.

9. Sigmund Freud, *Inhibitions, Symptoms and Anxiety* (1926), 20:7. (All references to Freud, unless otherwise indicated, refer to Sigmund Freud, Standard Edition [London: Hogarth Press, 1955]. Figures refer to volume and page number in this edition.)

10. A. Portman, *Animals as Social Beings* (New York: Harper and Row, 1964), pp. 75–76.

11. C. P. Snow, *Homecoming* (New York: Charles Scribner's Sons, 1956), p. 345.

12. M. H. Klaus and J. H. Kennell, *Parent–Infant Bonding* (St. Louis: C. V. Mosby, 1982).

13. Klaus, et al. as quoted in W. Gaylin, *Caring,* p. 62.

CHAPTER 3

1. Jeffrey M. Masson, *The Assault on Truth: Freud's Suppression of the Seduction Theory* (New York: Farrar, Straus and Giroux, 1984).

2. S. Freud, *Three Essays on Sexuality* (1905), 7:136.

3. W. Whitman, "Grand Is the Seer," *The Complete Poems,* p. 567.

4. W. Stevens, "Le Monocle de Mon Oncle," *Collected Poems* (New York: Vintage Books, 1982), p. 19.

5. This analysis of the nature of feelings and the adaptive purposes of emotions was begun in W. Gaylin, *Feelings: Our Vital Signs* (New York: Harper and Row, 1979).

6. Jonathan Edwards, *Representative Selections,* edited and with notes and bibliography by C. H. Faust and T. H. Johnson (New York: Hill & Wang, 1962), p. 60.

7. Peter De Vries, *The Blood of the Lamb* (Boston: Little, Brown and Co., 1961), p. 241.

8. Gerard Manley Hopkins, "Pied Beauty," *Oxford Book of Nineteenth-Century English Verse,* John Hayward, ed. (London: Oxford University Press, 1964), pp. 865–866.

9. Antonia White, *The Lost Traveller* (New York: Dial Press, 1978), p. 105.

10. A full discussion of the cultural role of anger can be found in W. Gaylin, *The Rage Within: Anger in Modern Life* (New York: Simon and Schuster, 1984).

11. Carol Gilligan, *In a Different Voice* (Cambridge, Mass.: Harvard University Press, 1982).

12. N. Scott Momaday, *House Made of Dawn* (New York: Signet, 1969), p. 191.

13. A. Trollope, *Can You Forgive Her?* (London: Oxford University Press, 1973), p. 49.

14. St. Augustine, *Confessions* (Baltimore, Md.: Penguin Books, 1961), p. 48.

CHAPTER 4

1. Walker Percy, *The Second Coming* (New York: Farrar, Straus & Giroux, 1980), pp. 240–241.

2. David Hume, *Of Self Love, Essays* (London: Ward, Lock and Tyler, 1924), p. 488.

3. Plato, *Symposium*, B. Jowett, ed. (New York: Tudor Publishing, 1956), pp. 315–318.

4. Sophocles, "Antigone," *The Complete Plays of Sophocles* (New York: Bantam Classics), p. 135.

5. Virgil, *The Aeneid*, translated by Robert Fitzgerald (New York: Random House, 1983), pp. 97–98.

6. Empedocles, W. K. Guthrie, *A History of Greek Philosophers*, vol. II (Cambridge: Cambridge University Press, 1975).

7. St. Augustine, *Confessions*.

8. William Aaron, *Straight* (New York: Doubleday, 1972).

9. Erica Jong, *Fear of Flying* (New York: Holt, Rinehart & Winston, 1973).

10. J. Breuer and S. Freud, *Studies in Hysteria* (1893–1895), 2:1.

11. Freud, *Totem and Taboo*, (1913), 13:1.

12. Abram Kardiner and Lionel Ovesey, *Mark of Oppression: Explorations in the Personality of the American Negro* (Cleveland, Ohio: World Publishing, 1962).

13. Plato, *Symposium*, p. 318.

14. Margaret Mahler devoted a lifetime to elucidating the nature of mother–child bonding. See Mahler, M. references in bibliography.

15. "You may call it madness, but I call it love," a ballad of the 1930s often associated with Russ Columbo.

16. Freud, *Civilization and Its Discontents* (1930), 21:64–65.

17. I. Singer, *The Nature of Love*, vol. II, p. 6.

18. Erich Fromm, *The Art of Loving* (New York: Bantam Books, 1963).

19. I. Singer, *The Nature of Love*, vol. II, p. 7.

20. For the best introduction to the works of Erikson, see Erik Erikson, *Childhood and Society* (New York: W. W. Norton, 1963).

21. Ernest Hemingway, *For Whom the Bell Tolls* (New York: Charles Scribner's Sons, 1940), p. 284.

22. I. Singer, *The Nature of Love*, vol. I, p. 221.

23. Ibid., p. 222.

24. *Life of St. Theresa*, J. M. Cohen translator, cited in *Bernini* by Howard Hibbard (New York: Penguin Books, 1965), p. 137.

25. S. Freud, *Group Psychology* (1922), 17:107.

26. S. Freud, *Mourning and Melancholia* (1917), 14:237.

27. Karl Abraham wrote the pioneering work on which all of modern psychoanalytic theory of depression was established. It is noteworthy as one of the rare times that Freud used an original theoretical construct of one of his disciples rather than his own. The original article may be found in *Selected Papers of Karl Abraham* (London: Hogarth Press, 1927), pp. 137–156.

28. W. Gaylin, *The Meaning of Despair* (New York: Science House, 1968).

29. D. Hume, *A Treatise of Human Nature* (London: Oxford University Press, 1949), p. 370.

30. W. Percy, *The Second Coming,* pp. 258–259.

CHAPTER 5

1. Thomas Hardy, *Jude the Obscure* (New York: Harper and Row, 1966), p. 393.

2. Ibid., p. 333.

3. H. Blossom, lyrics, as quoted by Singer, op. cit.

4. As quoted in W. Gaylin, *Feelings: Our Vital Signs* (New York, Harper and Row, 1979), p. 156, from W. B. Yeats, "For Anne Gregory," *The Collected Poems* (New York: Macmillan Publishing Company, 1956), p. 240.

5. Emily Brontë, *Wuthering Heights* (New York: Signet, 1959), p. 84.

6. Sir Walter Scott, *Ivanhoe* (New York: Penguin Books, 1984), pp. 440–441.

7. Ibid., p. 443.

8. Ibid., p. 506.

9. Ibid., p. 519.

10. Racine, *Phaedra,* translated by Bernard Grebanier (Woodbury, N.Y.: Barron's Educational Series, 1958), p. 33.

11. Ibid., p. 41.

12. Roberto Unger, *Passion: An Essay on Personality* (New York: Free Press, 1984), p. 287.

13. Marion J. King, *On Being Human: A Systematic View* (New York: Harcourt Brace Jovanovich, 1975), p. 125.

14. J. L. Singer, in Poke, K. S. and associates, *On Love and Loving: Psychological Perspectives on the Nature and Experience of Romantic Love* (San Francisco: Jossey-Bass, 1980), p. 190.

15. H. Fielding, *Tom Jones* (New York: Signet, 1963), pp. 226–228.

16. C. S. Lewis, *The Four Loves* (New York: Harvest/Harcourt Brace Jovanovich, 1960), pp. 134–135.

17. R. Unger, *Passion,* p. 176.

18. Ibid., p. 177.

19. W. Wordsworth, "She Was a Phantom of Delight," in *The Cassell Book of English Poetry,* James Reeves, ed. (New York: Harper and Row, 1965), p. 638.

20. Edward O. Wilson, *On Human Nature* (New York: Bantam Books, 1978), p. 146.

21. Ibid.

22. *Letters of John Keats,* Robert Gittings, ed. (London, Oxford University Press, 1970), p. 334.

23. Stendhal, *On Love* (New York: Liveright, 1947), p. 6.

24. Francesco Alberoni, *Falling in Love,* translated by Lawrence Verruti (New York: Random House, 1983), p. 3.

25. Ibid., p. 139.

26. Ibid., pp. 140–141.

27. G. B. Shaw, "Back to Methuselah," in *Complete Plays,* vol. II (New York: Dodd, Mead, 1962), p. 59.

28. C. S. Lewis, *A Grief Observed* (New York: Bantam Books, 1976), p. 71.

29. Ovid, *Metamorphoses,* translated by Frank J. Miller (Cambridge, Mass.: Loeb Classic Library), 1.7.

30. C. S. Lewis, *A Grief Observed,* pp. 69–71.

CHAPTER 6

1. James Agee, *A Death in the Family* (New York: McDowell, Obolensky, 1953), pp. 20–21.

2. W. Gaylin, *Caring.*

3. For the best introduction and summary of this work, see J. Bowlby, 1969, 1973; Renee Spitz, 1965; and Klaus et al., 1970.

4. W. Gaylin, *The Killing of Bonnie Garland: A Question of Justice* (New York: Simon & Schuster, 1982).

5. J. Agee, *A Death in the Family,* p. 305.

6. S. Kierkegaard, *The Sickness unto Death,* as quoted in W. Gaylin, *The Meaning of Despair,* op. cit., p. 15.

7. Jorge Amado, *Dona Flor and Her Two Husbands* (New York, Bard Books, 1977), p. 172.

8. Ibid., p. 206.

9. Institute of Medicine, *Bereavement* (Washington, D.C.: National Academy Press, 1984).

10. Ibid., p. 61.

11. Ibid., p. 80.

12. Ibid., p. 80.

13. Ibid., p. 80.

14. Ibid., p. 81.

15. P. De Vries, *The Blood of the Lamb,* pp. 150–151.

16. George Eliot, *Middlemarch* (Boston: Houghton Mifflin, 1956), pp. 570–572.

17. I. Turgenev, *Spring Torrents,* p. 168.

18. Philip Roth, *The Professor of Desire* (New York: Penguin Books, 1985), pp. 66–67.

19. John Herbers, "One-Person Homes Show Big U.S. Rise," in *The New York Times,* Nov. 20, 1985, p. A32.

CHAPTER 7

1. Arthur Schopenhauer, *Of Women,* in *Complete Essays of Schopenhauer* (New York: John Wiley and Sons, 1942).

2. Freud's attitudes toward women are apparent by scattered references throughout his writings. Two specific papers indicating these attitudes are: "Three Essays on the Theory of Sexuality." "The Transformations of Puberty." "The Differentiation Between Men and Women" (1905), 7:219, and "Review of Wilhelm Neutra's Letters to Neurotic Women" (1910), 11:238.

3. Jung, quoted in Philip Rieff, *Freud: The Mind of the Moralist* (Chicago: University of Chicago Press, 1979), p. 376.

4. C. Gilligan, *In a Different Voice.*

5. W. Gaylin, *The Rage Within: Anger in Modern Life.*

6. Margaret Harlow, in *International Encyclopedia of the Social Sciences* (New York: Macmillan Free Press, 1968), vol. I, p. 124.

7. Thomas Mann, *Death in Venice and Seven Other Stories,* translated by H. T. Lowe-Porter (New York: Vintage Books, 1966), pp. 92–93.

8. E. O. Wilson, *On Human Nature,* p. 170.

9. *The Gods Must Be Crazy,* movie produced by Jamie Uys, 1982, Twentieth Century-Fox, first reviewed July 1984.

10. This is best illustrated in the writings of T. Huxley, R. Dubos, and Th. Dobzhansky.

11. Gustave Flaubert, *Madame Bovary* (New York: Airmont, 1965), p. 123.

12. Ibid., p. 144.

13. W. Gaylin, *The Meaning of Despair* (New York: Science House, 1968).

14. Leo Tolstoy, *Anna Karenina* (New York: Modern Library, 1965), pp. 792–793.

15. Two powerful novels that build on an understanding of the power implications of maleness are James Dickey's *Deliverance* and Norman Mailer's *Why We Were in Vietnam.*

16. C. M. Turnbull, *The Mountain People* (New York: Touchstone Books, 1972).

17. Napoleon Chagnon, *Yanomamo: The Fierce People* (New York: Holt, Rinehart & Winston, 1968).

18. Bowlby, Spitz, Klaus, and Kennell were, as previously described, pioneers emerging from different disciplines.

19. Otto Kernberg, *Barriers to Falling and Remaining in Love,* presented at the annual meeting of the American Psychiatric Association in Dallas, May 1972, pp. 486–511.

20. Stendhal, *On Love,* p. 2.

21. M. G. Kinget, *On Being Human: A Systematic View* (New York: Harcourt Brace Jovanovich, 1975), p. 119.

22. As quoted by B. A. Farber in "Adolescence," in K. Pope et al., *On Love and Loving: Psychological Perspectives on the Nature and Experience of Romantic Love* (San Francisco: Jossey–Bass Publishers, 1980), p. 59.

23. Farber, op. cit., p. 60.

24. Ibid., p. 59.

25. J. Shore and J. Sanville, *Illusion in Loving: A Psychoanalytic Approach to the Evolution of Intimacy and Autonomy* (Los Angeles: Double Helix Press, 1978).

26. Stendhal, *On Love,* pp. 156–157.

CHAPTER 8

1. Francine du Plessix Gray, *Lovers and Tyrants* (New York: Pocket Books, 1977), pp. 83–84.

2. Ned L. Gaylin, in M. Farber, ed., *Human Sexuality: Psychosexual Effects of Disease* (New York: Macmillan, 1985), pp. 40–54.

3. Derek Parfit, "Later Selves and Moral Principles," in *Philosophy and Personal Relationship*, A. Montefiori, ed. (London: Routledge & Kegan Paul, 1973).

4. Susan Mendess, in *Philosophy*, vol. 59, April 1984. No. 228, pp. 243–252.

5. Ibid., pp. 251–252.

6. D. H. Lawrence, *A Propos of Lady Chatterley's Lover*, op. cit., afterword.

7. Justice Brandeis dissent in *Olmstead* v. *United States*, 277 U.S. 438, 478 (1928).

8. D. H. Lawrence, *A Propos of Lady Chatterley's Lover*, pp. 345–346.

9. Ibid., p. 347.

10. Ibid., p. 348.

11. Ibid., p. 345.

12. *Intimacy and Sexual Behavior* (New York: The National Hemophilia Foundation, 1985), quoted in *Hastings Center Report*, August 1985, Special Supplement, p. 10.

13. Christopher Lasch, *The Culture of Narcissism: American Life in an Age of Diminishing Expectations* (New York: W. W Norton, 1979).

14. P. Rieff, *Freud: The Mind of the Moralist* (Chicago: University of Chicago Press, 1979), p. 356.

15. Rachel Carson, *Silent Spring* (Boston: Houghton Mifflin, 1962).

16. John Rawls, *A Theory of Justice* (Cambridge: Harvard University Press, 1971).

17. V. Solovyov, *The Meaning of Love*, translated by Geoffrey Bles (London: Centenary Press, 1945), pp. 22–23.

18. Hume, *Of Self Love, Essays*, pp. 485–486.

19. S. Freud, "Contributions to the Psychology of Love I" (1910), 11:63; "Contributions to the Psychology of Love II" (1912), 11:177; and "Contributions to the Psychology of Love III" (1918), 11:19.

20. Milan Kundera, *The Book of Laughter and Forgetting* (New York: Alfred A. Knopf, 1981), p. 212.

21. S. Freud, *Civilization and Its Discontents* (London: Hogarth Press, 1953), p. 38.

22. W. Gaylin, *Feelings*.

23. R. Unger, *Passion*, p. 300.

24. William James, *The Writings of William James*, J. MacDermot, ed. (New York: Random House, 1967), pp. 618–619.

25. V. Solovyov, *The Meaning of Love*.

SELECT BIBLIOGRAPHY

The subject of love is distributed across such varied disciplines, from theology to biology, and is so extensive that a "complete" bibliography, even if possible, would be more confusing than helpful. I have therefore included here—under three sometimes arbitrary headings—books and articles that I have personally drawn upon and found useful.

Omitted from the bibliography are those works of fiction and poetry that often best illuminate the experience of love. While examples are utilized throughout this book, the world of literature is best appreciated within the special tastes and appetites of the individual reader.

PSYCHOANALYSIS, PSYCHOLOGY, AND SOCIOLOGY

Abraham, K. "Notes on the Psycho-Analytical Investigation and Treatment of Manic-Depressive Insanity and Allied Conditions," in *Selected Papers*. London: Hogarth Press (1911), 1927.

Ainsworth, M. D. S.; Blehar, M. C.; Waters, E.; and Wall, S. *Patterns of Attachment*. New York: Morley, 1978.

Aries, P. *Centuries of Childhood: A Social History of Family Life*. Translated by Robert Baldick. New York: Alfred A. Knopf, 1962.

Balint, A. "Identification," *International Journal of Psychoanalysis*, 1941.

Balint, M. *Primary Love and Psychoanalytic Technique*. New York: Liveright, 1953.

Bergmann, M. "Platonic Love, Transference Love and Love in

Real Life," *Journal of American Psychoanalytic Association,* 1982.

Berman, S. *The Six Demons of Love: Men's Fears of Intimacy.* New York: McGraw Hill Book Co., 1984.

Biegel, H. D. "Romantic Love," *American Sociological Review,* 1951.

Billow, R. M. "On Reunion," *The Psychoanalytic Review,* Summer 1980.

Bowlby, J. *Attachment and Loss,* vol. I, *Attachment.* New York: Basic Books, 1962.

———. *Attachment and Loss,* vol. II, *Separation: Anxiety and Anger.* New York: Basic Books, 1973.

———. *The Making and Breaking of Affectional Bonds.* London: Tavistock Publications, 1979.

Branden, N. *The Psychology of Romantic Love.* New York: Bantam Books, 1980.

Brazelton, T. B. and Als, H. "Four Early Stages in the Development of Mother–Infant Interaction," ed. Albert J. Solnit, et al. *The Psychoanalytic Study of the Child.* New Haven: Yale University Press, 1979.

Brody, S. *Patterns of Mothering.* New York: International Universities Press, 1956.

Bruner, J. S. *Beyond the Information Given.* New York: Norton, 1973.

Burlingham, D., and Freud, A. *Infants Without Families.* London: Allen & Unwin, 1944.

Caldwell, B. M., and Ricciuti, H. N., eds. *Child Development and Social Policy.* Chicago: University of Chicago Press, 1973.

Chagnon, N. *Yanomamo: The Fierce People.* New York: Holt, Rinehart & Winston, 1968.

Chasseguet-Smirgel, J. *Female Sexuality.* Ann Arbor: University of Michigan Press, 1970.

———. *The Ego Ideal.* New York: Norton, 1985.

Demos, J., and Babcock, S. J., eds. *Turning Points: Historical and Sociological Essays on the Family.* Chicago: University of Chicago Press, 1978.

De Saussure, R. "Identification and Substitution," *International Journal of Psychoanalysis,* 1939.

Dion, K. L., and Dion, K. K. "Correlates of Romantic Love,"

Journal of Consulting and Clinical Psychology, 1973.

Erikson, E. H. *Childhood and Society*. New York: Norton, 1950.

———. *Identity and the Life Cycle*. New York: International Universities Press, 1959.

———. *Youth Identity and Crisis*. New York: Norton, 1968.

Fairbairn, W. D. *An Object-Relations Theory of the Personality*. New York: Basic Books, 1952.

Farber, M., ed. *Human Sexuality: Psychosexual Effects of Disease*. New York: Macmillan, 1985.

Fine, R. *The Meaning of Love in Human Experiences*. New York: John Wiley & Sons, 1985.

Freud, A. *Infants Without Families*. New York: International Universities Press, 1944.

Freud, S. Standard Edition. London: Hogarth Press, 1955. Figures refer to volume and page number in this edition.

Three Essays on the Theory of Sexuality, 1905, 7:125.

Character and Anal Erotism, 1908, 9:167.

Contributions to the Psychology of Love, I, 1910, 11:163.

Totem and Taboo, 113, 13:1.

Mourning and Melancholia, 1917, 14:237.

Introductory Lectures on Psychoanalysis, 1916, 15:3.

Group Psychology and the Analysis of the Ego, 1921, 18:111.

Beyond the Pleasure Principle, 1920, 18:3.

Economic Problems in Masochism, 1924, 19:157.

Inhibitions, Symptoms and Anxiety, 1926, 20:77.

Civilization and Its Discontents, 1930, 21:5.

Female Sexuality, 1931, 21:223.

Fromm, E. *The Art of Loving*. New York: Bantam Books, 1963.

Fromme, A. *The Ability to Love*. New York: Pocket Books, 1965.

Gaylin, W. *The Meaning of Despair*. New York: Science House, 1968.

———. *Caring*. New York: Alfred A. Knopf, 1976.

———. *Feelings: Our Vital Signs*. New York: Harper & Row, 1979.

———. *The Rage Within: Anger in Modern Life*. New York: Simon and Schuster, 1984.

Gewirtz, J. L., ed. *Attachment and Dependency.* New York: Halstead Press, 1972.

Gilfillan, S. S. "Adult Intimate Love Relationships as New Editions of Symbiosis and the Separation Individuation Process," *Smith College Studies in Social Work,* June 1985.

Gilligan, C. *In a Different Voice.* Cambridge, Mass.: Harvard University Press, 1982.

Hamburg, D. A. "Observations of Mother-Infant Interactions in Primate Field Studies," in B. Foss, ed., *Determinants of Infant Behavior,* vol. 14. New York: John Wiley, 1969.

Harlow, H. F. "The Nature of Love," *American Psychologist,* 1958.

———. "The Maternal Affectional System," in H. L. Rheingold, ed., *Maternal Behavior in Mammals.* New York: John Wiley, 1963.

———. *Learning to Love.* New York: Aronson, 1974.

Harlow, H. F., and Harlow, M. K. "The Affectional Systems," in A. M. Schrier, H. F. Harlow, and F. Stollnitz, eds. *Behavior of Nonhuman Primates.* New York and London: Academic Press, 1965.

Institute of Medicine. *Bereavement.* Washington, D.C.: National Academy Press, 1984.

James, W. *The Writings of William James.* J. MacDermot, ed. New York: Random House, 1967.

Kahn, C. "Proverbs of Love and Marriage: A Psychological Perspective," *The Psychoanalytic Review,* Fall 1983.

Kernberg, O. F. "Barriers to Falling and Remaining in Love," presented at Annual Meeting of the American Psychoanalytic Association, Dallas, May 1972.

———. "Mature Love: Prerequisites and Characteristics," *Journal of the American Psychoanalytic Association,* 1974.

———. *Object Relations Theory and Clinical Psychoanalysis.* New York: Aronson, 1976.

———. "Boundaries and Structure in Love Relations," *Journal of the American Psychoanalytic Association,* 1977.

Klein, M. "On Identification," in M. Klein, P. Heinmann, and R. E. Money-Kyrtle, eds. *New Directions in Psychoanalysis.* New York: Basic Books, 1955.

Kohut, H. *The Analysis of the Self.* New York: International Universities Press, 1971.

———. *The Restoration of the Self.* New York: International Universities Press, 1977.

Liebowitz, M. R. *The Chemistry of Love.* Boston: Little, Brown & Co., 1983.

Lukeman, B. *Embarkations: A Guide to Dealing with Death and Parting.* Englewood Cliffs, N.J.: Prentice-Hall, Inc., 1982.

Maccoby, E. E., and Masters, J. S. "Attachment and Dependency," in P. H. Mussen, ed. *Carmichael's Manual of Child Psychology.* New York: John Wiley, 1970.

Mahler, M. S. "Symbiosis and Individuation—The Psychological Birth of the Human Infant," *The Psychoanalytic Study of the Child,* 1974

———. *The Psychological Birth of the Human Infant.* New York: Basic Books, 1975.

Masson, J. M. *The Assault on Truth: Freud's Suppression of the Seduction Theory.* New York: Farrar, Straus, Giroux, 1984.

May, R. *Love and Will.* New York: Dell, 1969.

Mellen, S. L. W. *The Evolution of Love.* San Francisco: W. J. H. Freeman and Co., 1981.

Modell, A. H. *Object Love and Reality.* New York: International Universities Press, 1968.

Morris, D. *The Naked Ape.* New York: McGraw-Hill, 1967.

Nance, J. *The Gentle Tasaday.* New York: Harcourt Brace Jovanovich, 1961.

Otto, H. A., ed. *Love Today: A New Exploration.* New York: Association Press, 1972.

Papousek, H., and Papousek, M. "Integration into the Social World: Survey of Research," in P. Stratton, ed. *Psychobiology of the Human Newborn.* New York: John Wiley, 1982.

Plutchik, R., and Kellerman, H., eds. *Emotion,* vol. II, *Emotions in Early Development.* New York: Academic Press, 1983.

Pope, K. S., et al. *On Love and Loving: Psychological Perspectives on the Nature and Experience of Romantic Love.* San Francisco: Jossey-Bass Publishers, 1980.

Reiss, I. L. *Family Systems in America.* New York: Holt, Rinehart and Winston, 1980.

Shore, J., and Sanville, J. *Illusion in Loving: A Psychoanalytical*

Approach to the Evolution of Intimacy and Autonomy. Los Angeles: Double Helix Press, 1978.

Skinner, B. F. *Beyond Freedom and Dignity,* New York: Alfred A. Knopf, 1971.

Spitz, R. A. "Hospitalism: An Inquiry into the Genesis of Psychiatric Conditions in Early Childhood," in A. Freud, ed. *The Psychoanalytic Study of the Child,* vol. I. New York: International Universities Press, 1945.

————. *The First Year of Life*. New York: International Universities Press, 1965.

Stern, D. V. *The First Relationship*. Cambridge, Mass.: Harvard University Press, 1977.

Stone, L. *The Family, Sex and Marriage in England 1500–1800*. New York: Harper Colophon Books, 1979.

Sudry, J. *The Social Context of Marriage*. Philadelphia: Lippincott, 1971.

Tennov, D. *Love and Limerence: The Experience of Being in Love*. New York: Stein and Day, 1979.

Turnbull, C. *The Mountain People*. New York: Simon and Schuster, 1972.

Valenstein, A.F. "The Earliest Mother-Child Relationship and the Development of the Superego," in S. Post, ed. *Moral Values and the Superego Concept in Psychoanalysis*. New York: International Universities Press, 1972.

Weiss, R. S. *Marital Separation*. New York: Basic Books, 1975.

Wheelis, A. *The Quest for Identity*. New York: Norton, 1958.

WHO Public Health Paper. *Object Relations, Dependency and Attachment: A Theoretical Review of the Infant-Mother Relationship*.

Winnicott, D. W. "The Theory of the Parent-Infant Relationship," *International Journal of Psychoanalysis,* 1960.

Zick, R. *Liking and Loving: An Invitation to Social Psychology*. New York: Holt, Rinehart and Winston, 1973.

BIOLOGY AND HUMAN NATURE

Beach, F. A., ed. *Human Sexuality in Four Perspectives*. Baltimore: Johns Hopkins, 1977.

Dobzhansky, T. *Evolution, Genetics, and Man*. New York: John Wiley, 1955.

_____. *Mankind Evolving*. New Haven: Yale University Press, 1962.

_____. *Genetic Diversity and Human Equality*. New York: Basic Books, 1973.

Dubos, R. *Man Adapting*. New Haven: Yale University Press, 1965.

_____. *So Human an Animal*. New York: Charles Scribner's Sons, 1968.

Hersher, L.; Richard, J. B.; and Moore, A. V. "Modifiability of the Critical Period for the Development of Maternal Behavior in Sheep and Goats," *Behavior,* 1963.

Huxley, J. *Man in the Modern World*. New York: Mentor Books, 1944.

Kinget, G. M. *On Being Human: A Systematic View*. New York: Harcourt Brace Jovanovich, 1975.

Klaus, M. H., and Kennell, J. H. *Parent-Infant Bonding*. St. Louis: C. V. Mosby, 1982.

Klopfer, P. H. "Mother Love: Whats Turns It On?" *American Science,* 1971.

Klopfer, P. H.; Adams, D. K.; and Klopfer, M. S. "Maternal 'Imprinting' in Goats," *Proceedings of the National Academy of Sciences,* 1964.

Portmann, A. *Animals as Social Beings*. New York: Viking, 1961.

Rheingold, H., ed. *Maternal Behavior in Animals*. New York: John Wiley, 1963.

Simpson, G. G., *The Meaning of Evolution*. New York: Mentor Books, 1950.

Skinner, B. F. *Beyond Freedom and Dignity*. New York: Alfred A. Knopf, 1971.

Wilson, E. O. *On Human Nature*. New York: Bantam Books, 1978.

PHILOSOPHY AND THEOLOGY

Alberoni, F. *Falling in Love*. Translated by Lawrence Verruti. New York: Random House, 1983.

Buber, M. *The Knowledge of Man*. London: Allen & Unwin, 1965.

_____. *I and Thou*. New York: Scribner's, 1970.

Capellannus, A. *The Art of Courtly Love*. New York: Columbia University Press, 1941.

Cassirer, E. *The Renaissance Philosophy of Man.* Chicago: University of Chicago Press, 1956.

D'Arcy, M. C. *The Mind and Heart of Love.* New York: Meridian Books, 1956.

DeRougemont, D. *Love in the Western World.* New York: Pantheon Books, 1956.

Empedocles in W. K. Guthrie. *A History of Greek Philosophers,* vol. II. Cambridge: Cambridge University Press, 1975.

Hume, D. *A Treatise of Human Nature.* Oxford: Oxford University Press, 1896

_____. *Of Self Love, Essays.* London: Ward, Lock and Tyler, 1924.

James, W. *The Writings of William James,* J. MacDermot, ed. New York: Random House, 1967.

Kierkegaard, S. *Works of Love: Some Christian Reflections in the Form of Discourses.* New York: Harper & Row, 1964.

_____. *The Sickness Unto Death.* Princeton: Princeton University Press, 1980.

Lewis, C. S. *The Allegory of Love.* New York: Oxford University Press, 1958.

_____. *A Grief Observed.* New York: Bantam Books, 1976.

Mead, G. H. *Mind, Self and Society.* Chicago: University of Chicago Press, 1934.

Moffett, J. *Love in the New Testament.* London: Hadden & Stoughton, 1929.

Nygren, A. *Agape and Eros.* Chicago: University of Chicago Press, 1982.

Ortega y Gasset, J. *On Love.* Cleveland: World Publishing Co., 1957.

Ovid. *Amores.* Translated by Guy Lee. New York: Viking Press, 1968.

_____. *Metamorphoses.* Translated by Frank J. Miller. Loeb Classical Library.

Plato. *Symposium.* B. Jowett, ed. New York: Tudor Publishing, 1956.

St. Augustine. *Confessions.* New York: Penguin Books, 1961.

Schopenhauer, A. *Of Women,* in *Complete Essays of Schopenhauer.* New York: John Wiley, 1942.

_____. *The World As Will and Idea.* New York: Dover, 1969.

Singer, I. *The Nature of Love,* vol. I and vol. II. Chicago: University of Chicago Press, 1984.

Solovyov, V. *The Meaning of Love.* Translated by Geoffrey Bles. London: Centenary Press, 1945.

Stendhal. *On Love.* New York: Liveright, 1947.

Tillich, P. *A History of Christian Thought.* New York: Simon and Schuster, 1968.

Unger, R. *Passion: An Essay on Personality.* New York: Free Press, 1984.

Williams, D. D. *The Spirit and the Forms of Love.* New York: Harper & Row, 1978.

INDEX

human vs. animal, 141–42,
144
imagination and, 89, 92
infantile, 46–47, 133, 138
Lawrence's elevation of,
11–12
trivialization of, 10–11,
17–18
women and, 11, 46, 184,
197–98
sexual revolution, 11, 17–18,
180
emptiness as aftermath of,
90
shame, 11, 55, 93–94,
96–97; betrayal of
parent and, 110; loss of
love and, 176–77
Shaw, George Bernard, 23,
149
Shelley, Percy Bysshe, 233
Sickness unto Death, The
(Kierkegaard), 170
Silent Spring (Carson), 242
Singer, Irving, 21–22,
101–102, 104–105, 121
Singer, J. L., 135
Skinner, B. F., 2, 29
Snow, C. P., 37–38
sociology, 2, 16
Solevyov, Vladimir, 244, 250
Sophocles, 86–87
space, condensation of, 240
Spitz, Renee, 160–61
Spring Torrents (Turgenev),
176–77
state:
family vs., 227–30
overvaluation of, 243
Stendhal, 144, 215, 220
Stevens, Wallace, 51, 78

Stevenson, Robert Louis, 66
stress, relief of, 79, 80
stroking, 61–62
Studies in Hysteria (Breuer
and Freud), 93
sublimation, 51, 94, 214
success, 237–38
suffering, 10, 87
of children, 36
see also pain
suicide, 196
in men vs. women, 194–95
superego, 108, 110, 238
survival, 26, 35, 54–55, 84,
177, 216
in groups, 95–96, 98
simple pleasures and,
62–63
Symposium (Plato), 9, 85–86,
98–99

taboos, 94–97, 130–31
Tarnower, Herman, 167
technological revolution,
13–18, 204
trivialization of sex and,
17–18
unfulfilled promise of,
15–16
teenagers:
parental death and, 161–
63
sex and, 98, 143
tenderness, 5, 217
theology, love and, 4
Theresa, Saint, 104–105
Thompson, Clara, 50
time, condensation of, 240
Tolstoy, Leo, 195–96
"Tonio Kröger" (Mann),
190–91

House Made of Dawn by N. Scott Momaday. Copyright © 1966, 1967, 1968 by N. Scott Momaday. By permission of Harper & Row, Publishers, Inc.

Metamorphoses by Ovid, translated by Frank J. Miller. Published by Harvard University Press.

The Second Coming by Walker Percy. Copyright © 1980 by Walker Percy. Reprinted by permission of Farrar, Straus and Giroux, Inc.

The Mind of the Moralist by Philip Rieff. Published by The University of Chicago Press. Copyright © 1959, 1961, 1979 Philip Rieff.

The Professor of Desire by Philip Roth. Copyright © 1977 by Philip Roth. Reprinted by permission of Farrar, Straus and Giroux, Inc.

The Nature of Love, Volumes 1 and 2 by Irving Singer. Published by The University of Chicago Press. Copyright © 1966, 1984 Irving Singer.

Homecoming by C. P. Snow. Copyright © 1956 C. P. Snow; copyright renewed. Reprinted with permission of Charles Scribner's Sons.

"Antigone" from *The Three Theban Plays* by Sophocles, translated by Robert Fagles. Copyright © 1982 by Robert Fagles. Reprinted by permission of Viking Penguin Inc.

On Love by Stendhal. Reprinted by permission of Liveright Publishing Corporation.

"Re-Statement of Romance" from *Collected Poems of Wallace Stevens.* Copyright 1954 by Wallace Stevens. Reprinted by permission of Alfred A. Knopf, Inc.

Passion by Roberto Mangabeira Unger. Copyright © 1984 by Roberto Mangabeira Unger. Published by The Free Press, a division of Macmillan, Inc. Used with permission.

The Aeneid by Virgil, translated by Robert Fitzgerald. Translation copyright © 1980, 1982, 1983 by Robert Fitzgerald. Reprinted with permission of Random House, Inc.

The Lost Traveller by Antonia White, published by Virago Press Ltd., 1979. Copyright © The Literary Executors of Antonia White 1980.

On Human Nature by Edmund Wilson. Published by Harvard University Press. Reprinted with permission.

Acknowledgment is made for permission to reprint "For Anne Gregory" from *Collected Poems* by W. B. Yeats. Copyright 1933 by Macmillan Publishing Company, renewed 1961 by Bertha Georgie Yeats. Reprinted with permission of Macmillan Publishing Company, Michael B. Yeats and Macmillan London.